THE FUTURIST

THE
FUTURIST

The Life and Films of
JAMES CAMERON

REBECCA KEEGAN

Crown Publishers

New York

For Dad,
my very first storyteller

Contents

Introduction
The Futurist

"First I just want to say that we're all doomed," the silver-haired director intoned. He was speaking to an Earth Day audience in Santa Barbara, California, in 2000, mocking his own predilection for spinning apocalyptic scenarios. James Cameron has spent his life looking ahead, warily, expectantly, and in the case of his chosen art form, movies, technologically and artistically. And he is constantly entreating the rest of us to join him there, in the perilous world of what's next.

Ever since he left the fate of the planet in the hands of a diner waitress in *The Terminator* in 1984, Cameron has shown a steady faith in ordinary people to handle extraordinary responsibilities. It could be you who has to save us from the machines, he tells any man or—remarkably—woman sitting in a dark theater watching his film. It could be you who has to decide how to live or die on the *Titanic*.

But there is not much that is ordinary about Cameron's own story.

He's a truck driver who directed the highest-grossing movie of all time before he turned forty-four and then ditched Hollywood to spend a decade of his life exploring the deep ocean and the heights of science. He's a tinkerer and a dreamer who pioneered tools that revolutionized the way stories are told, technologies that a generation of filmmakers now rely upon as surely as they do sound and color. He's a too-smart kid who spent his adulthood doing things other people called impossible, from filming a movie two and a half miles under the ocean to making a woman an action hero.

More than anything else, Cameron has muscled movies into the digital age, freeing filmmakers to tell stories that had once been possible only in their imaginations. It was he who first showed that computers could deliver not just sharp-edged images, but organic-looking forms, via the twenty computer-generated (CG) shots of a water tentacle rising in *The Abyss.* With the liquid-metal man in *T2,* he created a CG character, the T-1000, that stretched the rules of physics and the limits of storytelling. On *Titanic,* he was making a movie in which the special effects didn't draw attention to themselves but instead disappeared into the reality of a sinking ship, leaving behind only the visceral feelings of beauty, dread, and loss.

But it is *Avatar,* more than any of Cameron's previous films, that has the makings of revolution. He first laid out much of the technology he would use on the film in a digital manifesto in the early 1990s and labored to perfect it over the course of a decade and a half. For this movie, he created cameras that let him peer into virtual worlds and pushed for the industry's adoption of a digital 3-D format. The result is as if the director had broken through the screen, grabbed the viewer's hand, and pulled him or her into this exotic, never-seen world called Pandora, a planet of floating mountains, bioluminescent rain forests, and an elegant, tall, blue people called the Na'vi.

Cameron's fancy tools, however, are merely tools, just the latest iteration of the ape flinging the bone in *2001: A Space Odyssey*. Technology doesn't come with the wisdom to wield it, whether to make art or to make war. The dark side of our steady march of scientific advancement is a theme Cameron visits in each of his movies and puzzles over in his private life. His first cinematic "the end is nigh" warning was *The Terminator,* in which people had unwittingly surrendered our nuclear codes and our very humanity to machines, which waged war against us in 2029. By the time he got to *Avatar,* twenty-five years later, we were taking our bad habits, our rapacious treatment of the planet Earth, interstellar.

You have to walk fast to keep up with Cameron on one of his film sets. He moves in hyperspeed. After the first time I visited the stages in the Los Angeles warehouse where *Avatar* was filmed, I learned to wear my sneakers to work. I was there for a *Time* magazine assignment and was astonished by what I saw—a reinvention of how movies are made, a virtual set that existed only inside the director's camera, and in his mind. I knew Cameron to be an innovator, but this was clearly his magnum opus as a future-minded filmmaker. As I watched the director work, I became curious about a man who seemed interested only in doing things that were hard, and in doing them perfectly, and I was determined to follow his intriguing film's progress more closely.

I was a fly on the wall during the movie's performance-capture shooting and as Cameron teleconferenced with artists at Weta Digital in Wellington, New Zealand, to perfect *Avatar*'s 2,500 special-effects shots. I visited his production company, Lightstorm Entertainment, in Santa Monica as he conferred with scientists to shape the mythology of *Avatar,* and his home in Malibu as he edited the film. I talked to more than fifty of Cameron's friends, family members, and colleagues. I met his mother, who is an action heroine trapped in the body of a Canadian grandmother, and spoke to his friend Arnold Schwarzenegger, who has appeared as an iconic villain and hero in three of his movies and spends weekends riding motorcycles with him through the Santa Monica mountains. I talked to Dennis Muren, who helped achieve the stunning advances in computer graphics on *The Abyss* and *T2,* and to Peter Jackson, who stood on Cameron's shoulders to make the *Lord of the Rings* trilogy before lending his friend his special-effects house for *Avatar.* I interviewed Gale Anne Hurd, his second wife and first producing partner; Peter Chernin, the Fox executive who green-lighted *Titanic* and *Avatar;* Jon Landau, the producer who enables Cameron to realize his ambitious projects; and Rae Sanchini, who runs his company.

"You can't help but come away from spending time with Jim feeling that you're a little bit stupid," Jackson warned me early in my research. "He's got such a sharp mind, he's formidable." Jackson was right. Cameron's brain is formidable, fascinating, and equally developed on both sides—the scientist and the artist. I found a man who has both the ability to tease out esoteric engineering problems, like how a futuristic helicopter should land realistically, and to articulate a clear aesthetic vision to a team of artists, like how a lush alien forest should glow eerily at night. He also showed an uncanny ability to tune out a Greek chorus of naysayers and, just as amazingly, to convince lots of rational people to join him in pursuit of his daunting visions.

One of Cameron's oft-uttered phrases is, "I knew that would happen!" He says it with annoyance when a stunt goes wrong or a piece of technology fails, or with vindication when a championed actor delivers a strong performance or a crazy technical idea takes off. His movies, so many of which depict the future, have turned out to be far more predictive than your average sci-fi fare. Some of the ideas and images contained in them—robotic weaponry, exoskeletal suits for soldiers, massive domestic terrorism, economic ruin, a camera-driven culture— have come true in the years since they were made. So, too, have the filmmaking techniques he evangelized about, despite the skepticism of his colleagues. When he started work on a digital 3-D camera in 2000, most of the industry still thought of 3-D as an entertainment fad best left buried with Smell-O-Vision or disco. By 2010, every animated Disney and Dreamworks movie will be produced in digital 3-D, as will several live-action movies. Based on Cameron's track record as a futurist operating in a fictional world, it's entirely likely that 2029 will require our best survivalist skills.

But what all futuristic fiction, including Cameron's, does better than predicting what's going to happen next is mapping our present aspirations and fears. Cameron's movies provide us a place to imagine a path to a better future. Yes, we're all doomed, Cameron told that Santa Barbara crowd. "But on the positive side, we created this impending doom ourselves, with our brains, with our technology, and we can damn well uncreate it." Cameron's career has been built on questioning accepted wisdom and believing in the power of the individual. His outlook, that we can take fate in our hands, has implications far beyond making entertaining movies. It determines the very future we face.

1.

A BOY AND HIS BRAIN

The Beginning of the End

The end of the world was coming. And he was eight. That's when James Cameron found a pamphlet with instructions for building a civilian fallout shelter on the coffee table in his family's living room in Chippawa, Ontario, a quaint village on the Canadian shore of Niagara Falls. It was 1962, the year of the Cuban missile crisis, and Philip and Shirley Cameron felt they had reason to be concerned about the bomb—the Camerons lived just a mile and a half from the falls, a major power source for communities on both sides of the international border. But for their oldest son, discovering the brochure was a life-changing epiphany. Prior to that moment, the boy's only real care in the world had been getting home on his bike before the streetlights flickered on, the family rule. "I realized that the safe and nurturing world I thought I lived in was an illusion, and that the world as we know it could end at any moment," Cameron says. From that time on, he was fascinated by the idea of nuclear war, his fears fueled by the apocalyptic scenarios depicted in the science-fiction books he devoured at night, reading under his blanket with a flashlight. He may have been the only kid at his school to find the duck-and-cover bomb drills neither funny nor stupid. "Was this crazy or just a heightened awareness of truth?" Cameron wonders. "As the world turned out so far, it was a bit paranoid. But there's still plenty of time to destroy ourselves."

The pensive eight-year-old boy would grow up to tell vivid stories about worlds ending, from a machine-led war in 2029 to an unsinkable ship's descent into the deep in 1912. Each James Cameron movie is a warning against his darkest childhood fears and a kind of how-to guide for living through catastrophe with humanity and spirit intact. His own story begins with a long line of troublemakers.

Philip and Shirley

Cameron's great-great-great-grandfather, a schoolteacher, migrated from Balquhidder, Scotland, to Canada in 1825. "He was a bit of a free thinker. He didn't like the king," explains Philip, a plainspoken electrical engineer, understating things a bit. The Cameron clan is one of Scotland's oldest, a family of notoriously fierce swordsmen who were leaders in the Jacobite uprisings, the bitter Anglo-Scottish religious wars of the seventeenth and eighteenth centuries. Some were executed for treason, others exiled. Philip Cameron's branch ended up on a farm near Orangeville, Ontario, about fifty miles northwest of Toronto, where he attended a one-room school before following work north as a nickel miner to earn the money to enter the University of Toronto in 1948. "Pops is very male, strong. He was always bigger than everybody even though he wasn't bigger than everybody," says the Camerons' youngest son, John David. "He was the guy you didn't want to mess with. If it took you two turns of the wrench, it took Dad a half."

In high school Philip met Shirley Lowe, a slim, blonde-haired, blue-eyed dynamo who drove stock cars in the Orangeville powder-puff derby and won a countywide award for her war bond painting of a city in flames. "Do you want this to happen?" it asked ominously in red paint. While a mother with three kids under age eight, Shirley would join the Canadian Women's Army Corps, happily trooping off on weekends in fatigues and combat boots to assemble a rifle while blindfolded and march through fields in the pouring rain. She kept up her painting, in oils and watercolors, and one night a week she attended an adult education course in a subject of interest, such as geology or astronomy. "I did those things for me and nobody else," says Shirley, who professes bewilderment that she might be the inspiration for the gutsy maternal heroines in movies like *The Terminator* and *Aliens*. "I don't know why Jim thinks I'm so self-reliant," Shirley adds with a shrug, her blue eyes sparkling. Philip looks up from the dining table in their Calabasas, California, home, clearly amused by his wife of fifty-seven years. "Well, you are," he says wryly. Shirley is creative, impulsive, and fiery, Philip stoic, analytical, and precise. "It's tough to be diplomatic with stupid people," he confesses. Their wildly different dispositions would combine uniquely in their son, who became equal parts calculating gearhead and romantic artist.

When their first child was born, the Camerons were living in an apartment in Kapuskasing, a cold, remote company town in northern Ontario where Philip worked as an engineer at the local paper plant. Shirley had trained as a nurse in Toronto but was now a somewhat restless homemaker. On August 16, 1954, James Cameron arrived in the world one month late and screaming, an image Hollywood studio executives will have no trouble picturing. Because he was their first child, the Camerons didn't know there was anything unusual about Jim. When he strode into a doctor's office at eighteen months old, extended his hand, and said, "How do you do, doctor?" they learned their son was a little precocious.

Chippawa

When Cameron was five, Philip's job took the family to Niagara Falls, and from there they moved to a comfortable split-level in Chippawa, where they would live until 1971. The family kept growing—next came Mike, Valerie, Terri, and John David. The Cameron kids freely roamed the shores of Chippawa Creek, which is actually, by non-Canadian standards, a rushing river. There were fishing trips and daredevil hikes above the deep gorges. Cameron once slipped off an algae-covered board down a hundred-foot cliff, catching a tree limb and scrambling back up, a misadventure he never shared with his parents. "What happens on the hike stays on the hike," he says. He became a tinkerer, building and experimenting, often with his brother Mike. They made go-karts, rafts, tree houses. A favorite toy was the Erector Set, which Cameron had earned by selling greeting cards. (Shirley paid off the neighbors to buy them—mothers can keep secrets, too.) He used the Erector Set to construct Rube Goldberg contraptions for dispensing candy and Coke bottles. Once he built a mini bathysphere with a mayonnaise jar and a paint bucket, put a mouse in the jar, put the jar in the bucket, and lowered the bucket off a bridge to the bottom of Chippawa Creek. When he pulled it back up, the mouse was still alive, but probably not without having had a good shock. Another proud engineering milestone was the Summer Vacation Trebuchet, a siege engine Cameron constructed out of an old hay wagon at his grandparents' farm near Orangeville and used to launch twenty-pound rocks at spare-lumber targets he had dragged into the cow pasture.

The Cameron boys' handiness with tools was not always constructive. When some neighborhood kids stole their toys, Jim and Mike visited the lead suspects' tree house and sawed through the limbs. When the juvenile criminals climbed up to their woody retreat, it toppled to the ground. "That one they got in trouble for," says Shirley, nodding. "You don't do things where people can get hurt." Philip was the stern disciplinarian in the family, usually able to get his point across in few words. "My dad used to warn me, 'If you mess up I'll take you to the woodshed,'" remembers John David. "I was pretty confident I knew the house, and I didn't think we even had a woodshed. The threat was worse than any actual act."

Early on, Cameron demonstrated a knack for assembling large groups in service of his own goals. When her oldest son was about ten, Shirley noticed his younger siblings and several neighborhood children streaming into her side yard carrying scraps of wood and metal. "I said, 'What are you gonna do with all this junk?'" Shirley recalls. "Jim said, 'We're gonna build something.'" When Shirley checked on the project a couple of hours later, the kids had constructed an airplane. "Guess who was sitting in it being pulled?" Cameron was very good at telling people what to do. He took it upon himself to keep his younger siblings in line when the family went out to dinner. The oldest boy would fold his hands on the table and start twiddling his thumbs, a cue to the little ones to follow and not to grab the salt and pepper shakers.

Shirley encouraged her son's artistic side. At his request, some Saturdays they traveled eighty miles to the Royal Ontario Museum, where Cameron pulled out his sketchbook to draw helmets and mummies. "Everything I saw and liked and reacted to I immediately had to draw," he says. "Drawing was my way of owning it." He created his own comic-book versions of movies and TV shows he liked, from pirates inspired by the 1961 Ray Harryhausen fantasy *Mysterious Island* to spaceships he saw on the first season of *Star Trek* in 1966. He easily won all the local design contests—to paint a mural on the Seagram Tower at Niagara Falls or the bank windows at Halloween. At age fourteen, he painted a Nativity scene for the bank for one hundred dollars, enough to buy Christmas presents for his parents and siblings.

The Cameron kids are an intense bunch, biochemically turbocharged. Close in age and temperament, Jim and Mike were sometimes coconspirators, sometimes rivals, often both at once. Mike would grow up to be an engineer like his father, building the sophisticated filmmaking and diving technologies used on *The Abyss, Titanic,* and his older brother's documentaries. Both bright and convinced of their own opinions, the two oldest Cameron boys are a technically potent and often explosive duo. They could turn a theoretical conversation on space travel into a rowdy brawl. "When they'd mix, there would be fireworks, good and bad," says their youngest brother, John David, who likens the Cameron family dynamic to "Japan before warfare; everybody's got their own systems."

Dinner was served at 6:00 p.m. at the Cameron house every night and timed with military precision. "I make good carbon," Shirley says of her culinary efforts. "I burn things." Her sons talk glowingly of her chili and pot roast but say that it was best when Shirley didn't bring her adventuresome spirit into the kitchen. At a certain point, dinner with the Camerons would become a contact sport. "The more of the family that gets together, the more chaotic and loud and bright and crescendoed it gets, from who gets the goddamned dish," John David says. "There will always be a moment when somebody says something that shouldn't have been said. It's priceless. But it's participatory. If you sit idly by, you'll get chewed on."

"You Can't Read, Jim?"

As a child, Cameron was sometimes too smart for his own good. At the end of first grade, his teacher called Shirley in to explain that her son was going to be held back. "She said, 'He can't read. He can't do anything. He just sits and looks out the window,'" Shirley recalls. "I said, 'You can't read, Jim?' He gets this smirk on his face. He knows I know he can read." Shirley asked her son to pick up any book on the teacher's desk. He selected a science text and began reading aloud about the species of the Pleistocene era. "The teacher's jaw dropped. She said, 'Why didn't you tell me you could read?' He said, 'If you think I'm gonna sit there and read *See Spot Run* all day long . . .' I was so mad at that kid." In the fall of second grade, Shirley got another call. This time the teacher was skipping her son to grade three. In the middle of grade three, he was moved to grade four. Shirley had a rule that her kids weren't allowed to do homework when they got home from school. She felt they had spent enough time bent over books. But Cameron was a voracious recreational reader who pored over the latest comic books, especially *Spider-Man,* and loved science-fiction writers like Arthur C. Clarke, Robert Heinlein, Ray Bradbury, and Kurt Vonnegut.

He won every academic prize given out for grade nine at Niagara Falls' Stamford Collegiate High School. "We thought it was wonderful," says Shirley, "but the other kids didn't." Skinny and a head shorter than his classmates as a result of the two skipped years of grammar school, Cameron was an easy target. "I got pounded," he says. He eschewed sports and instead became president of the science club, which, he recalls, "consisted of me and one Czechoslovakian girl." In tenth grade, he was bitten by the history bug in a class on the ancients. "The Egyptians, Minoans, Greeks, Romans. I can picture every class, every slide show, and almost quote the lessons," he says. By then he had learned to do well enough to earn good marks without drawing too much attention to himself. The awards stopped. Cameron had enough smart, oddball friends that he didn't feel like an outcast. But sometimes the groupthink of his peers baffled him. "They thought they were being so rebellious by all wearing bell bottoms," he says. "I didn't get it."

First period meant singing the national anthem and saying the Lord's Prayer. In tenth grade, standing at the head of his row, Cameron listened to his classmates and felt a surge of defiance. "It struck me as this tribal chant." In the middle of the prayer, he sat down, opened his book, and started to read. When he looked up, his teacher's eyes were wide, but she didn't chastise him, and he never said the Lord's Prayer again. Shirley had brought her children up attending an Anglican church while Philip, agnostic since age sixteen, stayed home. One of the books Shirley found her son reading under his covers at night was a thick history of world religions. His Sunday-school teacher wanted to put him in the adult Bible class, but Shirley objected. As a teenager, Cameron's interest in religion was driven as much by intellectual curiosity as by any kind of spiritual questing. As an adult, his movies would be full of religious imagery. Today he calls himself a "converted agnostic"—"I've sworn off agnosticism, which I now call cowardly atheism," Cameron says. "I've come to the position that in the complete absence of any supporting data whatsoever for the persistence of the individual in some spiritual form, it is necessary to operate under the provisional conclusion that there is no afterlife and then be ready to amend that if I find out otherwise." By the way, Cameron's explanation for why he's *not* agnostic is similar to his father's reason for why he *is* agnostic. "An agnostic questions things," Philip says. "They don't have all the answers." It's easy to see how things can get cerebrally rambunctious with the Camerons.

Other Worlds

Growing up hundreds of miles from the nearest ocean, Cameron never so much as stuck a toe in salt water, but he was riveted by Jacques Cousteau's underwater documentaries. The French oceanographer's movies aired on TV regularly in the 1960s, delivering images of the richness and exoticism of life beneath the waves into the living rooms of landlocked families like the Camerons. Later in his life, Cameron would adopt Cousteau's deeply felt environmentalism, but at sixteen, it was the spirit of exploration that hooked him. "I began to think of the deep ocean as equal to outer space," Cameron recalls. "This was an alien world I could actually reach."

Inspired by Cousteau, Cameron begged and cajoled his parents into enrolling him in a scuba class at a Buffalo YMCA pool. At the Y, he learned diving military style, with harassment drills, in which the instructor pulls off your mask and rips the regulator from your mouth. The harsh training engendered in Cameron a confidence and resourcefulness that would help him survive two near-drowning experiences in his life, one of them while filming *The Abyss*. His first dive outside the Y pool was in 1971, in Chippawa Creek. He had been taught to dive with a buddy, but the only scuba-certified citizens of his town were the two guys who pulled bodies out of the Niagara River for the fire department. So Cameron dived alone with a rope tied around his waist, the other end held by his father, who was standing on a dock. "Unbelievably lame move, but it made sense to us at the time," he says.

Cameron's relationship with his father would strain in his teenage years. Philip wanted his son to be an engineer. "He didn't understand me very well 'cause I was into art and science fiction and fantasy and all this stuff he just couldn't hang with," Cameron says. "We were on this big disconnect." If Philip didn't always understand his oldest son, he kept holding the rope while he dived, literally and metaphorically. He would provide financial help in Cameron's hungry early years as an aspiring filmmaker, tacitly supporting the career choice no matter how grievous the odds that his son would succeed. After Cameron directed *Titanic*—his seventh movie, the highest-grossing film of all time and winner of eleven Oscars—Philip finally acknowledged verbally that this directing thing might just work out.

As a teenager, Cameron's twin interests in science and art didn't lead to any conventional career path that he could identify. "There didn't seem to be any reconciliation possible," he says. "You were either in science or you were in the arts. But I was interested in both." His dream was to write a science-fiction novel and illustrate it. Had the art form of graphic novels existed, Cameron says that's what he would have wanted to do, but it didn't yet. "I suppose it was pretty logical to say I want to be a filmmaker because as a filmmaker you're telling a story with pictures. But I hadn't really thought of it."

The first time he considered film as a career was in 1968, when he staggered out of a Toronto movie theater showing *2001: A Space Odyssey.* Stanley Kubrick's long, philosophical science-fiction film was performing poorly at the box office, and fourteen-year-old Cameron was one of only a handful of people in the giant, 1,500-seat room, sitting dead center in the front row of the balcony, alone. With its vast, allegorical story stretching from the dawn of man to a future where travel to Jupiter is possible, its realistic special effects and daring lack of dialogue, *2001* made a deep impression on Cameron. After it ended, he reeled outside into the sunlight, sat down on the curb, and threw up from the vertigo of the third act's psychedelic trip sequence. "I didn't know what to make of it," he says. "It was really exciting intellectually, but mystifying and powerful visually. It was everything I thought I liked, but it didn't really have any answers. But I felt viscerally that I knew what the answers were." It was the moment Cameron went from being a fan of movies to wanting to make films himself. Specifically, he was interested in special effects. He wanted to be the guy who made the spaceships look real.

Cameron and his friend Mike Nestler got their hands on Nestler's father's Super 8 camera. They galloped around Niagara Falls shooting everything in sight, splicing their footage together to make social commentaries about their hometown. They built spaceship models, lit them, and staged intergalactic battles in front of a strip of black velvet, wondering at their creative achievement. "It's all garbage, but you start to think in a visual, narrative way," Cameron says. He found a thick book about how *2001* was made, which taught him a few film-making terms but didn't really answer his questions, leaving him to solve the mystery of the movie's sophisticated special effects like an archaeological problem. He returned to the theater and saw the film several more times to try to understand how Kubrick had managed to place his actors so believably in space, his apes in their rocky, prehistoric world. The answer is a special-effects technique that Kubrick pioneered called front projection, in which the background image is projected onto both the performer and a highly reflective background screen, bouncing off the screen and into the lens of a camera. It would take about a decade before Cameron figured out how Kubrick did it, but knowing would eventually prove crucial to getting his first promotion in the movie business.

When Cameron was sixteen, Philip came to his family with some news. His company, the paper manufacturer Kimberly-Clark, was transferring him to a plant in Orange County, California. The next school year would have been Cameron's last—in Ontario at that time, students on a precollege track attended through grade thirteen. Moving would mean no prom and no graduation. But that didn't faze him. "Jim said, 'Can we leave tomorrow?'" Philip recalls. "He knew he was getting close to Hollywood."

Gone West

In the fall of 1971, the Cameron family moved to Brea, California, a onetime oil and citrus town, now a growing suburb south of Los Angeles. The weather was perfect, their new house on top of a hill spacious, the ocean Cameron had long dreamed about just a twenty-five-minute drive away. And he was miserable. He was only thirty miles from Hollywood, but he might as well have still been 2,500 miles away for all that living in Brea had to do with show business. He didn't know a soul. Cameron enrolled at nearby Fullerton College, a junior college with about twenty thousand students, planning to major in physics. He skipped Calculus 1 and went straight to Calculus 2, because that's how he had always done things. As usual, he got an A in physics, but not in calculus. "So I thought, 'Maybe this isn't for me,' and switched to English," Cameron says. This is sort of like slipping on ballet shoes for the first time, not getting up on pointe by the end of the day, and abandoning dance for accounting. But it made sense to him.

Cameron missed Niagara Falls and was starting to get itchy feet. When his Canadian friend Mike Nestler came to visit, they decided to spend the summer of 1972 hitchhiking together from Los Angeles to Vancouver to Niagara Falls. Cameron painted a gonzo freeway prop for their journey—a giant, photo-real hand with its thumb sticking out, which he wore on his arm. The superthumb worked—they never had to wait long for a ride. In the middle of Saskatchewan, they were picked up by a driver in a four-speed pickup truck. Cameron and Nestler didn't have their driver's licenses yet, but the pickup driver wanted to go to sleep. So at 2:00 a.m., on a rural Canadian highway, a stranger taught Cameron how to drive a stick shift. When the teenager finally got back to Niagara Falls, his beloved hometown was a bit of a disappointment. He realized his memories of the place were better than the reality. The next fall he would throw himself into making a life in California and finally grow to feel at home there.

Cameron was taking fourteen units at Fullerton College by day and working four to six hours a night as a precision tool and die machinist. He continued to tackle his own creative projects on the side, writing science-fiction stories and drawing. He painted an emotional portrait of a Vietnam prisoner of war gripping prison bars that would be selected to appear on POW/MIA billboards across the country. By this point, Cameron was getting tall, about six-two, and had long blond hair and a reddish beard. He was losing his Canadian accent but held on to the sincerity he had brought south with him. He started dating Sharon Williams, a pretty, down-to-earth Orange County girl a year younger than him. It was she who suggested Cameron meet Bill Wisher, another Hollywood hopeful and sci-fi fan just finishing high school in Brea. "Jim was very intense, very bright, full of ideas," Wisher recalls. "He was one of those guys that when you met him, you had the feeling he was going to do things." Soon another Fullerton College student, Randall Frakes, came into their orbit. He shared Cameron's passion for ideas, science fiction, and ancient tales. Frakes, who was seven years older and had been a journalist in the army, started out as a creative mentor. He read a postnuke survivor story Cameron was writing called "Necropolis." "It was so maturely written, the poetic use of the words and yet the sharpness of the mind behind it," Frakes says. "I said, 'You should write movies, science-fiction movies specifically.'" When Cameron had watched *2001*, he had thought about finding a job on the technical side of movie making. It had never occurred to him to be a writer, and he had never read a screenplay before. So Frakes started loading Cameron down with Paddy Chayefsky scripts, *Citizen Kane, Judgment at Nuremberg, Butch Cassidy and the Sundance Kid,* any example of a well-written screenplay to get his friend started.

In his early twenties, Cameron led a bifurcated life. He held a series of blue-collar jobs, working as a janitor, a truck driver, and a machinist and pumping gas in the hottest city in the United States, the tiny Mojave Valley town of Needles, California. He took a job driving the hot lunch truck for the Brea Unified School District and on breaks would curl up in the cab and write. His coworkers in the maintenance yard labeled Cameron "the mystery man."[1] His girlfriend, Sharon Williams, was a waitress at the hamburger chain Bob's Big Boy, an inspiration for Sarah Connor in *The Terminator,* who works at a diner. At night Cameron was painting, writing, and hanging out with Frakes and Wisher, often at the diner, drinking coffee and waiting for Williams to get off work, or at Kentucky Fried Chicken, talking passionately about movies for hours on end. On Saturdays, Cameron would stalk the library at the University of Southern California, photocopying graduate student theses on esoteric filmmaking subjects like optical printing and traveling matte processes. He filled two fat binders with technical papers. For the cost of a couple hundred dollars in photocopying, he essentially put himself through a graduate course in visual effects at the top film school in the country without ever meeting a single professor. Cameron and Williams married and rented a small house. Though passionately in love, they were often at loggerheads about the way his creative life took over both of theirs. Williams, whom Frakes describes as "smart in a streetwise way but not intellectual," held on for the ride. "As Jim became more interested in Hollywood, they drifted apart," Wisher says.

In 1977, *Star Wars* hit theaters, and the unprecedented success of George Lucas's space opera fired up the unofficial Brea film collective to get to work on a blockbuster of their own. "We were just kind of like our own little fan pod," Cameron says. "It didn't occur to us that there was a way to make movies where you started small, where you made independent films and you grew from that. We wanted to go straight to *Star Wars*." To that end, they began to craft a plan, writing a science-fiction treatment they called *Xenogenesis*.

Xenogenesis

Financing for the Brea filmmakers' space epic came about through a friend of a friend's dad, who was an accountant for a consortium of Orange County dentists looking for a place to invest some money. After introductions were made, the group delivered their pitch for a film about the search for a planet on which to start humanity's next life cycle. Cameron brought some of his paintings, and the novice group proposed a thrifty budget based on staged financing. "Jim being Jim, he basically took over," says Frakes. With thoughts of *Star Wars* dollars dancing in their minds, the dentists gave the earnest young men thirty thousand dollars to create a film illustrating a scene from their treatment. If it turned out well, there would be more money to come. "They didn't understand that we were so far out of the orbit of any normal filmmaking environment that a grip on the cheesiest film knew more than we did," Cameron says.

Inexperience didn't stop Cameron and his friends from planning a very ambitious movie. They rented space in an industrial park near the Orange County airport and combed bookstores and libraries for how-to books on old-fashioned special effects like forced perspective and miniatures. They spent hours constructing sets with X-Acto knives and cardboard, sometimes working so late they slept beside their futuristic cityscapes. When they rented the camera, they had to be shown how to thread the film. "We were young and broke and had all the enthusiasm in the world and everything in front of us," Wisher says. The special effects they accomplished are quite remarkable. In one shot, a character, played by Wisher, is running down a causeway being chased by a tank firing laser beams, while explosions blaze at his feet. To accomplish this, they had to rig the explosions and shoot Wisher's performance with them, film a miniature of the tank, and animate the laser beams. They then had to combine the three strips of film into one. The twelve-minute movie that resulted includes some design elements that would resurface in Cameron's later films—the tank is a prototype of the hunter-killer machines in *The Terminator,* and the robotic suit the heroine wears is a predecessor of Sigourney Weaver's power loader in *Aliens.*

The dentists never signed on for the feature-length version of *Xenogenesis,* but the experimental film served as a career stepping-stone for Cameron. It made a persuasive demo reel, showing that he knew how to build models and light and shoot in 35 mm with a special-effects camera. He would take *Xenogenesis* to Roger Corman's New World Pictures, the prolific B-movie house that happened to be staffing up for the next best thing to *Star Wars,* a guerrilla version called *Battle Beyond the Stars.* Cameron was about to land exactly where he needed to be, in a Darwinian environment for would-be filmmakers, a place that rewarded smarts and scrappiness and the kind of alpha behavior he had honed as the oldest boy in a creative and boisterous home.

THE ROGER CORMAN SCHOOL OF FILM

Roger

Cameron is not the first Hollywood director to arrive at filmmaking by way of a science background. Before he sent Douglas Fairbanks swash-buckling through *Robin Hood,* Allan Dwan studied engineering at Notre Dame. Howard Hughes and Frank Capra both attended classes at the science mecca that is now Caltech. Howard Hawks was an en-gineering student at Cornell University, and Alfred Hitchcock studied electrical engineering in London.

It was a Stanford University industrial engineering grad who would give Cameron his first job in the movie business—Roger Corman. "In engineering, one of the big things you do is plan," Corman says. "And it's the same with making movies. When the director is able to say 'cut, print' on the first day of shooting, that picture's half made." Corman should know. He has produced and/or directed some four hundred of them, with an efficiency and thrift that NASA would admire. Corman famously claims to have filmed the 1960 comedy *Little Shop of Horrors* in two and a half days, on a bet. When he went to England to shoot the Edgar Allan Poe adaptation *The Masque of the Red Death* in 1964, he saw some leftover sets from the just-wrapped *Becket* lying around and decided to use those. He is best known for exploitation films like *Candy Stripe Nurses* and *Death Race 2000,* but Corman's oeuvre stretches to the gothic horror of the Poe movies, inventive sci-fi like *X: The Man with the X-Ray Eyes,* and a thoughtful antisegregationist piece that was one of William Shatner's first starring roles, *The Intruder.* The prolific director-producer also distributed foreign art-house movies in the United States, like Fellini's *Amarcord* and Akira Kurosawa's *Dersu Uzala.* He even had the temerity to show an Ingmar Bergman movie at drive-ins, to the Swedish tragedian's delight.

But the most successful product of Corman's movie-making factory has been people. His low-budget productions have launched the careers of Francis Ford Coppola, Martin Scorsese, Ron Howard, Jack Nicholson, Peter Bogdanovich, Jonathan Demme, and many others in Hollywood. Corman recruited the young and eager—he was usually the only person working at his company over age thirty. "I was giving them training and an opportunity to make a picture that nobody else would give them," he says. "In return they were getting less money than someone with more experience." The hours were long and the working conditions far from glamorous—if an office had a leaky roof, its inhabitant was encouraged to look forward to the end of L.A.'s brief rainy season. But those were trade-offs most were happy to make for a chance to work at a company where, with enough pluck and talent, you could go from carrying light stands to directing your first picture in less time than it took to graduate from film school.

By the time Cameron came knocking on the door of Corman's New World Pictures in 1979, the independent film company was beginning to feel some pressure. Thanks to the success of *Jaws* in 1975 and *Star Wars* in 1977, Hollywood studios had suddenly discovered genre pictures, Corman's mainstay, and were making them with bigger budgets and higher production values. "They started making the exact type of film I had been making," Corman says. "They were taking away our bread and butter." In retaliation, Corman was about to embark on his most expensive movie to date, a $2 million nod to *Star Wars* called *Battle Beyond the Stars.* The story of space mercenaries trying to save a peaceful planet from a tyrant named Sador, *Battle Beyond the Stars* was a sci-fi version of Kurosawa's *Seven Samurai,* which had already been given a Western reenvisioning in *The Magnificent Seven.* Corman pulled out his big guns for the film. John Sayles, who would later write and direct the Oscar-nominated screenplays for *Lone Star* and *Passion Fish,* wrote the script, while the animator Jimmy Murakami directed. The cast included some name actors whose careers had crested: Richard Thomas, John-Boy from *The Waltons,* played the hero. George Peppard, moving from the *Breakfast at Tiffany's* to the *A-Team* stage of his career, was a space cowboy, and Robert Vaughn, the smooth spy from the 1960s TV show *The Man from U.N.C.L.E.,* essentially reprised his gunslinger role in *The Magnificent Seven.* A rookie film composer named James Horner wrote the score—he would go on to work with Cameron on *Aliens, Titanic,* and *Avatar.* After bids came in for the film's special effects that totaled more than the sum of his entire production budget, Corman decided to create his own effects department and hired a TV effects supervisor named Chuck Comisky to run it. It was Comisky for whom Cameron screened his *Xenogenesis* footage. He was hired on the spot as a model builder.

A Spaceship with Tits

New World's model shop was in a dusty former lumberyard in Venice, California, a few miles from Corman's office in Brentwood. The producer dispatched his twenty-four-year-old assistant, Gale Anne Hurd, to check on the progress of the model builders and the sets. A Phi Beta Kappa graduate of Stanford with a double major in economics and communications, Hurd was a classic Corman hire—bright, hardworking, and young. She was given far more responsibility than a studio executive's assistant would have—making offers to agents, scouting locations, preparing marketing materials, and keeping Corman up on the progress of his technical staff. A pretty, petite brunette, Hurd walked into the model shop, which was full of spaceships and builders hard at work. "This very tall blond guy came up to me and said, 'Hi, can I help you?'" She explained that she was there to make a report for Corman, and the tall blond guy gave her a tour. He showed her the designs for the spaceships, the various stages they were at, the time lines for finishing them. "I said, 'Wow, that's really impressive. You must be the head of the model shop.' He said, 'Oh, no, no, no, I'm just a model builder.'" Cameron had only been at Corman's for a matter of days, but he was already taking charge. He seems constitutionally incapable of doing otherwise. "He had a very commanding presence," Hurd says. "Even if his position was not running the model shop, he clearly seemed to be running the model shop."

When Cameron was hired, all of the spaceships for *Battle Beyond the Stars* had already been designed, except for one. The hero ship, Richard Thomas's vessel, was supposed to be run by a female robot named Nell. Corman held a design bake-off for the spaceship, soliciting ideas from his staff. Cameron had always won the art contests back in Niagara Falls, and, in his own way, he had been preparing for this moment for years. His *Star Trek* comic books, his *2001* Super 8 knock-offs, the concept art for *Xenogenesis*—it was all about to come in very handy. He threw himself into the design, deciding the ship should have a female personality to match the robot that was running it. He drew a warrior ship that was graceful and streamlined and resembled a twisted, almost cubist female torso. It had two big, round engine pods in the front. Corman made his way around the room looking at the proposed designs. The others were all geometric—rectangles and triangles. When he got to Cameron's design, Corman stopped. "He said, 'Now what's this?'" Cameron recalls. "I said, 'It's a spaceship with tits.' He said, 'I like this.'" Clearly Cameron knew his audience. Corman's films were as famous for baring breasts as they were for making money. "He said, 'This is the design. You are now in charge of this ship.'" All of a sudden, Cameron was in charge of something. "Intuitively, Jim understood that each spaceship had to have a personality of its own," Corman says. "He expressed it in his design, clearly and simply."

The young model maker was emboldened by his new responsibility. The next time Corman came through the shop, Cameron stopped him. "I said, 'You know, Roger, I've been studying the production and there's a fatal flaw.'" He explained to Corman that the filmmakers had no way of putting the actors in their movie inside the model environments in a realistic way. But there was a way to do it, Cameron said: front projection. It was what Stanley Kubrick had done on *2001: A Space Odyssey.* "And I know exactly how to do it," Cameron told him. He didn't tell Corman he hadn't actually done any front projection before. "I didn't lie, I just didn't tell the whole truth," he says. Cameron was made head of the New World Pictures' new Front Screen Projection Department. He hired a staff of one, his friend Randall Frakes. "I was like the guy in *Flight of the Phoenix* who knows exactly how to fix the plane. But they find out later he's only ever built model airplanes. I had a tremendous amount of theory and zero practical experience."

Just over a month before principal photography on *Battle Beyond the Stars* was to start, Corman made Hurd assistant production manager. She noticed that the art director, who had come highly recommended by Universal Studios, was moving awfully slowly. None of the sets had been designed. The art director was used to having a draftsperson design the sets for him, but on a Corman film, if you were the art director, you were the draftsperson. Hurd recalls, "I said to Roger, 'I'm really concerned. I haven't seen any blueprints. There are no hammers pounding nails.' He said, 'Why don't you go find someone who can pull it all together?'" Looking for advice, Hurd sought out someone who actually seemed to know what he was doing: Cameron. "Who do you think can do this?" she asked him. "Interiors need to match exteriors." Cameron immediately drew what the interiors would look like and gave Hurd the drawings to show Corman.

Cameron was so eager and the production so consuming that he had started sleeping at the model shop. Instead of going home at night, he pulled a prop gurney out into the hallway, away from the smell of the paint and Bondo, and grabbed a few hours of sleep there. That's where he was when Corman's new assistant, Mary Anne Fisher, woke him up at 3:00 a.m. Corman had just fired the art director, she told him. Did Cameron want to take his place? He had never been an art director and had no idea what was involved in the job. "Sure," Cameron said, and rolled over and went back to sleep. In a matter of weeks, he had jumped from a model builder on a film to its art director. Even by the accelerated career-advancement standards of New World Pictures, it was a breakneck promotion.

The Culling Process

The day after his prop-gurney recruitment session, Cameron entered into one of his first negotiations. "OK, let's talk about my salary," he said to Fisher. At the time, he was making $200 a week. Fisher offered him $300. "What did the other guy get?" Cameron wanted to know. $750, but he was very experienced. "I said, 'Yeah, but he fucked up. The show is in dire crisis. You fired him. You want me to do the same job. I want the same money.'" He nearly quadrupled his salary. There's a reason Cameron has spent much of his career without an agent.

Next he reported to the production manager's office. "He said, 'OK, here's your petty cash voucher. And here's your coke and here's your black beauties,'" Cameron says. It was January 1980. "I said, 'What's this for?' He said, 'Well, this is for the crew. It's part of the payment system.'" Cameron took the two bottles. He had never done either drug before, so he took a crew member aside and asked what he was supposed to do. "You just chop a little line, do it up with a spoon, and hand it to somebody," the crew member told Cameron. "You ask 'em, 'Do you need something?'" Cameron felt strange about his new responsibility. "Now I'm the production drug dealer all of a sudden? Do I get to do any art direction?" Drugs are one of the Hollywood minefields Cameron has managed to avoid. "Not with my personality," he says. "Me on drugs is not a good thing. Not a happy thing." His adrenal glands seem to secrete speed anyway. While working on *Battle Beyond the Stars,* he pulled an eighty-five-hour stretch with one hour of sleep, just drinking coffee.

Nearly thirty years later, Corman talks glowingly of Cameron's work on the space epic, of how inventively the young man used egg cartons and metallic paint to create believable spaceship interiors in hours. Time and success may have hazed Corman's memories. He actually fired Cameron twice. The shooting schedule on *Battle Beyond the Stars* was twenty-six days. One morning, after Cameron and his crew of three had been working all night building, dressing, and painting an interior, they were still finishing when the camera crew arrived. "God forbid it took us more than eight hours to build a set," Cameron says. "Roger comes in and says, 'Jim, this is just a shitty little set. It's just a shitty little set, and it's not done, and it's costing me production time. You're fired.'" Cameron stalked off, furious, and Fisher came running after him. "She said, 'Come back! Roger just does that.'"

Cameron learned that if Corman saw people painting and taping when a set was supposed to be done, the art director was toast. But if there was garbage all over the floor and the set was half painted, as long as the crew was gone, Corman didn't care. So Cameron posted a lookout with a walkie-talkie and held a "Roger drill." When Corman's Lotus sports car came down the street, the lookout was to notify Cameron, who would blow a whistle twice, and everyone was to leave the set, no matter what they were doing, and go get a cup of coffee. The next morning Cameron was wearing a gas mask, spraying copper-colored automotive lacquer, the only thing that would dry fast enough, when he got the walkie call that the Lotus had landed. He tore off his mask and blew the whistle, and his crew dropped their tools and scattered. Paint fumes still hung in the air when Corman walked in and looked around. "Very good," he said, and left. The crew came back in and finished the set.

Cameron's take-no-prisoners working style abraded some of his colleagues. The construction supervisor took visible joy in striking the art director's sets with a skip loader. And the quiet guys in the model shop and special-effects departments wondered at this skinny know-it-all who, after a month, had completely coopted their operation. "I ran roughshod over the place," Cameron confesses. "It's a culling process. Some people don't want to deal with it, the fact that so much relies on personality and not logic. That it's hype. That it's the pitch. I knew you had to sell and you had to make your move." Some of the Corman crew would go on to work for Cameron. Dennis and Robert Skotak, two brothers toiling in the relative peace of the special-effects and model departments when Cameron arrived, would receive Oscars for their work on *Aliens* and *The Abyss.* Thirty years after he screened *Xenogenesis* and gave Cameron his first paying job in Hollywood, Comisky was working on the visual effects for *Avatar.*

"There are two components to any filmmaker," Cameron says. "How you picture the movie in advance and how you make it happen in the real world." Cameron is exceptional both at dreaming up the vision and rallying people around it, assuaging their fears, and convincing them they're capable of seemingly impossible tasks. Some of that leadership ability is innate—the boy who had all the neighborhood kids pulling his junkyard airplane. But Cameron's already healthy sense of authority was boosted by the exuberant atmosphere of Corman's company. "There wasn't time for doubt," Cameron says. "We didn't know the twenty-seven reasons why we shouldn't be able to do exactly what we were in the process of doing. There was this blissful ignorance about the process of how films are really made that allowed us to do some pretty darn extraordinary stuff given the time and budget restraints. You come out of it with this feeling like you can do anything."

"Bring Me the Maggots"

After *Battle Beyond the Stars,* Cameron shuffled among different projects that made use of his design skills. *Halloween* director John Carpenter hired him to help create the grim future cityscapes in *Escape from New York,* a dystopian vision starring Kurt Russell in which the entire island of Manhattan has been turned into a maximum-security prison. It was a project for which Cameron was perfectly cast artistically—this was, after all, a guy who had been daydreaming about Armageddon since the fifth grade. Cameron took a plate of glass mounted with a photo collage of Central Park West buildings to the weed-strewn field in the San Fernando Valley where Carpenter was shooting, fine-tuned the Manhattan skyline with paint, and placed the glass in front of the camera, transforming the field into an overgrown Central Park.

His second movie for Corman was *Galaxy of Terror,* the producer's paean to Ridley Scott's *Alien,* the grittily realistic sci-fi/horror hybrid that Cameron adored and would five years later direct the sequel to, having essentially done a dry run of it for New World. In Corman's film, a spaceship crew meets with terrors created by their own imaginations. The cast includes Erin Moran (Joanie Cunningham from *Happy Days*), soon-to-be Freddy Krueger Robert Englund, and then blaxploitation film regular Sid Haig, who would become a favorite of director Rob Zombie more than twenty years later. Cameron was the production designer, charged with creating evocative biomechanoid sets like the ones Swiss artist H. R. Giger had designed for Scott, but on a Corman budget. He was also an active member of the visual-effects team on the picture. By the end of the movie, he would have finagled himself his first directing job.

Bill Paxton, a Texan transplant trying to launch an acting career, tagged along with a friend who was working on Cameron's night crew at the lumberyard in Venice. Paxton was looking for graveyard shift work, to keep his days free for auditions, and had done some set dressing on another Corman film. Cameron was looking for warm bodies to finish his sets on time. "Jim said, 'Can you start right now?'" Paxton recalls. "'Go paint that wall over there.' Typical Jim. Bang bang." They built spaceship interiors from dishwasher racks, Styrofoam, a Winnebago mold. "I would find drawings on the floor that were these amazing renderings," Paxton recalls. "These were just sketches Jim discarded. I hoarded away a couple of those." Along with the sets, they started to build a friendship. Paxton had directed a funny, bizarre short film called *Fish Heads,* essentially a music video for a novelty song by a band called Barnes and Barnes, about all the things fish heads can and cannot do (mostly what they cannot do, like wear sweaters, play drums, and drink cappuccino in Italian restaurants with Oriental women). Paxton invited Cameron to a screening of the short at a punk-rock club in the San Fernando Valley. *Fish Heads,* which would ultimately sell to *Saturday Night Live* and achieve early-eighties cult status, endeared Paxton to Cameron, who realized the affable Texan had ambitions beyond painting spaceships. Three years later, when Cameron needed a punk rocker to get beaten up by Arnold Schwarzenegger in *The Terminator,* he thought of Paxton. Over the years, the actor would appear in larger and more significant roles in *Aliens, True Lies, Titanic,* and *Ghosts of the Abyss* and become a diving buddy and confidant.

When Cameron's *Galaxy of Terror* sets were finished and the crew arrived to shoot them, he wasn't impressed. "They had no idea what they were doing," Cameron says. "I'm watching them shooting the sets and just blowing it, not getting the shots, not getting the performances." It was a lightbulb moment for Cameron. He had never thought of himself as a director. "I didn't think I had that much to offer as a filmmaker. Design, yes, absolutely, I knew that part of it. But I'm watching these guys just fail and I'm thinking, 'I can do that.'" He cornered Corman in the hall. "I think I should be the second unit director," he said. "I'll work at night and get inserts." Again Cameron made up a job for himself. And again Corman encouraged the enthusiastic young man. "He said, 'That's a good idea. Start tomorrow. Put your group together.'" Corman took ideas from any level. There was no grip too lowly to suggest a script change. It was one of the producer's trademarks. Cameron took the opportunity to propose a new scene that would involve Sid Haig's character cutting off his own arm with a crystal, and maggots swarming it. Corman liked it. "So my first task was to shoot the bullshit scene I had just made up," Cameron says. "An insert shot of an arm lying on the ground with maggots crawling."

The next day, when it came time to film his big scene, Cameron was completely focused. "Bring me the arm! OK, bring me the maggots!" For the maggots, he was using a box of mealworms from a pet-food store, where they're sold as reptile food. Mealworms are fine little larval sources of protein, but they're apparently a lot more sedentary than maggots. Cameron sprinkled the mealworms on the prop arm, and they sat there. Not even a wriggle. For the scene to work, he needed some serious writhing. "I wasn't about to go out to the town dump and find some cow carcass and get real maggots, plus I had to have the shot by ten," he says. "So I said, 'Let's see what happens if we juice these things.'" He got his hands on some methylcellulose, a viscous solution readily available on the set since it was a key ingredient in alien slime. He poured it over the arm and added the mealworms. Then he took a 110-volt cord, stripped it, split it, laid two copper ends in the methylcellulose, ran the cable behind the set, and buried it. He set up the camera and ran a test. A crewman behind the set plugged in the cord, the voltage zipped through it, and the mealworms came alive. It worked beautifully. They unplugged the cord, not wanting to kill their worm cast, and reset for the real thing. Just then, two visitors arrived on the set. They were producers working on a sequel to one of Corman's cult hits, *Piranha*. Someone had recommended Cameron as their special-effects supervisor, so they had stopped by to meet him. As they walked in, Cameron was rolling the camera. He called action, the man hidden behind the set plugged in the cord, and, right on cue, the worms began delivering their Marlon Brando–caliber writhing. Cameron panned the camera, got his shot, and called cut, and the worms stopped. The visitors were duly impressed. They hadn't seen the electrical cord or the crewman hidden behind the set. What they saw was a man who could direct maggots. Just imagine what he could do with actors.

Bad Story, Bad Piranha

Ovidio Assonitis, one of the two producers who swept through the miraculous maggot set, needed a director—and fast—for his $500,000 horror sequel, *Piranha II: The Spawning.* Assonitis's prior credits included a 1977 flesh-eating-octopus movie called *Tentacles* and a 1980 *The Omen* knockoff called *The Visitor.* Twice before, Assonitis had hired first-timers in order to secure a deal from a small label at Warner Bros. that allowed him to make cheap films as long as he used an American director. The feeling at the studio was that the Italian producer's florid tastes needed to be mediated by someone with more native sensibilities. But a few days into both of those productions, Assonitis had declared the directors incompetent as a pretense for taking over the movies himself. Now he was looking for another sacrificial director. This blond kid who got maggots to writhe on cue looked American (though he was really Canadian) and smart enough not to ruin the movie during the few days he would be in charge. Cameron was sitting in the crosshairs of a producer who had no real intention of letting him direct. But he didn't know that.

What he did know from the beginning was that *Piranha II* was not going to be *Citizen Kane.* Assonitis took Cameron out to lunch at Zucky's, a divey deli in Santa Monica, to offer him the job. He would be paid ten thousand dollars, five thousand now and five thousand when he finished. "It was the thing you did at Corman," Cameron says. "If a directing gig opened up, you just took it. It didn't matter if it was *Coed Nurse Zombies.* You didn't read the script. The simple fact that Roger was gonna spend money on it was all you needed to know. If there was a slot you took it. And then you learned how to direct." Cameron figured that whatever the movie was, he could make it better. By August 1981, he was in Assonitis's office in Rome immersed in preproduction, working on his storyboards, trying to fashion some decent-looking rubber fish, and rewriting the script. In *Piranha II,* a navy ship containing experimental piranha eggs has sunk, unleashing flying carnivorous fish on helpless beachgoers. "I had a bad story and bad piranha," Cameron says. "But I was going through all the steps."

Just about the only bright spot in the movie for Cameron was a couple of cast members, especially a grizzled New York actor named Lance Henriksen playing the besieged resort community's sheriff. Henriksen immediately struck Cameron as cool. The son of a waitress and a Norwegian seaman nicknamed Icewater for his cold personality, Henriksen had dropped out of school at age twelve and spent his adolescence riding freight trains across the country. He was a teenager in jail in Tucson for vagrancy when he got his first role, as an extra in a Lee Marvin TV movie being filmed at the prison. By the time Cameron met him, Henriksen had established a steady career as a character actor in movies like *Close Encounters of the Third Kind* and *Damien: Omen II.* Utterly devoid of pretension and always up for adventure, Henriksen would become a creative ally of Cameron's on the troubled *Piranha II* set, something of a muse for one of the director's iconic characters, and a regular weekend shooting buddy.

A week before the start of production, Cameron reported to the location in Jamaica, where Assonitis's team had supposedly been prepping the shoot. Cameron sat down to hold his first meeting and learned that the production manager had yet to secure a single location or set for the film. As chaotic as Corman's company seemed, his productions were always well organized. You can't make movies on a shoestring budget any other way. So Cameron was appalled. He ripped open the petty-cash drawer, grabbed all the money and a Polaroid camera, and stormed out. On the sidewalk, Cameron flagged down the first person he saw, a young Jamaican guy with a battered white car, and offered him some cash to drive him around for a day. They visited a police station, a school, a hotel, with Cameron cutting cash deals and hand-writing contracts for all the locations.

One of the spots they scouted was a morgue in St. Ann's Bay. It had an autopsy table and a cooler with two doors. Cameron visualized just how he would stream the light through the windows. "Yeah, this will work great," he thought, and made another deal. On the day of the morgue scene, Cameron showed up early with his fake piranha-chewed corpse. He saw a huge cockroach skittering across the floor that he wanted to catch and use in a shot. He was ready to go. Suddenly, Cameron realized he hadn't entirely thought through the details of the morgue location. "I guess I thought they would take the bodies and put them someplace else," he recalls. Instead, in the space where Cameron planned to film his fake corpse, was a real dead man, with another dead man stacked on top of him, and a little girl who had been hit by a car stacked on top of them. The bottom body had been autopsied, so there were gallons of blood lying in a tray beside it.

Cameron's cast had not yet arrived. He asked the morgue staff if he could move the bodies to the side to give him a place to shoot, and then had his art director cut a piece of plywood for a divider. He set up his fake body, and the cast and the rest of the crew trickled in. Steve Marachuk, who played resort employee Tricia O'Neil's biochemist boy-friend, got curious about what was behind the plywood. "Steve says, 'Hey, there's real bodies in here! I can use it for the scene.'" Cameron tried to dissuade his leading man from the Method approach, to no avail. Marachuk looked, stood silently for a moment, and excused him-self. He wouldn't return to the set for half an hour. When Cameron fi-nally got rolling, two dreadlocked hearse drivers walked in. They needed the bottom dead guy, who had been autopsied, so they would have to move the other dead guy and the little girl. "Can you come back when we break for lunch?" Cameron asked them. They did, but as they were removing the bottom corpse, one of the hearse drivers dropped his end and the overflowing blood tray splashed to the floor. "They're laughing, they get the guy back on the thing, push his guts back in, and go," Cameron says. Meanwhile, the first-time director was standing in a Jamaican morgue with gallons of real blood covering the floor and his cast and crew outside eating lunch. He stepped out to address them—"Take your time, guys! Have some more salad!"—grabbed a mop, a bucket, and some disinfectant, and started cleaning up.

While Cameron was directing *Piranha II,* he wasn't allowed to see his dailies, the raw, unedited footage of his shots. On his fifth day at work, Cameron learned from one of Assonitis's assistants that he was fired. "He says, 'Ovidio has viewed the dailies and he doesn't believe they'll cut together,'" Cameron recalls. Like the two directors before him, Cameron was out. "It bothered me that they said my scenes weren't any good. That bothered me more than getting fired, because it spoke to the whole issue of whether I really could be a director or not. I thought I'd covered them kind of well." He told Assonitis's representative that he didn't want his name on the film. Of course, Assonitis needed it for the Warner Bros. deal, and he knew Cameron was broke. "I literally didn't have the money to hire a lawyer to get my name taken off the movie," Cameron says. For the first time in his rocketing filmmaking career, Cameron was confronted with some self-doubt. Maybe he really wasn't that good. Maybe he should just stick to drawing spaceships, or even go back to trucking. Angry and disappointed, he left the *Piranha II* set and went home.

What felt like a career ending, however, was actually one beginning. The torment Cameron went through over his failed first directing effort would lead him exactly where he needed to be, into the dark recesses of his mind, for that's where he found *The Terminator.* But first he would have to confront the man who had fired him.

KICKING IN THE DOOR

The Nightmare

One long, miserable night alone in a Rome hotel room in March 1982, Cameron collapsed onto his bed with a raging fever and thought he might be dying. This was to be a life-altering night for the filmmaker, but not in the way he feared.

Cameron had come to Italy to see a rough cut of *Piranha II: The Spawning*. He was twenty-seven, broke, and depressed. Cameron wanted to know if Ovidio Assonitis was right, and if maybe he should abandon his Hollywood aspirations. "I felt I shouldn't go on with a directing career if I was deluding myself and my shot design and scene architecture didn't work," Cameron says. Not sure how exactly he would get home to California, Cameron had bought a one-way plane ticket to Rome, where Assonitis was in postproduction on the film.

When Cameron arrived in Assonitis's office in Rome, he must have been an intimidating presence, because the producer spent the meeting hunched behind his desk gripping a sharp letter opener. Eventually, Assonitis relaxed and allowed his visitor to see a rough assembly of the film. As Cameron had suspected, his scenes cut together just fine. Assonitis had fired Cameron so he could sit in the director's chair himself—it wasn't a coincidence that all the scenes of topless women bouncing on the decks of yachts had been shot in the last half of the schedule, and that Assonitis had cast those parts himself without Cameron's knowledge, using *Penthouse* centerfolds.

Horrified that his name would be attached to such shlock—even by B movie standards—Cameron decided to do some damage control. The next night he slipped the lock of the editing room with a credit card, crept in, and found himself surrounded by film cans labeled in Italian. Cameron spotted a can marked *fine*—at least he knew what that meant—and decided to recut the film himself, starting from the end. Every night for weeks, Cameron snuck back in and reedited the footage into something that, although he still considered it trash, at least was *his* trash.

Cameron had only collected half of his ten-thousand-dollar fee for *Piranha II,* and he had already spent that money. While in Rome, he couldn't afford food, so he snatched scraps from room-service trays at his *pensione.* Every morning a plate with two hard rolls was placed next to the door of each room. Cameron would take one roll from each plate and live on that for a few days. Eventually, his skinny, exhausted body broke down and succumbed to fever, and that's when Cameron had his nightmare epiphany. He dreamed of a chrome torso emerging, phoenixlike, from an explosion and dragging itself across the floor with kitchen knives. Cameron awoke and immediately started sketching the deathly figure on hotel stationery as ideas for a story line surrounding the image flooded his mind. A few days later, as he wandered the streets in the wind and rain, Cameron found a lire note worth about twenty dollars on the sidewalk. He bought himself an espresso and believed his fortunes were turning around. Indeed they were. Cameron's fever dream was a creative jolt that would become his first great movie idea.

Assonitis recut *Piranha II* his way, but Warner Bros. had tired of the producer by then and refused to accept the movie. Two years after it was completed, the flying-piranha sequel was released by a tiny company that was a front for a porn distributor. The version you can rent or buy on DVD today is Assonitis's, and although Cameron's name is on the movie, he doesn't consider it part of his filmography.

The Blood Oath

The Terminator introduces many of the themes and motifs that would come to define Cameron's career: a bleak future setting, an exploration of humanity's relationship to technology, a love story with a potent heroine and a stoic hero, and, oh yes, lots of cool explosions. Movie fans and film theorists have found in it everything from a retelling of the Christ myth to a reinvention of film noir. For Cameron it was simply a chance to tell a story of his very own.

Still youthfully enthusiastic despite the *Piranha II* debacle, and energized by his new story idea, Cameron returned to California with a loan and a beater car borrowed from his father. He camped out on Randall Frakes's floor in Pomona, California, in a squat, concrete house where he wrote the treatment for *The Terminator.* Even then, Cameron found writing a lonely, utterly unforgiving process. "Every thought, every gesture, is judged directly," he says. "And it's very hard to get started, and to stay focused." He prefers the dynamic aspect of making films, laboring on a set with actors and cameras. When he's writing, Cameron tends to bunker himself, working mainly at night and withdrawing from the outside world. He used to tell friends he'd like to buy the most uncomfortable chair he could find for writing, so he would finish as fast as possible just to get out of it. When it came time to turn *The Terminator* treatment into a script, Cameron enlisted his other friend from Orange County, Bill Wisher, as a collaborator and sounding board. Because he and Wisher had spent years talking about their favorite science-fiction books and movies together, they had a similar vocabulary and approach to storytelling. Cameron divided up his treatment—he gave Wisher, who was living fifty miles away in Brea, California, far from the Hollywood scene, the early Sarah Connor and police-department pieces. Cameron wrote everything else, including the future war and action sequences. Since this was before e-mail and home fax machines, every few days the two friends would compare notes on their high-tech thriller using a method just one step above two cans connected by string. Cameron called Wisher on the phone with a tape recorder on his end and had his friend read the new scenes into the receiver. Then he'd transcribe them.

The director shared his idea—a cyborg hitman from the future try-ing to change past events—with his agent, whom he'd landed thanks to the *Piranha II* job and some spec scripts submitted as writing sam-ples. The agent hated *The Terminator* and told Cameron it was a lousy idea, to forget it and start work on something else. So Cameron, who had no money and no prospects, fired his agent. In an industry where an agent is virtually the only path to paid work for an unknown writer, this was either recklessness or extraordinary self-confidence—something you can say about an awful lot of decisions Cameron has made in his career.

He did find someone else who shared his passion for the project, however: Gale Anne Hurd, Roger Corman's former assistant, who had plucked the blond-haired model builder from obscurity in New World Pictures' art department. Hurd and Cameron had worked well together in the low-budget pressure cooker at New World, and they decided to present themselves to potential financiers as a directing and producing team. The story of Cameron and Hurd's first contract is the sort that makes Hollywood deal brokers shudder. Cameron sold Hurd the rights to *The Terminator* for one dollar in return for a blood oath that she would produce the film only if he directed it, or it wouldn't get made. "I probably didn't really need to do this," Cameron says, "but I was naive and thought in expansive, theatrical terms." Also, having fired his agent, he didn't have any formal representation at the time. In any case, the first thing the financiers did was try to edge Cameron out, but Hurd said no. The blood oath worked. "And I have a career as a result," Cameron says. "So I've never really regretted that decision, although it was costly financially." (Cameron hasn't made any money off the two Terminator movies that followed his own, nor the accompanying video games, action figures, or theme-park ride.) "I chalked it up to the cost of a Hollywood education," he says. Cameron's partnership with Hurd was to become one of the most vital in his career, one that would evolve into a romance by the time they were in postproduction on *The Terminator* and ultimately a marriage, and would remain, he says, "pitch perfect" on the two strenuous shoots that followed, *Aliens* and *The Abyss*. However, Cameron was always disappointed that Hurd never corrected the record regarding her contribution to the writing on *The Terminator*. She had suggested edits on the script, which is part of the role of a producer, and took a "with" screenwriting credit to help their team-based sales pitch. "People more or less assumed that she was responsible for the strong female character," Cameron says. "Not the case. She did no actual writing at all."

When Hurd and Cameron were trying to raise the money for *The Terminator* in 1982, it was a terrible economy in which to be chasing a movie deal—unemployment topped 10 percent and interest rates hovered at 17 percent. But the duo had the advantage of selling a sci-fi script, a hot genre in the wake of the first two Star Wars films. And they had some other Roger Corman alumni pulling for them at Orion Pictures—Orion would distribute the film, it said, if Cameron and Hurd could get the production financed elsewhere. Eventually, *The Terminator* landed on the desk of John Daly at Hemdale Pictures. Hemdale picked up low-budget movies passed on by the major studios, like the breezy Farrah Fawcett vehicle *Sunburn* and Tony Danza's contribution to the primate comedy genre, *Going Ape!* "Hemdale didn't expect to make a movie that was a hit, or even a movie that was any good," says Hurd. "They just wanted to take their fee, and that's it." When Daly read the *Terminator* script, he was intrigued, not least because this script had already cleared the toughest hurdle, interesting a distributor.

Cameron wanted his pitch meeting with Daly to close the deal. So the director asked his friend from *Piranha II,* actor Lance Henriksen, to show up to the meeting early, decked out as the Terminator. Henriksen burst into the staid Hemdale offices with all the fearsome cyborgian drama Cameron had requested, literally kicking in the door. He was wearing a ripped T-shirt, a leather jacket, and knee-high boots and had gold foil from a pack of Vantage cigarettes smoothed on his teeth and special-effects cuts painted on his face. Henriksen's performance was convincing enough for Hemdale's poor receptionist, who screamed and jumped out of her chair. The actor sat waiting for fifteen minutes, saying nothing, simply staring icily. By the time Cameron arrived, entering the office in a more traditional fashion, the Hemdale staff were delighted to see him, if only to be freed from Henriksen's creepy gaze. Cameron delivered an enthusiastic pitch, aided by detailed sketches he had made of sequences from his screenplay. Daly was impressed by the young director's passion and persuaded by the sketches that Cameron had a clear, well-thought-out vision for the film. In late 1982, he agreed to back *The Terminator,* with help from Orion and HBO for the $6 million budget. Cameron was ecstatic and couldn't wait to start production. What he didn't know was that it would be nearly eighteen months before he got to step behind a camera.

Picking a Fight with Mr. Universe

One of Cameron's first tasks was to cast the actor who would play Kyle Reese, the heroic warrior from the future who visits the present to save humanity. Reese had to be believably butch enough to take on the Terminator but vulnerable enough to pull off an apocalypse-straddling crush on Sarah Connor. Orion wanted a star who was rising in the United States but also had a huge foreign appeal. The studio's cofounder, Mike Medavoy, had just met Arnold Schwarzenegger at a party and sent the bodybuilder's agent the script, with the lead role in mind. Schwarzenegger's representatives, who felt they were grooming an action hero, not a villain, thought "lead" meant Reese. A five-time Mr. Universe and seven-time Mr. Olympia, Schwarzenegger had already been in Hollywood for over a decade. He had played Hercules with a dubbed American accent in the often unintentionally hilarious *Hercules in New York* (credited as "Arnold Strong") and a conveniently speechless hitman in Robert Altman's *The Long Goodbye*. But most of the town had first glimpsed Schwarzenegger's glistening pecs and Teutonic charisma in George Butler's intelligent 1977 docudrama about the bodybuilding subculture, *Pumping Iron*. In one memorable scene, the future California governor likens the pump he gets from working out to the satisfaction of "having sex viz a woman and coming." It was this nuanced performance that earned Schwarzenegger some parts where he actually got to open his mouth, including the role of Conan in John Milius's *Conan the Barbarian* in 1982. The actor was now at a crucial moment in his career. Would he, like most bodybuilding stars, end up relegated to toga movies until he was too old to look good in a skirt? Or would he break out and get roles limited not by the width of his fifty-seven-inch chest but by the breadth of his charm? Cameron was skeptical—if this Austrian oak played Reese, he figured someone even bigger would have to play the Terminator. For that part, the studio had suggested another athlete-turned-actor: O. J. Simpson. In 1983, Cameron didn't see O.J. as a believable killing machine. He's a futurist, not an oracle.

Purely as a courtesy to the studio, Cameron agreed to take a lunch meeting with Schwarzenegger. As he walked out of his apartment that day, the director devised a plan to get this absurd casting idea dismissed. At lunch, he would pick a fight with Mr. Universe, and then head back to Hemdale and declare Schwarzenegger an asshole. The meal didn't go exactly as planned, however. Schwarzenegger was so entertaining and excited about the script that Cameron instantly forgot his hostile agenda. And while he was supposed to be lobbying for the role of Reese, Schwarzenegger kept talking about how the villain should be played. "I spoke much more enthusiastically about the Terminator character, about how he has to handle weapons, to be always like a machine," Schwarzenegger recalls. As the bodybuilder talked, Cameron noticed the sharp, symmetrical angles of his cheekbones and jawline and began sketching Schwarzenegger's face on a notepad at the table. He wanted to ask the gregarious Austrian to just stop talking for a second and be really still, but he was petrified. This guy even had muscles in his forehead. This guy, Cameron thought, would make a great Terminator.

Instead of clashing, Schwarzenegger and Cameron had bonded. These two Hollywood immigrants had a lot in common. Both men were abnormally capable—one with prodigious physical gifts, the other with intellectual ones. Though they had come to the United States from other countries, they shared a lot of qualities Americans often claim for themselves: self-reliance, creativity, energy, and an indefinable hunger. In Schwarzenegger, Cameron had met a man as preposterously confident as he was—how else do you walk out onstage in a bathing suit to the opening theme from *2001: A Space Odyssey*? And in a town full of girlie men, here were two men's men. They both liked motorcycles and guns and raising hell. Instead of a smackdown, this lunch had turned into an alpha male lovefest, one that would lead to a decades-long friendship. The awkward moment came with the check. Cameron had no money in his wallet, and the Hemdale executive who accompanied them was having trouble with his credit card, so Schwarzenegger paid. After the meeting, Cameron, still sick from Schwarzenegger's cigar smoke, went back to John Daly with bad news and good news. "Forget it," he said of Schwarzenegger playing Reese. "It's not going to work. But boy, he'd make a hell of a Terminator." The deal was closed the next day, when Schwarzenegger overrode his agent.

While *The Terminator* would become the movie that catapulted him from simple strongman into screen icon, Schwarzenegger didn't seem too optimistic about Cameron's passion project before shooting commenced, at least as described by a journalist who visited him on the *Conan* set in 1982: "As we sat there talking, he picked up the Conan sword, which weighed a ton, and went through all the movements he'd practiced. Then he picked up a pair of shoes and I said, 'What are those for?' And he said, 'Oh some shit movie I'm doing, take a couple of weeks.'"[1] The shit movie was *The Terminator.* Schwarzenegger prepared diligently for the role nonetheless. He spent three months training with weapons of all sorts—submachine guns, rifles, shotguns, pistols, revolvers, grenades—not just to know how to use them but to be completely comfortable around them. The truth is, casting Schwarzenegger as the Terminator shouldn't have worked. The character is supposed to be part of an infiltration unit, a supersoldier that insinuates itself into the human resistance movement fighting the machines in 2029. Cameron's first thought for the role was the man he had used to sell the film to Daly—Henriksen, with his lean build and world-worn face. What could a man who looked like Schwarzenegger infiltrate—a Greco-Roman wrestling team? "It made no sense whatsoever," Cameron says. "But the beauty of movies is that they don't have to be logical. If there's a visceral, cinematic thing happening that the audience likes, they don't care if it goes against what's likely."[2]

Other casting suggestions were floated for Kyle Reese—at one point Sting was even considered. But Cameron ultimately found his hero in a handsome twenty-seven-year-old actor named Michael Biehn, who had some TV under his belt and a film role as a psychotic fan stalking Lauren Bacall in 1981's *The Fan.* When Biehn's agent sent him the *Terminator* script, the actor was dubious—he was to audition for a time-travel movie made by some Roger Corman vets and starring Conan the Barbarian? "The project seemed kind of silly to me at the time," Biehn recalls. But any feature-film audition was an opportunity worth pursuing, and so, after a morning spent in rehearsals for a theater production of *Cat on a Hot Tin Roof,* Biehn drove up to Hurd's house in the Hollywood Hills. "From the moment I met Jim, my feelings about the project changed," Biehn says. Cameron had drawings of the Terminator and different sequences of the film tacked up at Hurd's house. Over the years, the director's way of describing his scripts—a mixture of animated verbal storytelling and detailed visual aids—has helped him woo actors and executives. "There's something clear about the way Jim thinks," Biehn says. "He wasn't looking for me to fill in the blanks for him. At that point, all of a sudden I really wanted the movie." Cameron and Hurd were impressed, too. The Kyle Reese role was a tricky one, with pivotal exposition delivered in the heat of a car chase—it's Reese who tells the audience that Sarah Connor is being targeted for assassination because in the future she's going to bear a child who will lead the human resistance. Biehn had delivered his lines with convincing strength. And he'd nailed the softer side of Reese—after all, we're supposed to believe this guy has been in love with a picture of Sarah Connor his whole life, that he's crossed time to be with her. "Michael was probably overly vulnerable for the role," Hurd says. "Almost everyone else who came in for the audition was so tough that you just never believed that there was gonna be this human connection between the two. They have very little time to fall in love. A lot of people came in and just could not pull it off." The only hurdle, the film-makers told Biehn's agent, was the actor's Southern accent. Could he get rid of it? Since Biehn grew up in Nebraska and had no accent to speak of, his agent was perplexed. Apparently a little of the Tennessee Williams drawl was left in Biehn's mouth the day of the audition. Once he returned, sounding as regional as Walter Cronkite, he got the part.

Do I Look Like the Mother of the Future?

In popcorn movies of the 1980s, if women existed at all, it was so the audience could learn more about the guys. Female characters were a ve-hicle for the hero's development—they raised the stakes by being en-slaved and forced to wear a metal bikini *(Return of the Jedi)*, getting kidnapped by heroin-smuggling Vietnam vets *(Lethal Weapon)*, or held hostage by radical German terrorists *(Die Hard)*. Or they inspired a man to greatness simply through the astonishing magnitude of their hotness *(Karate Kid, Top Gun)*. Hollywood didn't invent this reductive use of female characters—who was Helen of Troy but the motivation for some sensational battle sequences?—but in an era of films driven

by special effects and action set pieces, the movie industry let its female characters languish to new depths.

Starting with *The Terminator*, however, Cameron would flip the sex-
ist storytelling axiom on its end multiple times in his career and with
great success. The character who takes a real journey in *The Terminator* is the film's heroine, Sarah Connor. In the first few pages of his
script, Cameron describes Sarah Connor as "19, small and delicate features. Pretty in a flawed, accessible way. She doesn't stop the party when
she walks in, but you'd like to get to know her. Her vulnerable quality
masks a strength even she doesn't know exists." Sarah Connor begins
the film, which takes place over two days, as a sweetly flustered waitress. She doesn't immediately see herself as a likely caretaker of humanity's salvation. As she tells Reese when he delivers the news of her
burdensome fate: "Do I look like the mother of the future? Am I
tough? Organized? I can't even balance my checkbook." But by the
final scene, Connor is a fledgling guerrilla fighter, a woman who has
improvised explosives out of mothballs and corn syrup and rallied a
wounded Reese to his feet in a brutal fight scene. And, like the Virgin
Mary, she's pregnant with the child who will save us all—John
Connor.

Cameron wasn't making a feminist statement by giving a woman
the juiciest role in his film—nor was he making a religious one. He
was just trying to stand out from the crowd. "In writing I like to be
fresh, and at the time of *Terminator*, that kind of female character
hadn't really been done," Cameron says. It helped that Cameron didn't
give much credence to two Hollywood truisms—that an action movie
about a woman would inevitably fail with the young male audiences
who drive box-office receipts and that female audiences wouldn't turn
out for a film with cyborgs and car chases. Later on in his career,
Cameron's ability to tune out conventional wisdom would serve him,
and the field of filmmaking, well as he pioneered technical advances.

In his early movies, that indifference to popular sentiment was mostly a boon to his actresses. "He was fearless in thinking a strong woman is not gonna turn the men off," Hurd says. "Male audiences will still come. And they did." Over the course of his career, Cameron was to give women more power, authority, and strength than any other mainstream director has been able to get away with. To this day, the highest-grossing action film centered on a woman is still Cameron's *Terminator 2: Judgment Day,* which made $520 million worldwide in 1991. Unless, of course, you care to call *Titanic* an action film, which you certainly could, with its heart-pounding last hour devoted to the ship going down. In that case, the highest-grossing movie of all time is Cameron's action epic about a young woman finding the meaning of life thanks to some great sex on a sinking boat. Either way, it's hard to imagine the sinewy heroines of the decades that followed, in films like *Lara Croft: Tomb Raider, Crouching Tiger, Hidden Dragon,* and *Kill Bill Vols. 1 and 2,* without Sarah Connor's legacy.

Casting someone who could make the transition from everywoman to supermama was a challenge, however. Cameron needed an actress who was girl-next-door pretty but also athletic enough for the physical demands of the part. He watched prospective Sarah Connors run laps down Hurd's driveway to see how they'd look fleeing the Terminator. Cameron ultimately found his mother of the future in a little-known actress named Linda Hamilton, who was fresh off starring in the not-yet-released horror movie *Children of the Corn.* "Linda was believable as someone who felt she was completely unprepared for this responsibility and didn't want it, but at the same time, you thought she might be able to get away," says Hurd.

"Don't Be Stupid. Take Both Jobs."

With his cast assembled, Cameron prepared to start filming *The Terminator* in the spring of 1983 in Toronto. He found a role for Henriksen, his friend who had been so crucial to locking up the money on *The Terminator*, as Detective Hal Vukovich and continued to refine the script. But the production hit its first speed bump when Dino De Laurentiis, the producer of the Conan movies, exercised a preemptive option in Schwarzenegger's contract. That meant Cameron would have to wait nine months while his villain laced back up his moccasins for *Conan the Destroyer*. That wasn't enough time for Cameron to shoot another movie, but it was enough time for him to take on a writing assignment, so he started circulating his *Terminator* script as a writing sample and meeting with producers, including David Giler and Walter Hill.

Giler and Hill's Brandywine Productions owned the remake rights to *Spartacus*. Impressed by Cameron's *Terminator* script, the producers invited him to pitch them ideas for a futuristic treatment of the Roman slave drama. Cameron saw lots of potential in a *Spartacus*-in-space story and showed up for the pitch meeting full of ideas. It quickly became clear, however, that Cameron's high-concept sci-fi pitches weren't what Giler and Hill had in mind. The producers wanted to make a swords-and-sandals epic—with actual swords and sandals—that just happened to take place on another planet. The meeting was a bust. As the disappointed screenwriter headed for the door, Giler nonchalantly mentioned one other project that had been kicking around Brandywine for years—*Alien 2*.

There's a moment in an action film when the camera speed slows, when the director wants the audience to feel the hero's adrenaline surging, to see the bullet about to whiz past his head. Standing in the

Brandywine doorway that day, Cameron entered bullet time. He hadn't known that Giler and Hill had produced *Alien,* a movie he revered and had studied obsessively while creating creatures and spaceships for Roger Corman's *Galaxy of Terror.* Cameron had seen *Alien* on its opening night in 1979 with his friend Randall Frakes. Normally, at a movie he and Frakes would whisper and elbow each other in disbelief at some lame story element or cheesy gag. At *Alien,* neither one of them said a word. This movie was perfect. Instead of hewing to the *Star Trek* standard of space travel—a well-groomed crew in fitted jumpsuits piloting a shiny spaceship—Ridley Scott had depicted a band of oddballs in Hawaiian shirts and baseball caps rocketing through the galaxies on the dingy, lived-in *Nostromo.* The whole movie, including H. R. Giger's gruesome biomechanical designs for the alien, bore a patina of realism that terrified audiences, including the cocky twenty-four-year-old Canadian who saw it opening night. James Cameron and *Alien 2* were made for each other, he says, "like peas and carrots." But in front of Giler and Hill, he played it cool, not wanting to seem too eager. The producers gave Cameron a half-page description of their plans for the follow-up: a colony gets wiped out and the Marines are sent in. Giler and Hill's idea represented about the first twenty minutes of the movie, and, in case there was any doubt about how thoroughly they had thought it through, ended with the words "And then some bullshit happens." Cameron suggested that he write a treatment to show them what he might do with an *Alien* sequel. After the meeting, he raced home and got to work crafting a forty-two-page story outline, an adaptation of a spec script he had written about eighteen months earlier called "Mother."

"Mother" took place on a surface station on Venus—"Venus is hell" was its opening line. Cameron had first titled the script "E.T." but changed it when he heard Steven Spielberg had something cooking by that same name. The mother creature was a human-alien hybrid genetically engineered to live in an environment that was fatal to humans—Cameron would leave that story element in the desk drawer for a couple of decades, until he made *Avatar*. But the rest of "Mother" went right into his *Alien 2* treatment. The story climaxed with a battle between the titular mother alien and the film's male lead, who was wearing an exoskeletal loader called a power suit. For *Alien 2*, Cameron added a bunch of marines to "Mother" and swapped Sigourney Weaver's character into the male lead's role. Just a week after his meeting with Giler and Hill, he went back to them with, essentially, the movie. The producers immediately hired him to start writing the script.

The only problem was that on the very same day Cameron landed another, equally plum assignment—the script for the second *Rambo* film. He was also working on a *Terminator* rewrite, to be ready for the start of production in a few months. Cameron called Giler and asked what he should do. "Well, don't be stupid," Giler said. "Take both jobs." So Cameron took both jobs. This meant that, in a three-month period in 1983, he had to write three scripts. Cameron approached the dilemma schematically, as a Terminator might, scanning the scene with a computer readout in its head. He decided each script would be two hours long and 120 pages, for a total page count of 360. He divided the total number of waking hours he had during that three-month period by 360 and figured out how many pages per hour he had to write. "And I just wrote that many pages per hour," he says. Cameron wrote longhand on yellow legal pads, mostly starting in the evening and going into the early morning hours, so that he could attend to preproduction duties on *The Terminator* during the day. He listened to music—Gustav Holst's *The Planets* for *Alien 2* ("Mars, Bringer of War" was a favorite) and the *Apocalypse Now* soundtrack for *Rambo: First Blood Part II*. He downed pot after pot of coffee, ate plenty of junk food, and . . . didn't really finish.

With *Rambo*, Cameron had hoped to write a sophisticated action movie, one where the characters were motivated, the set pieces thoughtfully conceived. In Cameron's initial *Rambo: First Blood Part II* screenplay, Sylvester Stallone had a sidekick, and the prisoners of war Rambo rescued were fully drawn characters whose personal histories unfolded throughout the film. Stallone vetoed the sidekick, whom he felt got all the good lines, and reduced the POWs to symbols rather than human beings whose stories help explain his character's daring return to Vietnam. "It was almost like they were parachuting into 'Nam to pick up a six-pack of beer," Cameron told Canadian film critic Christopher Heard.[3] But after devoting time to four drafts of *Rambo,* Cameron had only been able to finish the first two acts of the *Alien* sequel before it was time to dive into shooting *The Terminator.* Fortunately, Twentieth Century Fox loved the first ninety pages of the script. The studio offered to do the unthinkable—wait until Cameron was available to finish writing. If *The Terminator* turned out well and Cameron demonstrated talent as a director, Fox said it would also let him direct. "Sometimes a director fits a movie like a glove," says producer Larry Gordon, who was president of Fox at the time. "Everything about him spelled right guy, right guy, right guy." Of course, Fox could have replaced Cameron at any time if another "right guy" appeared—he had no written contract. "But we chose to believe it," says Hurd. Sometimes when you're young in Hollywood, it pays to assume people actually are telling you the truth.

Stan

The effects shots Cameron had planned for *The Terminator* would have been ambitious on any budget—on a bare-bones shoot like this one, they seemed impossible. Cameron wanted full-sized robotic endoskeletons and human prosthetics that would look convincing even during lingering close-ups, as in a scene where the injured Terminator performs surgery on its own face in a bathroom mirror. Cameron felt he knew just the man for the job, Dick Smith, the makeup artist who had aged Marlon Brando for *The Godfather* and sploshed the fake blood in *Taxi Driver*. But when Cameron approached Smith with his lofty plans, the venerable special-effects man shook his head. This cyborg stuff was too much for him. Cameron should try his friend Stan Winston. "Stan does good robots," Smith said. Cameron persisted. "No, I want you." "*No,* you want Stan." Dejected, Cameron went to meet Winston, who had just received an Oscar nomination for his makeup work on a little robot love story called *Heartbeeps*. Winston had studied painting and sculpture at the University of Virginia and moved to Hollywood in 1968 to pursue an acting career. When he struggled to find acting work, Winston began a makeup apprenticeship at Walt Disney Studios, ultimately striking out on his own and racking up Emmy nominations for his makeup work on various TV projects. By the time Cameron met him, Winston was ready for a challenge. "Stan and I clicked early on because we both respect the artist, and he saw one in me and vice versa," Cameron says. "And we are both a little crazy and enjoyed each other's eccentricities." Winston was just nuts enough to take Cameron's outrageous ideas and execute them. The work he did for Cameron in subsequent films would earn Winston three of his four Academy Awards and would lead to their cofounding a visual-effects company, Digital Domain, in 1993. When Cameron resigned as chairman of that company in the middle of a tense board meeting in 1998, Winston stood up and walked out with him, quitting in solidarity. He was one of Cameron's closest artistic collaborators and friends until his death from cancer in 2008. But first, on *The Terminator,* the two had to learn to trust each other.

Normally, Winston would have started from scratch with a design— most directors have some concept of what they would like to see on-screen but rely on artists like Winston to realize and refine the image for them. But Cameron had already created several detailed pieces of concept art. Some artists might have been threatened by a director who could do their job as well as they could, but Winston saw it as an opportunity to up his own game. He and Cameron communicated by passing sketches back and forth, sharing a boyish zeal for the spectacular. Winston would later joke that Cameron was "one of the most talented artists who ever worked for me."[4] Ultimately, they settled on a design for the Terminator that was almost identical to the one Cameron had sketched that night in Rome. Now they just had to build the thing. Because this robot had its skeleton visible in certain places, it couldn't be played by a man in a suit. It had to be a full-sized puppet. Seven artists worked continuously for six months to build the Terminator puppet: First it was molded in clay, then plaster, then urethane. Then the mold was cast in epoxy and fiberglass and reinforced with steel ribbing. Those pieces were then sanded and painted to achieve a distressed look and then chrome-plated. Inside the robot's head, Winston's team placed a radio mechanism they would use to control the movements. In the end, the full-sized Terminator puppet weighed more than one hundred pounds, a bulk that would add to its on-screen appearance of unkillable strength. For the Terminator's tricky bathroom mirror scene, Winston painstakingly sculpted a lifelike reproduction of Schwarzenegger's face in various poses using silicone, clay, and plaster. Cameron was pleased—he felt he and Winston had built the definitive movie robot together.

The Do-It-Yourselfer

Finally, in March 1984, after two years of meticulous preparation, Cameron called action on *The Terminator.* "He had a kid-in-a-candy-store feeling about him," Biehn recalls. "Jim had been on the outside of the candy store looking in for a long time. He had been let in one tiny candy store once before—*Piranha II*—and been pushed out the door." But now Cameron had assembled all the people he wanted to work with, all the gadgets and the cameras and the lights. He had none of the burdens of studio or media expectations that hung over his later shoots, nor the responsibilities of massive budgets, army-sized crews, and groundbreaking technologies. "At that point he wasn't *James Cameron,*" Biehn says. "He was just Jim, and there was a great joy in him when he was making that movie." With most of the movie's complex action sequences to be filmed at night, Cameron was constantly fighting the clock, trying to accomplish as much as possible before the sun came up each morning. He had to make a quick adjustment just a week before filming started, when Linda Hamilton severely sprained her ankle and the production schedule had to be shifted entirely so that the actress's running scenes occurred as late in the shoot as possible. Even with the schedule change, Hamilton's ankle had to be taped every day, and she spent most of the movie in pain.

On *The Terminator,* Cameron established the hands-on working style he would take to an extreme in his later films. By the time he got to *Avatar,* Cameron would be holding the camera, editing the footage, mixing the sound—performing almost every technical and artistic task on the film himself except acting. At lunch, his crew half expected to see their director at the craft services table, manning the grill in pursuit of the flawless burger only he could achieve. Cameron's taking on every job, no matter how inconsequential or even dangerous it might appear to others, was a habit developed partly out of necessity in his Corman days. If a light needed to be moved on a Roger Corman movie, whoever was closest moved it. But the truth is, Cameron can do almost everything there is to do on a movie set as well as any specialist—and he knows it. Why bother struggling to explain something when you can just do it yourself? "Jim is actually as good as he thinks he is," says a crew member on *Avatar.* "It's kind of creepy." And then there's the machismo element of mastering tasks far outside his job description. On *The Terminator,* if an actor needed to have a stunt explained to him, Cameron demonstrated it, without padding. "He jumped on this Honda motorcycle I was supposed to be riding and accelerated and spun around, did a one-eighty to show me what he wanted," Schwarzenegger recalls. "I thought he was crazy." Cameron relied on all the low-budget tricks he had learned working for Roger Corman but delivered them at triple the scale. For a scene where a truck explodes on a downtown street, he cut from a long shot of a real semi to a miniature on the first burst of flame. "He had everything laid out in such detail that there was no room for error," Schwarzenegger says. "He got so obsessed and so into it, he lived the movie."

The Sleeper

The passion paid off—Cameron was proud of the end result he achieved on *The Terminator.* So it was a shock to him when executives at Orion dismissed the movie as just another down-and-dirty genre picture that would be gone from theaters within three weeks of its opening. Fearing critics would trash the film, Orion held just one press screening for it and spent the movie's small advertising budget on the week of release. Many influential critics who got to see *The Terminator,* however, raved about it. The *Los Angeles Times* called the movie "a crackling thriller full of all sorts of gory treats" and said it was "loaded with fuel-injected chase scenes, clever special effects and a sly humor." Critics at the *New York Times* and *Newsweek* were equally laudatory, and *Time* magazine put *The Terminator* on its "10 Best" list for the year. Audiences cheered, too. *The Terminator* became a sleeper hit, earning $78 million worldwide off its $6.4 million production budget.

It was one of the first films to find an even bigger audience in the home video market and over the years saw its reputation grow from trash classic to simply classic. In 2008, *The Terminator* was selected for preservation by the National Film Registry, which maintains prints of films it deems culturally, historically, or aesthetically significant.

One person who caught *The Terminator* while it was still in theaters was Harlan Ellison, the prolific and often contentious science-fiction writer. "I loved the movie, was just blown away by it," Ellison said. "I walked out of the theater, went home and called my lawyer."[5] Ellison alleged that the *Terminator* screenplay was based on two episodes of the TV show *The Outer Limits* that he had written, "Soldier" and "Demon with a Glass Hand." The episodes seem a plausible inspiration—in the first three minutes of "Soldier," as in the first three minutes of *The Terminator,* two mysterious warriors from the future materialize in the present. And the mechanized hand of "Demon with a Glass Hand" bears some resemblance to the translucent structure of the *Terminator* robot. But the *Terminator* script can hardly be called a straight rip-off of Ellison's work—in the *Outer Limits* episodes there's no one resembling the central character, Sarah Connor, nor any reference to preventing the birth of a future warrior. And in a genre in which countless books, movies, and TV shows tackle the same themes of time travel, robots, and future warfare, no one writer can claim ownership of them. But rather than wage a costly lawsuit, Orion gave Ellison an undisclosed sum and added a credit acknowledging the author in later prints of the film. Cameron objected to that decision at the time but felt he had little power to change it. "It was a nuisance suit that could easily have been fought," he says. "I expected Hemdale and Orion to fight for my rights, but they abandoned me. The insurance company told me if I didn't agree to the settlement, they would come after me personally for the damages if they lost the suit. Having no money at the time, I had no choice but to agree to the settlement. Of course there was a gag order as well, so I couldn't tell this story, but now I frankly don't care. It's the truth. Harlan Ellison is a parasite who can kiss my ass."

During postproduction on *The Terminator*, Cameron and Hurd's relationship had evolved from a professional partnership into a romantic one. In Hurd, Cameron had found a woman who could keep up with him—literally keep up with him: The two adrenaline junkies would race each other to meetings, he in the Corvette he had bought with his *Terminator* fee, she in a Porsche. They talked on their car phones as they topped 120 miles per hour on L.A. freeways. Their dates consisted of firing AK-47s and M16s at shooting ranges in the desert, riding horses together, and scuba diving. Once they crash-landed a hot-air balloon outside Palm Springs. Cameron's love interests, like his screen heroines, have tended to be highly capable women, and quite different from the armpiece wives favored by many powerful men in Hollywood. "I've always liked strong women, both in films and in life," Cameron says. "My mother was always very independent, so maybe it's just that the closest role model I had was like that." Of course, it would take him quite a few tries to get love right—it wouldn't be until his fifth marriage, to actress Suzy Amis in 2000, friends say, that Cameron found the right heroine for him.

Tech Noir

Like the film noir crime thrillers of the 1940s and '50s, *The Terminator* told a fatalistic tale in a shadowy urban setting. But instead of showing audiences the dark side of humanity, it revealed to them the dark side of technology. In *The Terminator*, a defense network computer has engineered a nuclear war. Machines called hunter-killers round up the few humans left in the bleak, ash-strewn world for orderly disposal. And robots that look like people—Terminators—infiltrate the population. *The Terminator* wasn't the first movie to raise questions about our reliance on machines—*2001: A Space Odyssey* and *Blade Runner* both posited futures in which humanity's mindless dependence on computers leads to grave consequences. But Cameron effectively coined the genre name "tech noir" when he chose that moniker for the nightclub where the Terminator first tracks down Sarah Connor. Since *The Terminator,* plenty of tech noir films have followed, such as Steven Spielberg's *Minority Report,* Terry Gilliam's *Twelve Monkeys,* and Andrew Niccol's *Gattaca.*

As far out as Cameron's vision of future warfare in *The Terminator* seemed in 1984, it was frighteningly prescient in many respects. Today robots are used as exterminators in Afghanistan and Iraq, where Predator drones do the killing once left to flesh-and-blood soldiers. Counterterrorism operations rely on robots to sniff for explosives and gather visual intelligence. And the U.S. Department of Defense has developed remotely operated robotic guns that can kill at a half-mile range—essentially the first hunter-killers. In 2009, a group of computer scientists were worried enough about the possibility of a high-tech coup to convene a special conference to assess the possibility of "the loss of human control of computer-based intelligences." Twenty-five years after he made *The Terminator,* the movie's admonitory themes still concern Cameron. "It is not the machines that will destroy us, it is ourselves," he says. "However, we will use machines to do it."

4.

THIS TIME IT'S WAR

Sigourney's Alamo

Aliens is Cameron's combat picture—and not just because it's about a band of Colonial Marines hunting down acid-bleeding, extraterrestrial predators with pulse rifles and flamethrowers. While filming the sequel to Ridley Scott's *Alien,* Cameron would go to battle in more earthly ways, fighting both a mutinous British crew and an anxious Hollywood studio for creative control. But first he had to beat back all the movie-industry well-wishers who were advising him to steer clear of Scott's iconic film.

In December 1984, Cameron was basking in the afterglow of *The Terminator*'s surprise success. Seemingly overnight, he had metamorphosed from a B-movie outcast into the hottest young filmmaker in town. After *The Terminator* opened at number one at the box office, the guy who had lived off room service leftovers two years earlier didn't have to buy his own lunch for two weeks. And just as suddenly, he didn't need the gig he'd wanted so badly—writing and directing *Alien 2.* Julia Phillips, the feisty producer of *Taxi Driver* and *Close Encounters of the Third Kind,* warned Cameron that if he directed the sequel, anything good in the movie would inevitably be attributed to Scott's vision and anything bad to Cameron's. "Yeah, but it'll be cool," Cameron said. "I was such a geek fan," he recalls. "It may have been hubris, but I never really considered how it could have been career suicide."

Cameron began calling *Alien 2* "Aliens" while working on the screenplay. He talked the film's producers, David Giler and Walter Hill, into that title by holding up the back of a torn-off script page where he had written "ALIEN" in Magic Marker. Cameron added the *S* and then drew two vertical lines through it, making a dollar sign. The producers agreed to the new title on the spot. In the 1980s, it was not yet a foregone conclusion that a sequel to a hit film would become a money tree. But Giler and Hill felt their concept of a war movie in space had real box-office potential. For Cameron, it was a chance to explore some fertile creative territory. As a kid he had liked war movies, and as an adult he admired the warriors themselves. For *Aliens,* Cameron envisioned something reminiscent of World War II combat pictures like *Sahara* or *The Dirty Dozen,* where a scruffy, ethnically diverse squad of soldiers find themselves trapped behind enemy lines and pull together to face an overwhelming foe. He also had in mind John Wayne's 1960 film *The Alamo,* in which Wayne, as Davy Crockett, galvanizes his overmatched, ragtag troops against the advancing Mexican army. As Cameron saw it, Sigourney Weaver's character, Ripley, was John Wayne, the unflappable leader in a hopeless battle.

There were a few advantages to packaging *Aliens* as a war movie. Cameron knew he couldn't do a better job at creating an atmosphere of claustrophobia and dread than Scott had with the original. The combat conceit was different enough from *Alien* that it would allow him to graft his own style onto Scott's and claim a sense of authorship. A military plot also provided the director an opportunity to layer Vietnam War metaphors into the story. Like any child of the sixties, Cameron had grown up surrounded by Vietnam imagery and themes, and he had further immersed himself in the conflict while researching his *Rambo* script. He watched *Apocalypse Now* and read Tim O'Brien's *Going After Cacciato* and Michael Herr's *Dispatches.* Cameron adopted the cocky attitude and lingo of U.S. troops in Vietnam for the Colonial Marines in *Aliens.* And he used the arc of the Vietnam story—the pride coming before the fall. "It was a definite parallel to Vietnam to tell the story of a technologically superior military force which is defeated by a determined, furtive, asymmetric enemy," Cameron says. For all their futuristic firepower, his soldiers would be obliterated by a giant bug.

"Get Away from Her, You Bitch!"

In the 1979 film, we don't learn much about Ripley, other than that she's smart, a junior officer, and an independent thinker and that she's got balls of steel. In fact, Ripley could be called a female version of a young James Cameron, which might help explain why he centered his script for the sequel on her character. In his *Aliens* screenplay, Cameron gives Ripley a backstory. He reveals that her first name is Ellen and that she had a daughter back on Earth who aged and died during Ripley's fifty-seven-year hypersleep. In the theatrical release of the film, the sequence that explains Ripley's motherhood was cut to trim the running time. But the maternal subtext plays out throughout the movie. Ripley takes on the little girl Newt, the lone survivor of the alien attack on the planet LV-426, as a surrogate daughter. Cameron had no children at the time he wrote *Aliens,* but he managed to tell a resonant parental love story. Looking back as a father of five, he says, "I'm surprised that I got it as right as I did, since it was not an emotion I'd ever felt. I had never even had my own dog." In *Aliens'* climactic fight scenes, a sweaty, dirty Weaver, clad in a baggy T-shirt and cargo pants, faces off against the slimy alien queen, each badass matriarch grappling to protect her young. Ripley isn't glamorous—she's a samurai. In one arm she cradles a little girl, in the other, a flamethrower. In making Ripley a mother and a warrior, Cameron managed to treat her gender as both the heart of her character and a complete nonissue. Even twenty years later, audiences who see *Aliens* in theaters at revival screenings yell loudest when Weaver delivers her memorable battle cry, "Get away from her, you bitch!"

Cameron had kept a picture of Weaver by his side while he wrote the script, which features her character in virtually every scene. So it came as some surprise to him when he learned his leading lady knew nothing of the sequel, wasn't under contract to make it, and had no real interest in revisiting the world of *Alien.* Cameron decided to call Weaver himself. "Look, you don't know me from Adam," he told the actress when he reached her in France, where she was filming a comedy with Gérard Depardieu. "But I just wrote this script I'm calling *Aliens.* And now I'm in an embarrassing situation. I've been working on this film for some time, but now I'm being told you know nothing about it. So—can I send you the script?"[1]

Weaver was dubious of what she thought was an attempt to cash in on the success of the original, but she agreed to read the script and was pleasantly surprised by Cameron's thoughtful take on Ripley. "He made her this renegade," she says. "It was a great beginning for this character to find this isolation and rage."[2] The actress agreed to meet with Cameron and showed up intensely prepared—she had marked her copy of the script with several different colors of ink and filled the margins with questions and notes. Weaver told Cameron some very specific things she wanted to see happen in the *Alien* mythos. "She wanted to die in the film, she wanted to not use guns, and she wanted to make love to the alien," Cameron says. When she attained a position of power as a producer of the third and fourth films in the *Alien* franchise, Weaver got to do all three of those things. But at their first meeting, Cameron vetoed her requests. "I thought she would bolt," he says. She didn't. And some of Weaver's ideas inspired Cameron to think more deeply about the character. He had seen *Aliens* as a straightforward revenge story. Weaver, more softhearted than her director, didn't think Ripley hated the aliens. "I said, 'No, no, no, she hates them,'" says Cameron. "'She hates the aliens that killed all her crew members and put her through the most traumatic event of her life, and she wants to see them destroyed.'" Ultimately, Cameron sold Weaver on the notion that there are colonists on LV-426 and Ripley would want to prevent the kind of trauma she had lived through from happening to anybody else. "That creative tug-of-war between us forced me to think outside of my limited box at that time and to see that her motivation was on a higher plane," Cameron says. "She was on a sense of duty."[3]

While Weaver loved the script, she made one other thing clear at the meeting: she still hadn't made her deal with Twentieth Century Fox. Weaver knew her own value as Hollywood's first real action heroine. After Scott made her a star, she'd gone on to earn lead roles in notable movies like *The Year of Living Dangerously* and *Ghostbusters.* Now that Cameron had crafted an entire screenplay around her character, Weaver felt she was ripe for her first fat paycheck. The studio didn't agree, however, and a stalemate developed in Weaver's contract negotiations. By now it was April 1985, and *Aliens* was set to go into production in September. Cameron had already tangled with Fox over one woman whom he considered central to the film—Hurd. Although she had delivered *The Terminator* on time and on budget, Hurd's youth (she was now twenty-nine), gender, pixielike appearance, and romantic relationship with Cameron led the studio to assume she was not a "real" producer. But Cameron insisted on the duo as a package deal, and won. After reinforcing their professional partnership, Cameron and Hurd sealed the personal one. The couple headed to Maui to marry. Before they left, Cameron told Fox, "We'll give you until we get back to lock in Sigourney's deal. If it hasn't happened by then, we're out."

When Cameron and Hurd returned from their honeymoon, Weaver and Fox still had no contract. And now Cameron had put himself in a spot. He felt he had to stand by the deadline he'd created, so he devised a ploy. Cameron called Arnold Schwarzenegger's agent at ICM, where Weaver was also represented. He told the agent he'd been thinking over his new place in the Hollywood pecking order and had decided to drop the character of Ripley altogether and build the story around Newt and the marines. That way *Aliens* would be 100 percent Cameron's, with no baggage from Scott's classic picture. He finished by telling the agent he was starting the rewrite immediately, and hung up. Cameron never had any intention of writing Ripley out of his script. But he knew what would happen next—Schwarzenegger's agent called Weaver's, who called Fox. And Weaver's deal was closed that day. In the end, she was paid one million dollars for *Aliens,* about thirty times her salary for the original.

The Garbage-Bag Test

Perhaps the most indelible image from the first *Alien* film is the gruesome moment when the creature violently explodes out of John Hurt's chest. Cameron knew he would include the "chest bursters" and "face

huggers"—the gory, parasitic life stages of the alien that had so horrified audiences of Scott's film. But he also wanted to take a design stand
of his own. The first unique design concept Cameron cooked up for
Aliens was the immense alien queen. He painted her himself as a super-
bug, sort of a cross between a black widow spider and a dinosaur, with
two pairs of arms and an egg-laying sac modeled on a termite queen's
ovipositor. Cameron references real animals and insects in his designs
for fantastical creatures like the alien queen for two reasons. Most important, he feels an image rooted in reality helps an audience suspend
disbelief. When you're asking people to travel with you to another
planet and time, it helps to give them vaguely recognizable forms to
latch onto along the way. But the other explanation for Cameron's
plagiarizing the natural world is that doing so feeds his Mr. Wizard
alter ego, the part of him that relishes any excuse to dive into scientific
esoterica like insect reproduction. Cameron's alien queen was only part
science, however. The other parts echoed H. R. Giger's designs for the
original *Alien* film: elegant, beastly, and begging for Freudian inter-
pretation. Some film theorists have called the alien queen Cameron's
version of Grendel's mother from *Beowulf*—"the female that is the
monstrous form beyond Grendel, and the real source of terror, as she,
unlike Grendel, could give birth to more beasts."[4] Cameron's mama
was fourteen feet of terrible, and she was dragging thousands more
hideous, chest-bursting babies in her distended sac full of eggs.

In the queen, Cameron had dreamed up another monster that
would require as much imagination to build as it had to conceive. For
that job, he recruited his pal Stan Winston. "I've got this great idea,"
Cameron told Winston. "We'll get a couple of guys. We'll put them in
a suit. We'll have puppeteers working the legs." Winston, who rarely
had trouble matching Cameron's enthusiasm for seemingly impossible tasks, didn't get it. "I'm looking at him going, 'This guy's completely out of his mind,'" Winston recalled years later on the DVD
commentary for a special edition of *Aliens*. But within seconds, the

special-effects artist thought back to their shared effort on *The Termi-nator.* "If Jim is imagining it, somehow he's got an idea of how he can make it happen. So my second thought was, 'Yeah, we can do that.'"[5] Cameron sketched how the two puppeteers would operate the four arms while lying back-to-back in a body tray inside the torso of the queen. To prove to Winston—and to himself—that his concept would work, Cameron proposed a test. He had Winston build a fiberglass tray mold to fit two workers from his shop. The crew then cut up foam core in the shape of a head, arms, and legs and covered it with black plastic garbage bags to approximate the black sheen of the alien. Then they dragged their hastily constructed queen out to the parking lot of Winston's San Fernando Valley studio. Using a crane, they suspended the two puppeteers inside the foam body. Cameron ran the camera for the test and called the shots. "Crane, raise up," he said. Up rose his Hefty-bag monster, gingerly at first. "All right, bob the crane up and down. Just a little bit, like it's shifting its weight. Try to keep the palms down." The goal was to see the total mobility and the silhouette of the creature. When they played back the video, to the surprise of everyone but Cameron, the potential of the design was clear.

Once the garbage-bag test proved successful, Winston's team set about building the real thing. Ultimately, it would take fourteen to sixteen operators to move the queen on set. The head, neck, and body were hydraulically controlled, the legs puppeted externally using rods, the face, lips, jaw, and tongue operated by cables. "The queen alien is probably the only actress that could take direction from Jim Cameron, get pissed, and back him off," says Winston. She was also the most complicated creature Winston had ever constructed at that point in his career. Seven years later, Steven Spielberg would seek out Winston's help for *Jurassic Park.* "He said, 'Well, you built a fourteen-foot alien and it worked. Why can't you do a dinosaur?'" Winston recalled. "Everything leads to something else."[6]

With the queen in the works, Cameron and Winston tackled the army of warrior aliens. The alien in the original film was played by a seven-foot-two Nigerian design student named Bolaji Badejo, who was discovered in a pub in England by a member of Scott's casting team. Unlike Scott's movie, Cameron's called for dozens of aliens. Unless the entire NBA showed up for auditions, Cameron knew he couldn't find enough seven-footers to cast his alien army. But in studying *Alien,* Cameron realized that the creature almost never appears in the same frame as a person for scale, so Badejo's freakish height wasn't all that important. Cameron decided to use normal six-foot-tall people instead. He also wanted his aliens to have more mobility than Badejo had had in his rubber suit. So Winston's team created costumes out of spandex that stuntmen and dancers could wear as they jumped, crawled, and skittered. This was one of the many times when Winston's background as an actor came in handy in his special-effects work—intuitively, he understood that creatures had to be not only wonderful to look at but capable of delivering a compelling performance.

Ugly, Battered . . . Functional

The art of H. R. Giger had been crucial to the first film, enormously influential in creature and movie design, and inspirational to Cameron personally. Over the course of his career, Cameron has sought out some of the best artists in the world to collaborate with, but he didn't invite Giger to help on *Aliens,* a decision he later regretted. "He sounded like an eccentric who might be difficult to work with," says Cameron. "Maybe, at the time, I was afraid of giving up too much visual control. That comes from lack of confidence." Cameron did muster the courage to seek out some other artists he idolized, Syd Mead and Ron Cobb.

Mead, a onetime designer for Ford Motor Company, had reinvented himself as Hollywood's "visual futurist," concocting wildly imaginative vehicles for sci-fi movies like *Blade Runner* and *Tron.* Cameron tracked Mead down in Miami, where the artist was engaged in another act of ocular fantasy—judging the 1985 Miss Universe contest. He FedExed Mead a copy of the *Aliens* script and asked the artist to tackle the *Sulaco,* the hulking spaceship that transports Ripley and the Colonial Marines to investigate what happened on LV-426. Mead stayed up all night reading the script and meditating on Cameron's description of the ship's first appearance on-screen: "Metal spires slice across frame, followed by a mountain of steel. A massive military transport ship, the *Sulaco.* Ugly, battered . . . functional." Mead completed several sketches of the *Sulaco,* first designing it as a massive sphere. The spherical idea didn't work for Cameron, however. Instead, he sent Mead a quick sketch of his own in which the *Sulaco* resembled a giant gun drifting through space. Mead expounded on the giant-gun design, which was ultimately what appeared in the film. Mead also worked on the drop ship the marines would use to descend into LV-426's atmosphere. Here Cameron wanted a vehicle that could dive down onto hostile planets and deposit ground troops, like the helicopters that plopped American GIs into the jungles of Southeast Asia. But again, the final drop ship would be based upon a design Cameron constructed himself, using parts from a model kit of an Apache helicopter that he bashed together on a Sunday afternoon and spray painted gray. "Syd had some great ideas, but his stuff was too sleek for the gritty, used future look we were doing," Cameron says.

Cobb, an accomplished illustrator who had worked on *Alien* and *Star Wars,* often packaged Cameron's rough designs, adding the finishing touches. Though he was working with artists whom he respected in Mead and Cobb, Cameron relied on his own design aesthetic for *Aliens* more than anyone else's. Rare among directors, he has the artistic ability to sketch, paint, and build things himself—and he prefers to. This is largely because Cameron knows better than anyone else what he envisions in his own mind. But there's also a part of him that seems to deal best with the stresses of life and moviemaking by using his hands. Some directors drink, some smoke, some screw—Cameron moseys off to the model shop and gets dirty.

The climactic third-act confrontation between Ripley and the alien queen makes use of one of Cameron's signature designs—the power loader, a piece of full-body construction equipment Ripley wears during her hand-to-claw battle with the alien mother. The power loader was inspired by Robert A. Heinlein's military sci-fi novel *Starship Troopers,* in which infantry troops don an exoskeletal suit in combat. Heinlein's vision of future warfare has proved especially prophetic and was a major inspiration to Cameron in the making of *Aliens*—Bill Paxton's character's reference to a "bug hunt" is a nod to the book's influence. For *his* exoskeletal suit, Cameron needed something that Ripley might have been trained to use, so he came up with a construction version. To create the appearance that Ripley was manipulating her giant metal outfit, Cameron had Weaver stand on the feet of a burly stuntman hidden behind her. A combination of cables and the stuntman's strength moved Weaver and the suit together. Cameron also has a variant of the power loader in his 1978 film *Xenogenesis,* and he has a military model of it—called an AMP suit—in *Avatar.* "I like the idea of giving a character great power to fight a big, fierce enemy in mano-a-mano combat," he says.

Robotic suits like the power loader that lend humans extraordinary strength are no longer just the stuff of fantasy. In 2000, the Pentagon launched a seventy-five-million-dollar program called "Exoskeletons for Human Performance Augmentation," and the army has already built working prototypes that provide soldiers ten times their natural brawn. In 2004, a Japanese robotics company produced a power loader–like model that nurses could use to lift their patients. The Japanese roboticists are obviously Cameron fans—that company is called Cyberdyne, the same name as the firm that builds the robots in the Terminator films.

Boot Camp

Cameron's casting on this film reflects one of his dominant traits—loyalty. Michael Biehn, the future warrior from *The Terminator,* plays Hicks, the Colonial Marines' squad leader. Lance Henriksen, whom Cameron had met on *Piranha II,* was cast as Bishop, the movie's heroic android. And Bill Paxton, who had hammered sets beside Cameron at New World Pictures, is a hyped-up marine named Hudson. Cameron's allegiance to his friends on this film is particularly remarkable given that the production was obligated to audition and hire a certain number of UK-based actors. He did take a few, including Jenette Goldstein, a freckle-faced bodybuilder who darkened her hair and complexion to play the squad's tough Latina, Vasquez. And for Newt, Hurd found Cameron a nine-year-old army brat named Carrie Henn, one of the only children who showed up for the audition without any acting experience. That turned out to be an asset, as all the other kids had been trained to smile after delivering every line—helpful for a soda commercial, but not for playing a victim of extraterrestrial post-traumatic stress.

Months before casting began, when Cameron had just been hired to write and direct the film, Paxton ran into his old friend at the Los Angeles airport. "I was just kidding him, and I said, 'Hey, I hope you write me a good part in it,'" Paxton says. Since his Corman days, Paxton had been getting more acting work. He was fresh off a well-received performance as the obnoxious big brother in *Weird Science* when he got a call in the summer of 1985 to audition for Cameron. "Jim put me through my paces," Paxton recalls. "He handed me a long cardboard tube to pretend like that was the plasma pulse rifle I was holding. I left thinking I wasn't gonna get the part. I thought I was too over the top." But Paxton's energy was just what Cameron wanted. Hudson would become the film's comic relief, a break from the constant tension of the combat scenes.

Cameron decided that some kind of military training was necessary for his Colonial Marines to lend authenticity to their speech and movement and to bond the cast as a group. All the actors playing marines had to participate in a two-week boot camp, humping backpacks in the rain, learning how to use weapons, and enduring the yells of a drill sergeant. Actor Al Matthews, who had earned two Purple Hearts as a marine in Vietnam before Cameron cast him as Sergeant Apone, conducted the drills. "I enjoy actors in general, and forming such a tight-knit group before we started shooting gave us all a sense of being on a team, doing something fun and important," Cameron says.

Weaver was kept out of the training so that she would be the outsider, just as Ripley is in the film. She and Cameron would slip away to the sets after the workmen left for the day and rehearse. One of the issues the director and his leading lady had to overcome was their differing ideologies on guns. When Cameron wants to blow off some steam, he drives into the desert and shoots, usually aiming at soda cans and watermelons, targets he considers "especially visual, ballistically speaking." Cameron doesn't collect guns, but he does know how to use them. He trained with a champion shooter for two years and at his peak could shoot a "double tap"—two rounds hitting the target in under fifteen hundredths of a second. "I believe in gun control for everyone but me," he says. So for Cameron, all the futuristic weaponry in *Aliens* was good fun. But for Weaver, who had donated money to antigun causes, the notion of spending two-thirds of a movie with her hand on some kind of trigger was upsetting. To accustom Weaver to weapons, Cameron took her out behind the stage and gave her a .45 Thompson submachine gun. Weaver fired off a fifty-round magazine from the hip. "I knew from her grin that she was at least temporarily converted," Cameron says. "Another liberal bites the dust."

The Tea-Trolley Mutiny

Production on *Aliens* took place at Pinewood Studios, the historic soundstages about twenty miles outside London where *Fahrenheit 451, The Shining,* and the James Bond movies were filmed. In some respects, England in the fall and winter was the perfect place to shoot this movie—the cold, windswept weather matched the bleak atmosphere on LV-426. But the location posed some unique challenges for Cameron. In England in the 1980s, studios came with a crew attached, unlike the current "four-wall" studio system, in which a soundstage is simply an empty space and producers hire their own crews. Many of the employees at Pinewood were lifers, locals who viewed their film jobs as they might factory work—a paycheck and nothing more. The Pinewood crew was an abrupt change from the young, eager, nonunion film crews Cameron and Hurd had labored with at New World Pictures and on *The Terminator.* "Gale and I were shocked to be working with people who simply couldn't care less about the film they were working on," says Cameron. "The Pinewood crew were lazy, insolent, and arrogant. There were a few bright lights amongst the younger art-department people, but for the most part, we despised them and they despised us."

By the standards of an American film crew at the time, twelve hours was an average day. In England, twelve hours was a very long day. Cameron was accustomed to pushing his crews through fourteen-hour marathons. "Jim was like a tornado hitting Pinewood Studios," says Paxton. "The crew guys, they were used to their breaks at ten and two. They'd go to the pub on the lot at lunch. They're ready to knock off by five." One ritual that was particularly hard for the Americans to understand was a twice-daily set-clearing fury that accompanied the union-mandated arrival of a woman pushing a tea trolley. "I was shocked when at a particular time of the morning everybody would be gone," Winston recalled. "Hello? Where is everybody?"[7] In the middle of filming a scene, the giant stage doors would swing open, letting the special-effects smoke spill out, so the crew could rush the tea lady, with her urn of hot water and plate of cheese rolls.

No one in England had seen *The Terminator* yet, so as far as the Pinewood crew was concerned, Cameron was a young, upstart Yank with no credits and no business directing the follow-up to Ridley Scott's masterpiece. Of course, he was actually a young, upstart Canadian, but no one ever seems to remember that. When Cameron did try to hold *Terminator* screenings for the crew, they didn't bother to attend. "There was a lot of resentment and really very little understanding of what Jim was trying to accomplish," says Hurd. "At the time, there was a sense that you don't get to the top of your profession through talent, you get there by paying your dues and putting in your time." To the Pinewood veterans, Cameron, at thirty-one, was an undeserving kid and Hurd, as a female producer married to the director, was a joke. When Hurd interviewed crew members for various positions, they would inform her that they didn't take orders from a woman. Forget LV-426; Cameron and Hurd had found a hostile environment right here on Earth.

Every day, the tension between director and producer and their crew escalated. At the heart of the conflict was the film's first assistant director, Derek Cracknell, well respected among the crew because he had been Stanley Kubrick's AD. Cracknell took to calling Cameron "guv'nor" and "Grizzly Adams" for his bushy beard. These were not terms of affection. Cracknell felt he was better qualified than Cameron to direct the film. "Jim would ask him to set up a shot one way, and Derek would say, 'Oh, no no no, I know what you want,'" says Hurd. "Then he'd do it wrong and the whole set would have to be broken down." Cracknell was seriously undermining Cameron and Hurd's tenuous authority. The director of photography, Dick Bush, also wasn't working out. And Cameron and Hurd were falling behind on their ambitious seventy-five-day shoot. In film parlance, they weren't "making their days," so they decided to make some changes. They replaced Bush with Adrian Biddle, a DP from Scott's commercial production company who had shot Apple's groundbreaking "1984" ad. And they gave Cracknell his notice, causing the festering hostility of the *Aliens* set to erupt into a full-blown mutiny.

At Cracknell's urging, in the middle of the shooting day, the Pinewood crew downed their tools and stopped work in protest. Cameron and Hurd were in a delicate situation. At the time, England was busy with film shoots and there wasn't another crew they could bring in immediately. They called Twentieth Century Fox and tried to decide what to do. Cameron wanted to move the entire production out of England, but Hurd tried to talk him out of it. "It was, to this day, the most difficult moment of my entire career," says Hurd. Instead of attempting to replace their crew, the young filmmakers gathered everyone together on the set for a summit. Cameron addressed the group with characteristic frankness. "Look, this is a really important movie to me," he said, as Hurd and Paxton remember it. "This is my first studio movie. We have an almost impossible shooting schedule, and I need everyone's help. I can't do this on my own. But I also can't have a situation where it seems like the crew is working to prove that the endeavor is gonna be a failure. If you have a problem with that, you've gotta step forward 'cause we've gotta replace you." The meeting lasted for hours, as crew members aired their grievances about the long hours. At the end of the day, the AD staff agreed to be more supportive of Cameron, and he to be more sensitive to teatime. But no real warm feeling ever developed between the director and his British crew. When he finally wrapped at Pinewood, Cameron stood up again to address them. "This has been a long and difficult shoot, fraught by many problems," he said. "But the one thing that kept me going, through it all, was the certain knowledge that one day I would drive out the gate of Pinewood and never come back, and that you sorry bastards would still be here." He never did return.

Five More Cases of Lube, Please

The tricky task of translating Cameron's designs into practical sets and locations in England fell to British production designer Peter Lamont, who had created the sets for several of the Bond films and *Fiddler on the Roof*. Among Lamont's first great finds was a decommissioned coal-generating plant in Acton, an industrial neighborhood in West London. The Acton plant was the perfect place to house the alien queen's giant, gooey nest. "What Jim really liked about it was all the walkways and stairways were grille, so when you looked down you could see from top to bottom," says Lamont. "There was so much old equipment. It was all rusty and horrible. They said, 'You can do anything you want with it.'" The only problem with this abandoned industrial dream set was that it was covered in asbestos. So before Lamont and his team could start construction, a firm had to clear the plant of contaminants, and readings of the air quality had to be taken multiple times a day during production. To dress the set with alien slime, Winston's crew arrived with their magic formula. The English must have thought the Americans were having an awfully good time there, because every week, several cases of K-Y jelly were shipped to the set. The lubricant was not for recreational use, however—it was an important ingredient in extraterrestrial spit, giving the aliens' drool that special glisten.

Lamont seemed to have a knack for procuring good-looking junk. To build the full-sized version of Cameron's Vietnam-evoking drop ship, he used the undercarriage of an old Vulcan helicopter that was being dismantled. For the armored personnel carrier, Lamont got his hands on a vehicle that British Airways used to tow its 747s. The aircraft tow truck weighed seventy-eight tons—even after Lamont's crew pulled thirty-eight tons of lead out of it, they had to reinforce the floor at the power station so it wouldn't fall through. Lamont's inventiveness would help save a scene that at one point looked financially unfeasible—the moment when Ripley and the marines emerge from their hypersleep chambers inside the *Sulaco*. By the time the chambers were to be built, the production was already running out of money. Hurd and a producer from Fox determined that the hypersleep scene had to go. Since it was a production-design issue, Hurd asked Lamont to deliver the bad news to the director. "I'm not telling him," Lamont said. "You're married. You tell him." Lamont shuffled back to his office and reread the script, trying to determine what to do about the costly chambers. Cameron, normally a kinetic bundle while he's working, stopped by Lamont's office and did something unusual—he sat down. "You look worried," he said to Lamont. "Are you OK?" Instead of telling Cameron he'd have to cut the scene, Lamont proposed an old-fashioned idea for shooting the chambers. He could build just four, he said, and, with mirrors, make the *Sulaco* interior appear vast. It was a simple solution that allowed Cameron to keep his set piece and appease his budget-conscious producers, an idea that might have come

from one of Roger Corman's striving crew kids. In this Pinewood jour-
neyman, Cameron had found a scrappy ally. A decade later, he would
call the sixty-five-year-old production designer out of retirement to
build him his most audacious set—the *Titanic*—a job that won Lamont his first and only Oscar.

Cameron's vision of the future in *Aliens* is surprising for how much
it looks like plain old 1985 in certain scenes. He wanted some of his
sets and costumes to feel familiar to his audience, especially the portions of the film that take place at the space station in Earth's atmosphere. "Since we never actually set foot on Earth in *Aliens,* the station
needed to stand in for it," the director explains. "We needed to go from
the familiar and safe to the distant and alien." When Ripley is whisked
from her hypersleep capsule to the space station maintained by her
employer, the Weyland-Yutani Corporation, she reports to a staid conference room that could just as well be 1980s IBM, except for the
Nehru collars on the suits. "I wanted her return to Earth to feel like a
return to a corporate bureaucracy we could recognize," Cameron says.
"So the 'suits' still wore suits."

Weyland-Yutani is Cameron's version of that durable sci-fi trope,
the evil multinational corporation, and Paul Reiser's character, Carter
Burke, is Cameron's company man. Burke will stop at nothing to retrieve an alien superpredator for his firm's weapons division. Appro-
priately, Burke ends up cocooned in alien slime. In a scene that was cut
from the film because Cameron didn't like it visually, Ripley hands
Burke a grenade as an act of mercy, so he can blow himself up before
becoming host to another chest burster. At this point in his career,
Cameron had little experience with corporations. Looking back, he
says, "I don't think Burke is a very realistic character. Most corporate
people are spineless and would not go as far out on a limb as Burke
does for a proactive reason of greed." By the time Cameron got to
Avatar, his company man would be more nuanced, a character whose

evil is banal and is informed by Cameron's additional years of tangling
with big corporations.

A Cutting Dilemma

Cameron hired Ray Lovejoy, Kubrick's craftsman who had cut *2001:
A Space Odyssey,* to edit *Aliens.* Because *2001* was the movie that had
inspired Cameron to make movies, he was prepared to be awed by
Lovejoy's gifts. But Cameron's techniques and Lovejoy's were of completely different eras. Lovejoy was deliberative in his cuts and in his
working pace. Cameron liked staccato editing, especially in his action
sequences, where he inserts blank flash frames to accelerate the tempo.
Splicing those little white frames into the film was maddening work,
however—a negative cutter told Cameron he had more cuts in *Aliens'*
reel twelve alone than in any complete film he had ever worked on before. "Ray Lovejoy is a terrific editor, but he didn't know what hit him
with Jim," says James Horner, who, as the film's composer, had the unfortunate role of being the next man in the postproduction line.
Cameron's post crew faced other delays. The sound mixers weren't sure
how to tackle the scene where the drop ship flies onto LV-426, since
the special-effects artists were still working on it. So Cameron ran down
in front of the screen the mixers were using, held up a broom, and said,
"Follow this," as he ran in the path of the drop ship. The timing
worked perfectly.

But the film was still falling behind, causing serious problems for
Horner, who was supposed to have seven weeks to compose the score
at Abbey Road Studios. Horner was another Roger Corman grad who
had met Cameron when they were both working on *Battle Beyond the
Stars.* Born in Los Angeles and educated at the Royal College of Music

in London, Horner speaks with an indefinable Anglo accent. As a trav-
eler in both artistic cultures, he had anticipated the clash between
Cameron's hyperactive American working style and Lovejoy's more
measured English pace. But he'd had no idea how bad it would get.
By the time Lovejoy had locked reels for Horner to compose to, it was
less than two weeks before the film's scheduled scoring session with the
London Symphony Orchestra. The session couldn't be canceled without forfeiting the entire fee. "I have to write a score, but I don't have
the film," says Horner. "It was horrible. It was just too hard. I think Jim
and Gale thought I was just being an asshole and I didn't get it. I completely got it. I knew it wasn't going to satisfy everything they wanted."
When the second-to-last day of the scoring session arrived, Horner still
hadn't composed the last action cue of the movie. He wrote the final
piece of the score overnight, and the orchestra recorded it on the last
day of the session. Additional music was added after Horner left to
score another film. "I didn't really know how to work with an orches-
tral composer, and I don't think James knew how to work with directors," Cameron says. "He had a lot to learn, and I had a lot to learn."
As disappointing as their process was on *Aliens,* Horner and Cameron
both admired each other's creativity and drive and would end up finding a better way to collaborate later in their careers, on *Titanic* and
Avatar.

Once Cameron had a finished film, he had some difficult decisions
to make. His movie was way too long, nearly two hours and forty-five
minutes. Cameron couldn't figure out where to cut—a minute here or
there wouldn't get the film down to the running time he needed to satisfy Fox. Hurd made what seemed like a wild suggestion—dropping all
of reel three, the portion of the film where Ripley's daughter is revealed
and the LV-426 colony is shown before the aliens attack. "I thought she
was nuts at first," says Cameron. "It would remove the only images of
the derelict ship, which was the only tether to the first picture."

Cameron thought about it for a day and decided that Hurd was right. The reel was a clean cut. By excising reel three and two other scenes, they could slash almost half an hour and reach a length of two hours and seventeen minutes, still long by the standards of the day but defensible to studio bigwigs. It was a tough call, and one that home video made reversible in 1992, when Cameron restored reel three in its entirety in a 154-minute special edition.

The Aftermath

In 1986, Twentieth Century Fox desperately needed a hit. A year earlier, Rupert Murdoch had bought the studio, and Barry Diller, made chairman by its previous owner in 1984, had yet to prove he could make and release movies that worked there. When it came time to show *Aliens* to the studio brass, Cameron proudly toted his film cans into the screening room. "Here it is," he told the executives. "It's done." Tom Sherak, who was handling marketing for Fox at the time, remembers someone suggesting the film might be too long. "No, it's not too long," Cameron said, awfully sure of himself for a guy handing over his first studio movie. Halfway through the screening, Sherak knew Fox had something special on its hands. When it was released on July 18, 1986, *Aliens* did something unusual for a sequel at that time— it built on the audience of the original. Thanks in part to a demographic Cameron reliably entices to the box office, young women, *Aliens* earned more than $130 million worldwide. "*Aliens* helped save the studio," says Sherak. "I don't even think Cameron knew what the impact was on us. It's one of those rare times when one movie can change almost everything." The movie changed everything for Weaver, too. Although she was crestfallen that Cameron edited out Ripley's motherhood, Weaver's performance in *Aliens* made her the first actor to be nominated for an Oscar for a sci-fi film, a genre historically ignored by the Academy.

Aliens remains the highest-grossing film in the franchise. The movies that followed it opened strong but never managed to hold on to their audiences after the first weekend or to win over the die-hard fans of Scott's film as Cameron had. To hear Cameron talk about the last two movies in the quadrilogy is to hear the voice of the fourteen-year-old fanboy in him more than the director. *Alien³* was the first feature film by David Fincher, who got the job based on his stylish music videos and went on to make *Fight Club* and *The Curious Case of Benjamin Button.* "Fincher pissed me off by killing off Newt, Hicks, and Bishop, essentially trashing the entire ending of *Aliens* in the first few minutes of *Alien³*," Cameron says. "His photography is always so good, so I've come to see it as an interesting failure, at least an admirable film." The director of the fourth movie, *Alien: Resurrection,* was a curious choice—Jean-Pierre Jeunet, the Frenchman behind the black comedy *Delicatessen.* Jeunet would later make *A Very Long Engagement,* a war romance that Cameron admired a lot more than his farcical take on the *Alien* story. "Some of the imagery is fun, but the film is ridiculous," Cameron says. "However, I have to say I did shed a tear for Ripley finally returning to Earth, at the end of a four-film cycle and hundreds of years, including death and rebirth each time (either symbolically or actually), thus ending her epic struggle. Of course it was just for the idea of that, not the execution. I wish the film had been better."

If he were making *Aliens* in 2010, Cameron says he would use computer graphics to create the queen. The director is an advocate for all-CG creatures now, which saddens some in the old-school special-effects world who look to his alien queen as the pinnacle of the art form. But Cameron concedes it would probably be best to mix prosthetics and CG to maintain the textural reality of glistening, dripping alien slime.

"Prosthetics is a dying art," he says, "but an *Alien* film would be the exception."

With the release of *Aliens* in 1986, Cameron closed act one of his career. He had delivered a hit, a studio film, on time and close to budget. *Aliens* cost Twentieth Century Fox $17.5 million to produce, nearly $2 million more than it had planned to spend but an overage that would seem downright quaint by the time Cameron and Fox got to *Titanic.* He had shown he could hold his own with Ridley Scott's classic material and with a truculent crew. He had helped a struggling studio stay afloat and earned the underappreciated sci-fi genre some respect with *Aliens'* seven Oscar nominations. For his efforts, Cameron got to enter that rarefied Hollywood club, directors with final cut. The first thing he would do with his new power was turn to a story he'd wanted to tell since he was sixteen. It was the movie that would drag him to his depths physically and emotionally, into *The Abyss.*

5.

STARING INTO *THE ABYSS*

A Human with Gills

As a boy in Chippawa, Cameron lived about a mile and a half upstream from Niagara Falls, the roar of the water crashing over the limestone cliffs a constant soundtrack in his ears. Water and its mysteries would be an abiding source of fascination and creative stimulation for Cameron throughout his life—one that would inspire him to make his most grueling and personal movie, *The Abyss. The Abyss* began as a short story Cameron wrote at age sixteen, when he was devouring Jacques Cousteau's underwater TV documentaries. Because he earned top grades in science, Cameron was invited to attend a series of weekly lectures just over the U.S. border at a university in Buffalo, New York. One lecture was delivered by a diver who showed film of an experiment in which he had breathed liquid oxygen while lying on an operating table. Among the researchers' goals was to send humans deeper into the oceans; with liquid rather than air oxygenating the lungs, a diver's body could more easily accommodate changes in the pressure of the surrounding water. The research hadn't gotten very far—the test had been terminated when the diver wasn't getting the right mix of gases. But the experiment stunned Cameron, whose mind reeled with the possibilities. This diver was like a human with gills—imagine the places he could go. The next day, Cameron started scribbling a short story about an underwater science lab perched on the edge of the Cayman Trough, the deepest point in the Caribbean. In the sixteen-year-old's story, scientists testing experimental fluid-breathing gear made dives down the wall, going deeper and deeper and, one after another, failing to return. The last of the dive team had to decide whether to follow the others and see what had happened to them or to abort the experiment. He dived and experienced a kind of rapture, ending up in a depth-induced psychosis. "It was a simple story, more of a psychological metaphor than a thriller," Cameron says. Nevertheless, this was pretty heady stuff for a teenager—a statement on the attitude of exploration and the lure of the unknown.

Since Cameron's first diving adventures as an adolescent in Chippawa Creek, he has logged more than 2,500 hours underwater, including 550 hours in diving helmets and 500 in deep submersibles. The drive to go ever deeper, which sent the divers in his short story into the Cayman Trough never to return, is one Cameron understands at his core. While making *Avatar* in 2009, he was also at work on an engineering project, designing and building a one-man sphere to dive to the Mariana Trench, the deepest point in the world's oceans. The last manned vessel to reach the 36,000-foot depths of the Mariana Trench was a U.S. Navy boat called the *Trieste* in 1960. One of the *Trieste*'s Plexiglas windows cracked under the pressure, and the two men inside spent just twenty minutes on the ocean floor before turning back. That no one has bothered to try again in fifty years doesn't deter Cameron—

it makes the journey irresistible to him. He plans to dive into the abyssal depths, alone in his submersible, in late 2010.

"I like doing things I know others can't," Cameron says. That's part of what attracts him to shooting movies in water, an arduous, almost masochistic endeavor that he does better than any other Hollywood director by a factor of about a zillion. "Nobody likes shooting in water," Cameron says. "It's physically taxing, frustrating, and dangerous. But when you have a small team of people as crazy as you are, that are good at it, there is deep satisfaction in both the process of doing it and the resulting footage." To Cameron, journeying deep into the ocean is as close as he can get to rocketing into outer space. To go where almost no man has gone before and fail to bring a camera? Well, that would be like Buzz Aldrin and Neil Armstrong planting the flag on the moon and never stopping to take the picture. When Cameron explores the deep ocean, he feels a responsibility to bring it back for the rest of us, just as Cousteau did for him. "I love the experience of being underwater," he says. "As a filmmaker I want to share that."

Truckers, Aliens, and God

Triumphant after the July 1986 release of *Aliens,* Cameron and Hurd departed for a well-deserved honeymoon in the south of France, their first having been cut short by the film's preproduction schedule. When the couple arrived to find the region swamped by European tourists, they quickly changed their travel plans and flew to the Cayman Islands instead, where they chartered a boat called the *Cayman Aggressor* and spent their days scuba diving, exploring, and enjoying some of the first low-pressure moments in their marriage, all just miles from the site of Cameron's high-school short story. When they returned to L.A.,

Cameron decided that rather than scramble to set up deals capitalizing on his growing heat in Hollywood, he would take time to contemplate his next move. While her husband brainstormed story ideas, Hurd signed on to produce her first non-Cameron movie since her Roger Corman days, a sci-fi thriller starring James Caan and Mandy Patinkin called *Alien Nation*. After working elbow to elbow under stressful conditions for the last three years, Cameron and Hurd were taking a break from each other professionally. It seemed like a good idea at the time.

In December, urged by Hurd to tackle a project he'd long dreamed about, Cameron began working on a treatment for *The Abyss*. The scope of the movie would be much grander than his high-school idea, involving loose nukes, submarine chases, wise aliens, and Cameron's most sophisticated love story. Although his original piece had followed a group of researchers working underwater, Cameron felt scientists weren't commercial enough protagonists for the big budget he would need to realize this wildly ambitious underwater action film. So he turned to another archetype he knew well and felt he could sell to a studio—blue-collar heroes. He knew he could create a compelling story around some of the real-life characters who had labored beside him in his twenties—he just needed an excuse to get them underwater. Around this time, Cameron hired Van Ling, a recent USC film school grad who became such an indispensable assistant that the director began calling him his "extra RAM"—it was Ling who first showed Cameron how to use a Mac, so he could ditch his yellow legal pads and typewriter and write *The Abyss* on a computer. Cameron and Ling researched possible underwater gigs for the movie's heroes—harnessing thermal-vent energy, mining undersea manganese nodules. They were all too technical, Cameron thought, but undersea oil drilling, a technology that is possible but isn't practiced in the real world due to its prohibitive cost, would be easy for an audience to understand. So Cameron decided to set *The Abyss* on a civilian underwater oil-drilling rig called Deepcore. And he conceived of Deepcore's crew, led by the foreman or "head tool pusher" Bud Brigman, as the kind of no-nonsense good ol' boys and gals who could just as easily be driving an eighteen-wheeler across the desert as piloting a submersible across the deep ocean. In an early scene that establishes the Deepcore family, the actors sing along to Linda Ronstadt's trucking anthem, "Willing," as they twist knobs and pilot subs. It's just another workday under the sea. That is, until the Deepcore crew is drafted into taking aboard a group of Navy SEALs to rescue a sunken U.S. submarine carrying Trident missiles. And in case that isn't enough drama, a hurricane is blowing in, and so is Lindsey Brigman, Deepcore's designer and boss and Bud's soon-to-be-ex-wife.

Just as in Cameron's high-school short story, Deepcore is perched on the edge of the abyssal Cayman Trough. That's the literal meaning of the movie's title. But Cameron was interested in exploring the multiple interpretations of the word "abyss." He was taken with the idea of a psychological abyss—a pit of madness, of fear, of the unknown. His script started with a quote from Friedrich Nietzsche: "And if you gaze for long into an abyss, the abyss gazes also into you." The quote was omitted from the theatrical release of the film because it had been used in another movie that opened just before *The Abyss,* but it got to the heart of what drew Cameron to this story, the idea that his characters would go to the deepest, darkest part of the ocean to confront a monster, and find out the monster was them.

Under the sea, along with that missile-bearing submarine, the Deepcore and SEAL teams were to discover mysterious, glowing creatures—aliens that Cameron called NTIs, for "nonterrestrial intelligence." As always, the director's sci-fi here is heavy on the sci—the rationale for the NTIs living so far below sea level is that the high ambient pressure of the abyssal depths might be similar to the gravity on denser planets. The NTIs are neither hostile and gruesome like the creatures of *Aliens,* nor cute and cuddly like E.T. They're ethereal, resembling underwater butterflies, with giant eyes and no mouths. This is just the opposite of H. R. Giger's alien, which had a giant mouth and no eyes—this time, Cameron wanted to inspire wonder rather than fear. Here's how he described the NTIs in his *Abyss* treatment: "An extraterrestrial creature, bioluminescent like the deep-sea fish. It has four arms and two legs, all long and slender, moving with a slow balletic grace. Its body and limbs are translucent, and it resembles a figure made of blown glass. . . . The head is refined and strangely anthropomorphic, with large eyes that convey a cold, dispassionate wisdom without malice. It is stunningly beautiful."[1] The NTIs are sage, peaceful inhabitants of our universe, carrying a message of warning to Earth. Their closest filmic predecessor may be Klaatu, from Robert Wise's 1951 sci-fi parable, *The Day the Earth Stood Still.* Klaatu views humans as misbehaving children with a choice to live in harmony or face obliteration. While Klaatu delivers his message verbally, the mouthless NTIs do so via a video screen playing a kind of montage of evil's greatest hits—nuclear bomb footage, Holocaust scenes, Vietnam newsreels. With all that destruction in humanity's wake, the NTIs are mulling whether we're worth saving.

Just as he had in *The Terminator,* Cameron infused his script with religious metaphors. One of Deepcore's crew refers to an NTI as "that angel comin' toward me." Bud Brigman's meeting with the NTIs at the bottom of the Cayman Trough is like a meeting with God—he symbolically dies on the edge of the abyss and is taken by the angel of death into heaven. Cameron doesn't believe in God, he says, "but I believe in religion. We are all wired with the need to feel that there is some greater sense of purpose and order, that it all somehow makes sense, and that some great force is watching over us." As far as he's concerned, belief in UFOs and intelligent aliens originates in the same part of the brain as religion. Some of us choose heaven, some of us outer space, but most of us need to feel there's something out there smarter and more benevolent than we are.

Wet for Wet

With *The Abyss,* Cameron wanted to bring a new level of authenticity to underwater filming, photographing real actors in an underwater soundstage complete with sets, lights, and sound. No one had ever attempted this kind of filmmaking before, which made it even more attractive to the director. After trying something new with the fourteen-foot queen in *Aliens* and succeeding, he was learning to listen to his instincts, not the prevailing wisdom about how movies should be made. Historically, underwater scenes in movies have been shot on a soundstage using the "dry-for-wet" technique. With smoke and slow-motion photography, the director creates the illusion of submersion. Another method is to rely on stunt divers doubling as the characters for any scenes that are shot in deep water and to film the close-ups of the real actors in the safety of a swimming pool. Few feature films ever manage to capture the wonder of the ocean as Cousteau's documentaries did. One undersea movie that stands out, however, is *The Deep,* a 1977 diving thriller starring Nick Nolte and Jacqueline Bisset. Generally written off as a shameless attempt to capitalize on the success of *Jaws* two summers earlier, *The Deep* contains a few stunning underwater scenes, all of them shot by Al Giddings, a six-foot-two, 240-pound cinematographer who had started out as a spear fisherman and competitive swimmer in the 1960s. Giddings had photographed a number of award-winning underwater nature documentaries and was beginning to develop a reputation as a latter-day Cousteau when Cameron flew to meet him at his Oakland, California, studio in 1987. The burly cameraman engineered his own equipment and had a can-do spirit that matched his technical competence and athleticism. Like most people who get along with Cameron professionally, he regarded the director's formidable plans as an exciting challenge. Older than Cameron, he inspired a confidence in the filmmaker, assuring him that he was not crazy, that what he wanted to accomplish could be done. Giddings was soon hired as underwater director of photography on *The Abyss.*

Early on, Cameron ruled out shooting *The Abyss* on the ocean. Even before *Jaws* tripled its $4 million budget, Hollywood had dismissed filming on open water as foolhardy. Storms and tides destroy sets, underwater wildlife can both endanger and be endangered during filming, salt water corrodes everything, and visibility is a day-to-day concern. Cameron needed a tank, a controllable environment in which to build Deepcore and his other underwater sets. But despite surveying available tanks everywhere from Europe to the Caribbean, he couldn't find one big enough to create the grand-scale realism he wanted. At least until he got an invitation from Earl Owensby, the so-called drive-in king of the South and producer of such regionally successful B movies as *Rottweiler: Dogs of Hell* and *Chain Gang.* Owensby had recently bought the never-completed Cherokee Nuclear Power Plant (outside Gaffney, South Carolina), which he intended to turn into an independent movie studio. The producer thought the plant's large, rectangular turbine pits might be just the place for Cameron to construct his underwater sets, so the director and Giddings flew to South Carolina to assess the site.

Gaffney is ninety minutes from Charlotte. It has one main drag with a few fast-food restaurants, one movie theater, and the local landmark— a water tower in the shape of a giant peach. The day Cameron and Giddings arrived was cold, windy, and spitting rain. Owensby toured his guests around the power plant, which was composed of several warehouses and offices connected by weed-strewn concrete paths and littered with hunks of never-installed equipment. Cameron, by now a veritable connoisseur of forgotten industrial sites, was impressed enough by the turbine pits Owensby was proposing for his film. But in the distance he could see something really intriguing—a giant concrete bowl. From afar it looked something like the Roman Coliseum. Would Owensby take them over there? The massive cylinder half a mile away was to have been the nuclear reactor's containment vessel. Only half finished and still studded with rebar, it was 240 feet in diameter with eighty-foot-tall walls and no entrance. Parked beside the enormous tub was the construction crane that had been used to build it. Cameron and Giddings, who had his Nikon camera slung around his neck, exchanged a look and started climbing up the 110-foot crane. In the rain and wind, the two men clambered out onto the jib and took in the view of what would eventually become known as A Tank, their home for ten harrowing weeks. The longer they stared, the more certain they were that this massive basin could work. They discussed building the Deepcore set, where they could put the cliff face, constructing a dive platform, and how they could create a viewing and a control room. Before they climbed down off the crane, they had their plan all mapped out. It would involve pouring thousands of yards of structural concrete and installing enormous filtration systems and pumps and a row of twenty-thousand-Btu heaters to warm the 7.5 million gallons the tank would hold to a comfortable temperature. What they were planning wasn't just the largest underwater set ever built; it was a feat of industrial engineering. When Cameron returned to L.A., he showed Hurd his photos from the trip. "Isn't this great?" he enthused. "Great for what?" Hurd asked, bewildered by a picture of a bowl filled with red, muddy water. "To make the film," Cameron said. By now, Hurd knew Cameron well enough to think, *This is crazy, and he can probably do it.* But neither of them had any idea how hard it would be.

Bud and Lindsey

At the heart of *The Abyss* is a relationship rare to find in any studio movie, an absolute curio in the action genre, and, in the late 1980s, the last thing anybody expected from a sci-fi technician like Cameron: a realistically troubled marriage. This guy was supposed to be dreaming up the next intergalactic war, not penning a fable about the complexity of human connection. And yet, somewhere between meeting aliens and preventing World War III, *The Abyss*'s estranged spouses, Bud and Lindsey Brigman, take one last look at each other and rediscover the goodness they had forgotten after years of laboring side by side on Deepcore.

It's a testament to the brilliant performances of the actors who play the Brigmans, Ed Harris and Mary Elizabeth Mastrantonio, that the most electrifying moment in this movie involves not extraterrestrials or careening subs, but Bud trying to revive his drowned wife. The lone special effects are Harris's pleading blue eyes and Mastrantonio's unflinching brown ones. A long list of actors were floated for the role of Bud—Mel Gibson, Dennis Quaid, William Hurt, Harrison Ford, Kurt Russell, Patrick Swayze. Though Harris had proved his heroic mettle as John Glenn in *The Right Stuff* in 1983, he had no real marquee value and Twentieth Century Fox didn't see him as a leading man. The studio was concerned about the actor's receding hairline, a trait Cameron thought added to his everyman appeal. "I don't much care what an actor's past roles have been or what his star power might be," Cameron says. Wearing a motorcycle helmet doubling as a dive helmet, Harris delivered a screen test that sealed the deal. "He was Bud, from the second he started to read. He had the relatability, the strength of character, the physicality to play a diver." And of course there were those piercing blue eyes, which lent Bud intelligence and depth beyond his aw-shucks first impression.

Lindsey would be another one of Cameron's spiky heroines, whose arrival on the rig is heralded by a Deepcore crew member as the coming of the "queen bitch of the universe." The actress who played her would have to be believable as someone smart enough to have designed an oil rig and open-minded enough to receive the alien communiqué everyone else is too blocked to see. She would need to be photographed wet and disheveled with very little makeup. And she would have to be willing to spend six months paddling around in tanks. Casting suggestions included Kathleen Quinlan, Jessica Lange, Debra Winger, Jamie Lee Curtis, and Barbara Hershey. But Mastrantonio had turned in two recent performances that suggested she possessed the strength the role required—as Al Pacino's fiery sister in *Scarface* in 1983 and as Tom Cruise's tough-talking pool-hall gal in 1986's *The Color of Money.* As Lindsey, Mastrantonio had to play a huge spectrum of emotions—courage, terror, awe, loss. Both she and Harris would have to learn to dive and would film many of their own underwater stunts. Both actors were deeply impressed by Cameron when they were cast and excited to get to work. By the end of the movie, they would have wanted to kill him at least a dozen times.

The authenticity of the Brigmans' marriage also owes quite a bit to Cameron's writing. This is a love story from someone who knows how working next to your partner day after day can somehow simultaneously breed both respect and contempt. As he prepared to film *The Abyss,* Cameron's own marriage to Hurd was falling apart. While he researched underwater cameras and gear and rewrote drafts of his script, she produced *Alien Nation,* and husband and wife retreated into their own separate projects. By the time he was fully into preproduction on *The Abyss* in December 1987, Cameron and Hurd had separated. Their personal relationship had suffered irreparably. But Cameron could think of no one he would rather have produce his demanding underwater action film than his soon-to-be-ex-wife. "So we wound up working together under pressure," Cameron says. "But I didn't meet any aliens and we didn't get back together."

The rest of the Deepcore oil-rig crew were mainly character actors cast out of New York City. A month before the start of production, they underwent diving training on the same boat Cameron and Hurd had chartered on their honeymoon, the *Cayman Aggressor*. The goal was to get the actors working as a team before they had to play one on camera. One cast member, it soon became clear, had lied at his audition and didn't actually know how to swim. But most were like giddy young soldiers about to march off to war—anxious to get their hands on the gear and learn how to use it. Harris, who had been cast last and was still filming another movie, couldn't attend the training in the Caribbean and so got scuba-certified in a lake near his other film location. By the end of the shoot, Harris would be the most accomplished of the cast underwater, strong enough, Giddings says, to hold his own with professional divers, and all without having spent one minute in the actual ocean.

For his villain, Lieutenant Coffey, the leader of the Navy SEALs, Cameron cast old friend Michael Biehn, who had played heroic characters for him in *The Terminator* and *Aliens*. Biehn read an early draft of the screenplay and sought an explanation for Coffey's increasingly reckless behavior. He convinced Cameron to add that Coffey was falling victim to high-pressure nervous syndrome—a disorder from breathing high-pressure gases that results in tremors, nausea, and decreased mental functioning. Biehn grew a mustache to look more menacing than the baby-faced good guys he had played before. Along with the three other actors cast as the SEALs, he underwent a different training, to learn discipline and a military mind-set. Cameron had now assembled his two families—the Deepcore crew and the SEALs—and he wanted each bonded as a unit.

Endless Night

Much of the equipment Cameron would need to realize his vision for *The Abyss* didn't yet exist. The director wanted his actors' faces clearly visible in the underwater sequences, but conventional diving gear covers the whole face, revealing just the eyes. Ron Cobb, who had helped Cameron design many of the memorable vehicles in *Aliens,* drew a concept dive helmet with a clear faceplate, so the actors' every subtle facial movement would show. A Santa Barbara company called Western Space and Marine (WSM) manufactured Cobb's design. One of the things Cameron wanted to achieve on *The Abyss* was the first recorded underwater dialogue in a motion picture. For a number of reasons, this was going to be a knotty problem. A typical regulator—the piece of dive gear that supplies the air—fits into the diver's mouth and wouldn't allow the actors to speak their dialogue. For *The Abyss,* WSM built the regulator into the side of the helmet Ron Cobb had designed, cycling fresh air as needed without a mouthpiece, freeing the actors to talk. To record the dialogue, microphones normally used in fighter aircraft helmets were incorporated into the WSM helmets. The special helmets were made for all the principal actors and for Cameron. To distinguish the director's helmet from the others, the company painted it with multiple colors and a big star on each side. Wearing it, Cameron resembled Captain America's skinny, scuba-diving sidekick. An underwater PA system was created so that Cameron—and only Cameron—could be heard by the cast and crew. "Jim enjoyed that," says Giddings. "It was a total dictator system." The cast and crew heard not just Cameron's orders but his every Darth Vader–like breath on his regulator. At a twentieth-anniversary screening of *The Abyss,* the production's sound mixer, Lee Orloff, recalled that for months after filming finished, "I would wake up in a cold sweat, hearing Jim's breathing." When the crew needed to communicate with Cameron underwater, they did so through hand signals. Since the clapping of the film slate—the traditional way moviemakers synchronize the picture and sound in a scene—couldn't be heard in the tank, a crew member would instead crack the slate on an actor's helmet. It was one of the milder indignities the cast would endure on this unusual shoot.

Before *The Abyss,* underwater motion-picture lighting was purely a practical consideration—was there enough illumination to get a good exposure? A cinematographer, who was primarily expected to rely on ambient light, could rarely consider aesthetic sensibilities about shadow, balance, or mood. But this movie was to take place in the black depths of the ocean, where no light penetrates. Ambient lighting would ruin that illusion and reveal the confines of the tank that housed the sets. Therefore, all lighting in *The Abyss* had to appear to come from practical sources on Deepcore, the subs, or the divers themselves. For help determining how to light the deep ocean realistically, Cameron dispatched his friend John Bruno, a visual-effects artist who had helped create the apparitions in *Poltergeist* and *Ghostbusters,* to the Cayman Islands with some still cameras and a couple of subs. Bruno dived down seven hundred feet and acquired images of the blue-black undersea world. These would serve as inspirational documents for Cameron and his crew, which now included Mikael Salomon as the director of photography on land and the underwater lighting supervisor. Now they just had to get their hands on hundreds of lights bright enough to illuminate the massive sets and safe and reliable enough to stick in a giant bowl of water with thirty people swimming around in it. Most of the existing lights designed for underwater use didn't have enough candlepower for the job. Richard Mula and Pete Romano, two engineers at an El Segundo, California, company called HydroImage, created for Cameron a powerful 1,200-watt metal halide lamp called the SeaPar. After *The Abyss,* the SeaPar went on to be used in countless other movies, from Michael Bay's *Armageddon* to National Geographic nature films. It became the only underwater lighting NASA allows in the indoor pool in Houston where it trains its astronauts in weightlessness. And it earned Mula and Romano a special Oscar for technical achievement. Of course, back on *The Abyss* set no one had much time to think about making movie history. It was on to the next technical problem, of which there were plenty.

A still body of water reflects everything. Once A Tank was filled, the entire set would be mirrored on the underside of the surface, ruining the illusion of being thousands of feet underwater. The filmmakers needed some kind of cover to help maintain the appearance of endless night. Several different ideas were considered—a canvas tarp of some kind, it was assumed, would be the best approach. But the winning plan was an unusual one that passed a test on a sunny afternoon in Giddings's swimming pool in Berkeley, California. Giddings got his hands on a giant barrel of black propylene beads about the size of BBs, which are normally used as filler in molding fiberglass products. He built a small, floating grid to contain the beads on the surface of his pool. From above, they looked like fresh blacktop road cover. From below, the beads blocked out all the light and blue sky. This cover allowed a diver to burst through in case of an emergency; if a lighting cable or a steel I beam penetrated the surface, the beads would immediately collect around the form, blocking any light. The production ordered forty thousand dollars' worth of the little black beads. It was a novel and ingenious solution. The only problem Giddings's swimming pool test failed to predict was that the crew would be pulling beads out of their ears, their noses, and every conceivable fold of their bodies for the next three months.

Early on, clearing the film's countless engineering hurdles was fun for Cameron. Making *The Abyss* was when he rediscovered just how much he enjoyed hands-on science. Although he had abandoned the subject as a vocation in college, the director was now returning to the family trade with the help of his brother Mike, who had spent the past fourteen years as a mechanical engineer. Mike's biggest contribution to *The Abyss* was something called the SeaWasp. Cameron needed a way to move the camera underwater smoothly and quickly, to achieve the kind of dramatic tracking shots for which filmmakers normally rely on dolly track or cranes. He tried mounting his camera on various diver propulsion vehicles but found them limited—he wanted to be able to aim the camera separately from the path of the scooter. As a solution, Mike Cameron built a vehicle powerful enough to tow two divers at nearly three knots and nimble enough to rise or descend while allowing the camera operator to stay on the subject. The SeaWasp DPV would earn the Cameron brothers their first of five patents on technical filmmaking equipment. Not much had changed since the Cameron boys' raucous, competitive youth. On *The Abyss,* the director cast Mike as a drowned corpse. At twenty-five feet below the surface, Mike had to lie with his eyes open and a live crab in his mouth. When his brother called action, Mike was to let the crab out. The shot took five takes. "Two times, I had to crush the crab because Jim was taking too long setting the lights," Mike says. "I'm sure it was a sheer delight for him."[2]

"Welcome to My Nightmare"

The art department moved to Gaffney in April 1988 to start building Deepcore. The turbine pits, which Cameron had originally come to Gaffney to scout, would be used to shoot miniatures and subs and would be referred to as B Tank. Production was supposed to begin in A Tank on August 8, but thanks to engineering delays in preparing the tank, Deepcore was nowhere near done. While he waited, Cameron started shooting what he could in B Tank and on dry sets. "Hello, boys," he greeted the crew on the first day of production. "Welcome to my nightmare." By early September, Deepcore—the main set and the site of the most complex underwater action sequences—still wasn't finished. Since it would take five days just to fill A Tank with water from a nearby lake and additional time to heat and filter it, Cameron decided to start pouring water into A Tank with the workers still inside it. As the water rose beneath them, painters stood on skiffs, working day and night to finish the set before it became submerged. When construction finally finished, the crew faced maddening new delays—thunderstorms, pipe ruptures, water clarity problems. A Tank was so big that it actually had its own weather. Some mornings the crew would arrive to find it too murky to shoot. Some local Gaffney goats even showed up, wandering into B Tank, chewing equipment, tumbling off the walls, and relieving themselves—fate was literally pissing all over this production.

Shoot days on *The Abyss* averaged fifteen to eighteen hours. When filming underwater, the crew was typically at about thirty feet deep, or two atmospheres. An underwater filling station was built to enable Cameron and the cast—with their unusual and cumbersome dive helmets—to fuel up on oxygen underwater, saving time and hassle and enabling them to stay down for up to five hours at a time. It took a while to get the pH levels in the tanks right—initially, there was too much chlorine, and crew members' hair started falling out and changing colors and their skin was burning. During breaks, the cast and crew emerged from the tanks shaky and unstable, like moon men readjusting to Earth's gravity. Immediately, they climbed into plastic hot tubs that were set up topside to warm them back up. After that many hours in the water, even in wet suits, they were chilled and clammy. Twentieth Century Fox considered the hot tubs an indulgence and gave Hurd a hard time about purchasing them, but as production moved into fall and winter, the hot tubs became the only place at the desolate industrial site that was warm enough for the crew to eat lunch or hold meetings. People grew exhausted and irritable and started coming down with ear and sinus infections. Someone erased the words "The Abyss" from a blackboard on set and instead wrote "The Abuse."

Decompression was a concern, especially for the principals like Cameron and Giddings, who were spending the most time under water. Their long daily immersions at relatively shallow depths were unusual and not something covered by standard navy dive tables. Dr. Peter Bennett, an expert on the physiology of diving, visited the set to advise the filmmakers on how much their bodies could take. At the end of the day, Cameron and Giddings often had to hang ten feet under the surface for an hour to adjust to the pressure difference. Never one to waste time, Cameron asked the crew to install a monitor in the control room so he could watch his dailies through the acrylic window while suspended on a line. When his neck was sore from his helmet, he hung upside down and had the crew invert the monitor. He asked Orloff to patch phone calls from the studio through to his helmet so he could to talk to Fox executives while he decompressed. After a draining eighteen-hour day, the few lingering cast and crew members heading home would stop and take one last look in the viewing room window at their director, clinging to the line like a bat on a branch and still at work. "I was stunned by Jim's allegiance to the project and the extent of his physical abilities," says Giddings, who had worked in the water all his life and was about sixty pounds heavier than Cameron. "I'm a big guy, strong and capable, and this was my world. Jim was there for every minute of it. It was beyond belief his commitment to what we were doing." Bennett recommended that the crew who were spending the longest hours underwater breathe pure oxygen through a mask for half an hour every night when they got home. So Cameron would sprawl on the bed at the house he had rented in Gaffney, eating his dinner and breathing pure O_2. Often he'd wake up the next morning fully dressed, in exactly the same position, with his dinner plate on his chest and the mask on his face.

"A Classic Clusterfuck"

The space-age helmets the actors wore were unwieldy—they weighed up to forty pounds and required a dive-tech assistant to remove them at the surface. When underwater, each actor had a dedicated safety diver watching his or her every move. The safety divers, or "angels" as they were known on the set, wore long fins and could swim in from off camera in a second or two to provide air if something went wrong. There was only one diver working in a helmet with no angel— Cameron. The director was also weighted with an extra forty pounds at his waist and ankles so that he could walk around the bottom of the tank with the camera. Cameron could go for about an hour and fifteen minutes on a single fill of oxygen. Because he tended to get absorbed in his work, he asked his assistant director to warn him when it had been an hour since his last fill. A few weeks into the production, Cameron was talking Mastrantonio through a shot; the actress was about twenty feet away. Giddings, about thirty feet away, was lining up the shot with his back to Cameron. All the other divers were at the surface or rigging lights off in the distance. As Cameron spoke to Mastrantonio, he took a breath and got no air. Perplexed, he looked down at his pressure gauge, which read zero. The AD had forgotten to give Cameron the requested one-hour warning. The director's helmet was attached to his buoyancy vest. He knew if he removed it, it would lose its bubble of air and become a forty-pound anchor—between the helmet and the waist and ankle weights he was wearing, Cameron would be eighty pounds negative. With the extra weight and no fins, there was no way he could swim to the surface. Hmm. This didn't look good. But he still had the microphone in his helmet linked to the underwater PA system. And Giddings was down there with him. So Cameron called to him, "Al . . . Al . . . I'm in trouble." The running joke on the set had been that all the other divers had to cover their ears all day long while Cameron yelled, "Al! Al! Pan left!" because the DP had ruptured both eardrums in a diving-bell accident twenty years earlier and was all but deaf from the scar tissue. Funny, but not this time. Unable to rouse Giddings, Cameron looked around for the support divers. "Guys, I'm in trouble," he said, using up the rest of the air in his lungs. He made the sign for being out of air, a cutthroat motion across the neck and a fist to the chest. Nothing. At the bottom of a 7.5-million-gallon tank, in the dark, thirty-five feet from the surface, Cameron really was in trouble. He knew he had to ditch his rig or die.

Up in the control room, Orloff had noticed the director wasn't sounding like himself. Suddenly the sound mixer heard Cameron's helmet being popped off and all the expensive electronics inside it flooding. Back in the tank, with his heavy helmet now off and fastened to his buoyancy vest by a braided steel hose, Cameron couldn't see anything but a blur. By feel, he located the release of his buoyancy vest and shrugged out of it, dropping the helmet to the floor of A Tank. Then he began what divers call a "blow and go," a free ascent. If a diver fails to breathe out during a free ascent, the compressed air in his lungs will expand as the pressure in the water around him decreases, and eventually his lungs will explode, a very painful way to die. Cameron was blowing out a stream of bubbles as he ascended and kicking like crazy because of his ankle weights. Finally, a safety diver named George raced to the director's aid. And that's when things got bad.

Safety divers are trained to stop panicking divers from ascending so they don't blow their lungs. So George stopped Cameron about fifteen feet from the surface, as he was schooled to do, and shoved his backup regulator into Cameron's mouth. And Cameron did what he was supposed to do, which is purge, then inhale. But the backup regulator was broken, a useless piece of junk disguised as lifesaving equipment. So Cameron inhaled water. Thinking he had purged incorrectly, Cameron repeated the procedure, as George held him down, and got another blast of water in his lungs. Now he was choking, about to black out, and he had a guy preventing him from ascending. With no way of explaining that he wasn't getting air, Cameron tried to pull away. Thinking the director was panicking, George held him even tighter and tried to make him breathe on the regulator. "A classic clusterfuck," recalls Cameron. It was then that Cameron's rough scuba training in the Buffalo Y pool really came in handy—either that or having brothers. He punched George as hard as he could, right in the face. George let Cameron go, and the director made it to the surface without blacking out. He swam weakly to the dive platform and dragged himself from the tank. By the end of the day, he had fired George and his AD. And he ordered the divers at the surface to fish out his helmet and fix the microphone so he could get back down in A Tank.

Wussies

The Abyss is the movie on which Cameron first earned a reputation for running a brutal set. Only half joking, he would yell, in the midst of yet another endless day in wet suits, "I'm letting you breathe. What more do you want?" Loyalists like Biehn knew Cameron could be harsh one minute, jolly the next, and they shook off the bad days. On *The Abyss,* though, there were mostly bad days. For newcomers, the director's relentless pace and harsh criticism of anyone who couldn't keep up were jarring. "Wussies," he called them. "He's so possessed and maniacal," Giddings says. "He's always a handful, always stressful, a mad hatter, moody, but I say it softly because of the load he's carrying. Tough to work with? The toughest." At the time, Cameron wanted to be the kind of leader he had written for Ed Harris to play. Bud Brigman commands the respect of his team and doesn't abuse his authority. He delegates to people based on their strengths. He's sensitive to morale. Cameron's leadership style has evolved over his career, particularly on the expeditions he took after *Titanic,* but on *The Abyss,* he still had a lot to learn. "Bud expressed the qualities I believe are critical to leadership, in any environment, business or hazardous," Cameron says. "Even though I knew these things during the making of *The Abyss,* I found it personally hard to lead that way."

There were plenty of moments on the film when Cameron pushed his team to the brink—and beyond. One dangerous sequence called for Harris and supporting actor Leo Burmester to complete a long, helmetless free swim—more than forty feet underwater without their own sources of oxygen. The safety divers had to stay far enough away to keep out of the shot. When Harris or Burmester made the cutthroat "out of air" sign, it seemed to take forever for their angels to glide in with the life-giving regulators. They finished the free-swim footage without incident, but after multiple takes, the actors were utterly drained. For another nerve-racking scene where Harris descends the wall of the abyss, the actor had to hold his breath inside a helmet full of liquid while he was towed the entire length of the set, some two hundred feet. Harris wore special contact lenses to be able to see underwater, but the chlorine left his eyes stinging and his vision blurred. During one take, the actor's safety diver got hung up on some cable, so when Harris signaled that he was out of air, his angel was nowhere to be found. Another diver swam in, opened Harris's faceplate, and shoved a regulator into his mouth—upside down. Instead of air, Harris got a gulp of water, and then another. "For a split second I really thought I was a goner," he said in a documentary about making *The Abyss.*[3] Finally Giddings rushed in, ripped the regulator out, and inserted his own, right side up, so Harris could breathe. In the car on the way home that night, Harris wept in frustration and fatigue. During the press junket for the film, when a reporter asked how he was treated on *The Abyss,* the actor said that was "like asking a soldier how he was treated in Vietnam."[4]

The most notorious story from *The Abyss* is somewhat misunderstood, having been told out of context in Hollywood for years. It's known as the day that drove Mastrantonio to scream, "We're not animals here!" and storm off the set. It was November, three months into the grueling shoot, and there had been a bomb threat called in that morning that halted production in A Tank. Just another day on *The Abyss,* people thought. Maybe it was the goats. The dry-set scene on the schedule was Bud's revival of Lindsey, the movie's emotional climax. For this scene, Mastrantonio would have to lie on the floor of Deepcore's sub-bay, wet, her shirt ripped open and breasts exposed, her eyes unblinking as Harris administered CPR and the rest of the Deepcore crew formed a concerned circle around her. She used eyedrops to dilate her pupils, giving her a lifeless stare but preventing her from seeing very well. The actors delivered a strong first take, but the shot wasn't well positioned—Harris's arm was blocking Mastrantonio's face. The second take was what directors pray for: magic. Crew members describe the hair on the backs of their necks standing up at the power of the performances. Mastrantonio, Harris, and the four other actors played the long, white-knuckle scene brilliantly. But this take was running longer than the one before it. Mastrantonio was just beginning to revive when suddenly the sound of a negative end flapped inside the camera magazine. The camera had run out of film. "Rollout!" the cameraman said, and cut the take—as well as all the hard-won tension in the room. That's when Mastrantonio jumped up, screamed the animal line, and left the set. "I understand the pressure and how it got to her," Cameron says. "It was our fault." It would be hours before the actress returned, after apologies from Cameron and Hurd and understanding words from Harris, to finish the scene. "I can be as hardy as the next person but only for a limited period of time," Mastrantonio told the *New York Times* in 1989 of the stress of making *The Abyss.* "I don't have the stamina."[5]

While she was gone, Harris filmed his close-ups. The script called for Bud to yell, "You never backed away from anything in your life. Now fight! Fight!" and slap his dying wife across the face. When Harris turned in the take that Cameron used in the final film, there was actually nobody there. He was slapping a sandbag. "I'm still in awe of that," says Cameron. The scene as it plays from beginning to end is riveting, and preview audiences and critics alike would praise it as their favorite. No one ever seems to notice that in the take Cameron selected, a cameraman quickly wipes his steamed-up lens. The director guessed, correctly, as it turns out, that this was one take that didn't need reshooting.

Another performer who would deliver above and beyond the call of duty was the white rat—or rather, five white rats—cast as Beany, beloved pet of the Deepcore crewman played by Todd Graff. In the years since Cameron first saw the liquid-breathing diver in that Buffalo seminar, scientists had continued to research the plausibility of the technology on various animals, from rats to dogs and chimps. Cameron sought out the main researcher, Johannes Kylstra, who turned out to be at Duke University in Durham, North Carolina, not far from Gaffney. Kylstra, at first a bit surprised that Hollywood was even interested in his work, briefed Cameron on all his research in the intervening seventeen years. Cameron told him he wanted to show fluid respiration with a rat on camera. "He told me exactly how to do it, like giving me a recipe for a pie," Cameron says. The director ordered the materials and followed Kylstra's method. He heated the fluid to rat body temperature, bubbled oxygen through it with an aquarium bubbler for twenty-four hours, and then shot the scene, with five live rats in five takes breathing the fluid. The actors' reactions are natural, because the experiment was really happening in front of them on set. After each take, Cameron picked up the rat by the tail to drain the fluid from its lungs. The first four times, the experiment went flawlessly. A production assistant would dry off the rat and take it to the vet for an antibiotic shot, since the fluid stripped out the protective mucus in the lungs, leaving the rats susceptible to infection. But when Cameron pulled the fifth rat out, it hung limply by its tail, completely inert and not breathing. The cast and crew watched silently. "I thought, 'Oh, shit, I'm not going to be able to get that little disclaimer at the end which says no animals were harmed in the making of this film, not with all these witnesses,'" Cameron says. So the director performed CPR on the rat, rhythmically pumping the little rodent's sternum, not unlike Bud reviving Lindsey. Within moments, rat number five came back to life in front of the crew. Cameron kept it as a pet until it died more than a year later of old age. "We were good friends," he says. "I like rats."

As the underwater photography portion of the shoot wound down, the crew members found themselves working in comically smaller and smaller tanks. After Christmas 1988, they gladly moved from Gaffney to C Tank, the Harbor Star Stage in Long Beach, California, for insert shots. After that, there was a miniature shoot in the 1932 Olympic swim stadium in Los Angeles, and then a close-up shot of a flare going off in Hurd's pool in the Hollywood Hills. The last shot of the film— the Brigmans embracing after the aliens rescue Bud—is actually two body doubles standing in a puddle in a parking lot at Cal State Dominguez Hills.

The Pod Squad

One of the innovations that came out of *The Abyss* was actually a process—this was the first film to divide its visual effects among multiple vendors, seven to be exact. The multishop model is now common practice in Hollywood, a way of guarding against a bottleneck in the production schedule, saving money, and allowing different companies the opportunity to do what they do best. *The Abyss* called for all kinds of complex shots utilizing miniatures, rear-projection screens, green-screen technology, puppets, opticals. But the sequence that had Cameron stumped was the alien water tentacle, the shifting, shimmering liquid pseudopod that rises out of the ocean and reveals itself to the Deepcore crew. Cameron wrote a detailed letter to effects houses that would be submitting bids for the work, explaining each shot and the method he thought best to complete it. For the pseudopod, he wrote, "Allow for testing to determine a technique. CGI has been suggested but due to the extremely long lag time between start-up and demonstration of positive (or negative) results, I am shying away from this." At the time, computer graphics was considered a crapshoot. "Digital was kind of corny," says John Bruno, who was supervising the effects on the film. "Everybody was doing stick figures with shiny heads and cue-ball faces. I hated the look of the stuff. It wasn't real." The early movies that employed some kind of CG were 1982's *Tron,* which takes place inside a computer, and 1984's *The Last Starfighter,* which is about a video game—both stories where the graphic, linear look of CG is an asset. But the pseudopod was supposed to feel organic and lifelike.

In northern California, Dennis Muren, one of the founders of George Lucas's special-effects empire, Industrial Light & Magic, was looking for a game-changing project. With *Star Wars,* ILM had broken new ground in motion control and miniatures, enabling cinema's most complex, perfectly synchronized spaceship battles. But by the mid-1980s, Muren was convinced the future of his industry lay in computer-generated effects, and he wanted ILM to get moving on the new technology. "I had the feeling that our tool-chest way of doing effects was just repeating itself," Muren says. Lucas had also started up a little computer division, a company tantalizingly located right across the parking lot from ILM. To Muren, the computer division seemed to be taking forever to get off the ground. It was called Pixar. In 1985, ILM and Pixar collaborated to create the first-ever CG film character, for the Steven Spielberg–produced *Young Sherlock Holmes.* The six or seven shots of a knight made of stained glass—all hard edges and no facial expression—were a good way to test Pixar's new software. In 1986, Steve Jobs bought Pixar from Lucas for $5 million. While perhaps not the best financial move for Lucas—twenty years later, Disney bought Pixar from Jobs for $7.4 billion—losing Pixar freed up Muren to press ahead with a CG division at ILM. He knew whom he wanted to work with first—the guy who had directed *Aliens,* which had deeply impressed him.

Muren showed Cameron a rough but promising animation test of how the CG pseudopod would move. He assured Cameron ILM could do it. It would take the company nine months to deliver twenty shots, amazing when you consider that twenty years later on *Avatar,* Cameron's crew would produce more than two thousand shots in the same time period, each of them many orders of magnitude more complex than the water tentacle. But this soft-surface, biotic-looking water weenie, which morphed into the actors' faces, was a lot harder to accomplish than the stained-glass knight. Cameron and Bruno had a couple of other ideas about how to shoot the water tentacle if CG didn't work out—at one point, Claymation was discussed. But ultimately they took a huge leap of faith with ILM. When Cameron got his first shots back from ILM, of Mastrantonio's face imposed onto the water tentacle, he knew he had made the right decision. It was a darn good thing, too, because by then it was too late to do anything else. In the end, ILM produced twenty pod shots totaling about seventy-five seconds of screen time. Cameron's water tentacle became the proving ground for realistic CG. For the first time, someone had created a life-like, natural character—not some shiny, sharp-edged effect—using computers.

The Wave

For years, Cameron had suffered a recurring nightmare about a wave, miles high, rolling toward him. A wave is a symbol of inevitability—once it rises, it always breaks upon the shore. Like death, nothing can stop it. In the third act of *The Abyss,* a wave of biblical proportions threatens everyone on Earth. Angry with humanity for playing at nuclear war, the NTIs have raised the wave to teach us a lesson. The image of the standing wave looming over beaches and cities required the use of miniatures and freeze-frame technology. The tricky sequence still wasn't finished by the time Fox held its first test screening of *The Abyss* in Dallas in May 1989—instead, the crowd saw a drawing of the wave. The test audience had a strong but strange reaction to it—members listed the wave sequence either under "scenes I liked most" or "scenes I liked least." By now the release date had been pushed back multiple times due to delays on the effects. Cameron, as was becoming his habit, had a movie that was way too long and an ending that in some ways felt like it belonged in another film entirely. "People didn't get it," says Tom Sherak, who was in charge of marketing the film for Fox. "Jim was trying to deal with past aggressions by society, the Holocaust, cruelty, how precious life was. He was trying to delve deep inside the psyche, and we were just looking for a commercial movie." Fox head

Barry Diller told Cameron *The Abyss* was "too much movie for today's audiences."[6]

Cameron elected to remove the problematic wave sequence, which diminished his defining theme of nuclear peril but brought the film down to a manageable two hours and twenty minutes. To their credit, executives at Fox questioned whether that was the right answer. But they knew the film had to come down in length, and Cameron had final cut. This was the director's first experience with the test-screening process. "I believe we misinterpreted the results, due to my inexperience," Cameron says. "I made cuts to the film that I shouldn't have made. I now know how to better interpret the cards. And I also know, never, ever preview a movie with unfinished effects." *The Abyss* opened on August 9, 1989, with the new, truncated ending. Reviews were mixed, and for the first time in his career, Cameron's box-office performance was underwhelming. On a production budget of $45 million, the movie made $54 million domestically, $90 million worldwide. It won the Oscar for best special effects and earned three other nominations, for art direction, cinematography, and sound. Riding in a limo with Cameron after the Academy Awards, special-effects supervisor John Bruno tried to get the director to hold the trophy for the film he had worked so hard on, nearly died for, in fact. Cameron refused to take the Oscar.

In 1992, he reedited the film for a special edition, adding twenty-seven minutes of material, including the wave sequence, which would appear in a new theatrically released print in early 1993 as well as on laser disc and DVD. "I like the wave version," he says. "I like the idea that we are judged and found wanting by rational, godlike aliens, but then saved by one good man. As a mob, we're a lost cause. As individuals, there is hope." More than twenty years after he first began it, Cameron's long journey into *The Abyss* was over. He never had the nightmare about the giant wave again.

6.

AND THEN THERE WERE TWO

Rebooting

When Cameron had first sketched out the *Terminator* story, his plans were too grand for the era—1982—and for his stature—a no-name crashing on his friend's floor in Pomona, California. Cameron's initial outline had called for two Terminators sent sequentially to our present from the future. The hero, Kyle Reese, was able to dispatch the first—essentially the T-800 model that Arnold Schwarzenegger played—at about the midpoint of the story. Then the future enemy reluctantly sent the second killer. This was the Terminator even the bad guys feared to deploy, because of its power and potential effect on history's time line. It was a tenacious liquid-metal robot that couldn't be destroyed by any conventional weapon—shoot it or blow it up and it would just reform and come after you again. Cameron tried to think of ways to depict the liquid-metal man using the filmmaking techniques of the day.

He thought Claymation might work, if it was shot carefully and in shadows. But he wasn't sure. "I was seeing things in my head which couldn't be done with existing technology," Cameron says. "Eventually, I realized I had too much story and nobody would fund it anyway." So he cut the narrative down to just the T-800 idea, which made *The Terminator* less an effects picture and more a conventional shoot with actors on street locations, an easier sell to financiers. But the liquid-metal villain always stayed in the back of his mind.

After *The Abyss* had underperformed at the box office, Cameron figured he'd better get back in the game right away. Within months he would get a chance to return to the story that had launched his career. It was just before Christmas in 1989 when he received a call from Mario Kassar and Andy Vajna at Carolco Pictures, the fast-growing independent production company behind the first three *Rambo* movies. Kassar and Vajna wanted to become major players in Hollywood, and they were spending money accordingly, buying up talent and irritating the studios by upsetting the value placed on stars and filmmakers. Carolco had bought the rights to *The Terminator* for ten million dollars, and the investors asked Cameron to write and direct a sequel. "They offered me a lot of money," Cameron says, six million dollars, to be exact. "I can be bought." Schwarzenegger could, too—for the action hero's participation, Kassar gave him a twelve-million-dollar Gulfstream jet. After he signed on, Cameron's first thought was of the liquid-metal villain he had dreamed about seven years earlier. Thanks to the pioneering CG work on *The Abyss,* now he knew just how to accomplish it.

This was a period of professional and personal new beginnings for Cameron, who was, for the first time since *Piranha II,* working without Gale Anne Hurd by his side. In early 1990, he founded his production company, Lightstorm Entertainment, so named for the lightning effect in *The Terminator* that accompanies the arrival of the

future warriors in the present. The director bought a building next to
the Burbank airport as headquarters and hired Larry Kasanoff, an executive from Vestron Pictures, which had produced *Dirty Dancing*, to
run it.

Before starting production on *The Abyss*, Cameron had begun dating a woman who could have strutted right out of one of his action
films, director Kathryn Bigelow. Strong, lean, and nearly six feet tall,
with a pretty, angular face, Bigelow resembles a female Clint Eastwood—
enough that she sort of played him in a spaghetti Western–style video
that Cameron directed for Bill Paxton's band, Martini Ranch. Like
Cameron's mother, she was a painter. She studied at the Art Institute
of San Francisco and later at the Whitney Museum in New York with
Susan Sontag before earning her master's degree in the film division at
Columbia University. Artistically, Bigelow was a good fit for Cameron.
Her movies are both macho and high-minded, starting with her 1978
short film called *The Set-Up*, in which Gary Busey and another actor
fight each other while cultural critics deconstruct the violence in voiceover. Her second feature, the 1987 Western-horror hybrid *Near Dark*,
became a cult hit and starred a number of Cameron regulars—Paxton,
Lance Henriksen, and Jenette Goldstein. While Cameron was in South
Carolina shooting *The Abyss* and Bigelow was in New York directing
the Jamie Lee Curtis cop drama *Blue Steel*, they would fly to see each
other on weekends. After *The Abyss* was released, they married and
bought a cliffside house in L.A.'s Coldwater Canyon.

Since he had worked successfully with Hurd, it seemed natural to
Cameron to work with his third wife. In this case, their roles were re-
versed, with Cameron producing and Bigelow directing. Bigelow had
found a mediocre action script about surfers called "Johnny Utah,"
which she wanted to make darker and more psychological. She enlisted
Cameron to rewrite as much of the script as he could while he prepped
Terminator 2. "I wound up going to studio meetings with her, pitch-
ing it, and pretty much woke up as producer one day," he says. Bigelow

was convinced she had found the next big action star to play her lead, an actor then best known for his dopey role in the teen comedy *Bill and Ted's Excellent Adventure*—Keanu Reeves. "She was determined to make him a star," Cameron says. "I didn't see it. But she insisted she would dress him, cut his hair, teach him to walk, to move. To this day I have no idea how she saw this in him." Executives at Columbia, which originally had the film, didn't get it either, and they passed on "Johnny Utah" with Reeves as lead. But it was Cameron's job as producer to back Bigelow's play. So he helped her set the film up with his old friend from Fox, Larry Gordon, who had by now launched the independent production company Largo Entertainment. The film's title was eventually changed to *Point Break,* and it became a surprise hit, launching Bigelow as a maker of big-boy action films and minting Reeves as the next big thing in Hollywood. Cameron's role as producer was mainly as Bigelow's guardian angel with the executives, including Gordon, with whom he engaged in at least one tense shouting match on Bigelow's behalf. "I'm not sure I've ever enjoyed producing that much," Cameron says. "But with Kathryn it was always a fun partnership. She is so committed to making great films, without compromise."

"Hey, Can We Really Do That?"

When Cameron signed on for *T2,* it meant returning to his old torment—writing. To have someone to share the agony with, he recruited Bill Wisher, his friend from Brea who had collaborated with him on the script for the original film. This time, Wisher and Cameron sequestered themselves in the director's tiny home office. The writers decided the T-800 would be the hero and would arrive in the present to protect John Connor, not to kill him. "We thought, 'If we make

Arnold the good guy, that'll surprise people,'" Wisher says. "That was a daunting decision at the time." Schwarzenegger as the Terminator was considered one of the film's great villains. If they turned him into a cyborg humanitarian, Cameron and Wisher wondered, "Will people hate us for doing this?" The first person they had to convince was the actor himself. When the writers got Schwarzenegger on the phone and pitched him the idea, he was dubious at first. At the end of the day, as Wisher recalls, Schwarzenegger gave in to their enthusiasm, saying, "Just don't make me gay."

Next the writers turned to their villain, the mimetic poly-alloy T-1000, the second Terminator Cameron had envisioned in his original telling of the story. Working late into the night as the coyotes howled in the canyon below, Cameron and Wisher kept trying to top themselves with crazy things the T-1000 would be able to do—what if he could shape-shift into a knife or fit through prison bars? It was an intensely creative period, as Cameron and Wisher pushed each other out of the way at the computer to get their ideas down in words. They were writing with the potential of CG in mind, but sometimes they wondered, "Hey, can we really do that?" So Cameron called Industrial Light & Magic, the company that had created his pseudopod in *The Abyss,* and asked. "They'd always say yes," Wisher recalls, "whether they knew they could or not. And we said, 'Well, it's going in the script, so you'd better figure out a way to do it.'" It was one thing to tie a single scene in *The Abyss* to the unproven computer graphics technique. But to make the nemesis in this big-budget action picture dependent on CG was a whole other gamble. This time Cameron would need ILM to push the technique further, to create not just faces but full body motion and even dialogue.

After a few weeks, Cameron and Wisher had a forty- to fifty-page treatment with a beginning and an end and all the beats Cameron felt it needed. The writers cut the treatment in half, with Wisher taking the first chunk and Cameron the second, and each headed off to turn his portion into a real script. This early 140-page draft contained plenty of sequences that didn't make it into the shooting script—there is an expanded future war at the beginning of the film where an adult John Connor defeats Skynet, breaks into the time-displacement lab, and sends young Kyle Reese through time, as well as a scene where Connor finds a cold-storage room full of racks of unactivated Terminators. The scenes created a vivid backstory for the first film, but with finite resources and bold plans for the T-1000, Cameron felt he had to focus the story on the present. He added a new character, Miles Dyson, the inventor of the neural net processor that would lead to the development of Skynet. Though he had mostly stuck to soldiers and blue-collar types as his brave characters in the past, Cameron's personal idols have always been scientists. With Dyson, he got his first lab-coat hero.

Cameron had set for himself the somewhat arbitrary deadline of finishing the script in time for his flight to the Cannes Film Festival in May, where Carolco would be announcing *Terminator 2: Judgment Day* along with the rest of the company's slate. Kassar had chartered a jet to take Cameron, Schwarzenegger, and a number of other big names, including Oliver Stone and Paul Verhoeven, to the festival for Carolco's press conference and legendarily extravagant yacht party, at which the titles and stars of the new films would be spelled out in fireworks. As the deadline drew closer, Cameron's nights of writing got longer. After one last thirty-six-hour-straight writing push, he finished in the nick of time. As Cameron hit "print" on his computer, the airport limo idled in his driveway. The last of the hundred passengers to arrive, Cameron was booed as he boarded the Carolco jet for delaying the flight. He gave copies of the script to Kassar and Schwarzenegger and passed out in his seat for the rest of the long, turbulent ride. As Cameron slept, Schwarzenegger read and was riveted. He liked the script, but he was nervous about not getting to kill anybody. "Can't I

just kill a few, at the beginning, before John tells me not to?"
Schwarzenegger asked Cameron. "I said what I always say when actors
have ideas for changing the script," Cameron says. "No."

Rambolina

Cameron quickly signed Linda Hamilton onto *T2* with a simple
pitch—it's twelve years later, your son is the target, and you're in a
mental hospital. Like Sarah Connor, Hamilton had become a single
mother in the years since the last film, and she found the character
easy to grasp. The actress had struggled with mood disorders and depression throughout her life, and three years after filming *T2,* she
would be diagnosed with bipolar disorder. Hamilton felt she could access those troubled parts of herself in playing Sarah Connor, a woman
emotionally burdened by knowing the apocalypse is coming when no
one else does. The biggest challenge of the role would be physical. The
T2 script called for Sarah Connor to have become a kind of feral warrior in the years since her innocent waitressing days. She was supposed
to have begun preparing herself for the bleak future by learning
weapons and combat techniques and training her body into peak physical shape. To get her in futuristic fighting form, Cameron paired
Hamilton with Uzi Gal, an ex–Israeli commando who was as far from
the usual sycophantic Hollywood personal trainer as could be. The actress worked out three hours a day, six days a week, for four months,
lifting weights and performing aerobic exercises. "Linda is blessed with
a muscle system which responds at the mere sight of weights,"
Cameron says. "So her physical transformation was dramatic."

More than just building biceps, Gal forced Hamilton to focus her
mental energy. He made the actress strip and reassemble the three
weapons she was to use in the film, in the dark, repeatedly, every day.

He threw tennis balls at her while she loaded her guns and fired them without ammunition over and over, for hours on end. Hamilton became machinelike in her precision of movement. And yet she had never fired a single round, not even a blank. The power of the training was demonstrated when Cameron and Gal finally took her to a range for live firing. Hamilton stood silent and still, ten yards from a human silhouette target with a Colt .45 automatic pistol and two loaded magazines. On a command from Gal, she smoothly slammed a magazine into the weapon, cocked it, and emptied the gun rapid-fire. Then she reloaded and did it again. "It was all thunder and smoke and flying brass, and it was over in seconds," Cameron says. The woman who had never fired a weapon in her life landed every round in the torso area of the target. "The gun guys at the range were duly impressed," Cameron recalls. "They did not believe her when she said she'd never shot before. They couldn't process how that was possible." Hamilton's hard hours of preparation paid off. On the first day of shooting, out in the Palmdale desert, Schwarzenegger took one look at her in her tank top and said what everyone else was thinking: "Linda! You are ripped to shreds!" There's no endorsement like Mr. Universe's. The training would help Hamilton make it through the grueling shoot, in which she was battered and chased and slammed into walls. "Every day was a physical challenge, but I was prepared for it," Hamilton said. "I was as much of an Arnold Schwarzenegger as I could be."[1]

In an era when women talk covetously about the First Lady's triceps, it's easy to forget how revolutionary Hamilton's chiseled physique and untamed performance were. It was 1991. Madonna still ate bread. A decade earlier, Robert De Niro had won an Academy Award for transforming his body to play boxer Jake La Motta in *Raging Bull*, but Hamilton's muscles threw some critics for a loop. In an article headlined "Why Can't a Woman Be a Man?" *Time* magazine dismissed Sarah Connor in *T2* as "Rambo in drag." The article stacked Sarah up against old-school tough gals like Joan Crawford in the noirish *Mildred*

Pierce, claiming Hamilton's performance lacked Crawford's "ingenuity, humanity and mother wit."[2] Mildred Pierce is an apt cinematic ancestor of Sarah Connor—as a single working mother in the forties, Mildred presented a strikingly strong image, the cultural equivalent of the sinewy lady who stockpiled weapons in the desert fifty years later. If Mildred is wittier, it's because she never carries the fate of the world on her giant shoulder pads. As for Sarah lacking Mildred's ingenuity— the woman breaks out of a mental hospital with a paper clip and *saves humanity.* There may never be a better screen metaphor for the resourcefulness of single moms. The truth is, there had never before been a female character like Sarah Connor in *T2.* Cameron had edged closer to her with each of his films, from young Sarah's reluctant acceptance of her awesome responsibility in the first movie to Ripley's ferocity fighting the queen in *Aliens* to Lindsey Brigman's courage in the face of death in *The Abyss.* With *T2,* Cameron and Hamilton went all the way and created the ultimate female action hero. For the first time, saving the world was woman's work, too. Sarah Connor owes as much to John Wayne roles as Joan Crawford ones. That idea may have shocked some people in 1991, but it doesn't now, when any would-be action heroine is expected to know her way around a weight room.

Hamilton's performance did lose a layer of depth in the editing room, however. Cameron, as usual dealing with an overstuffed movie, cut out a tender dream sequence that paired Sarah Connor back up with her lover from the first film, Michael Biehn's Kyle Reese. The sequence is restored in a longer version of *T2* available on DVD, but its removal from the theatrical release meant Sarah Connor was all warrior. During the making of *T2,* Cameron and Hamilton would become romantically involved, a point they both refused to acknowledge publicly, as Cameron was still married to Bigelow at the time. The director had always been drawn to women who resembled his fiery heroines, and this time he went for the genuine article. The two intense personalities were pulled to each other like celestial bodies, as almost anyone working beside them could see. Despite their love affair, Cameron kept his decision about cutting the dream sequence to himself until the last minute. "I was sleeping with the man and he didn't tell me, until we were looping," Hamilton told Canadian film critic Christopher Heard. "There was so much that had gone into that love scene with Michael Biehn. You were brought into the open heart of the character, which is just never that wide open throughout the rest of the movie."[3]

Mali and the Boy

With Schwarzenegger and Hamilton on board, Cameron's toughest casting job was finding young John Connor. The boy needed to resemble the actors who play his parents, Hamilton and Biehn, and had to talk and act like a kid, not a little adult. Young John Connor had to show enough strength of character that the audience would buy his leading the human resistance against the machines as an adult in 2029. And yet he had to look like he needed the protection and stand-in father of the T-800. Luckily, Cameron embarked on the search with the best kind of help—a casting director as driven as he was.

Mali Finn had spent her early life as an actress in local theater in the Midwest and had toured with the USO before settling down as an English and drama teacher with her husband, Donn, a theater professor, in Michigan. In 1981, the Finns moved to Southern California. Mali applied for casting assistant jobs but was dismissed as underqualified, overqualified, or too old, so she volunteered to help established casting directors for free, eventually earning credits on movies like *The Untouchables* and *Outrageous Fortune*. Cameron was one of the first directors to hire Finn after she hung out her own shingle at age fifty-one. She would go on to cast nearly eighty movies and TV shows, including *L.A. Confidential* and *The Matrix*, but it was the work she did for Cameron on *T2* and all his subsequent feature films until her death in 2007 that earned Finn a reputation as Hollywood's most indefatigable talent bloodhound. In 1995, Finn hunted down 1930s film star Gloria Stuart, then age eighty-five and without an agent, and suggested her to Cameron to play Kate Winslet's centenarian counterpart in *Titanic*. At eighty-seven, Stuart became the oldest nominee ever for a competitive, nonhonorary Oscar.

Finn undertook a nationwide search to find Cameron his John Connor, looking at hundreds of professional child actors. Not one to sit in her office sifting through head shots, she was watching kids play at the Boys and Girls Clubs of Pasadena when a pale, thin youngster caught her eye. Edward Furlong, then twelve, had some things in common with John Connor. He had never met his dad, didn't live with his mom, and was at once streetwise and needy. Finn smiled and approached Furlong, who thought he was getting in trouble for something and snarled at her. "I was intimidated by him," Finn told *People* magazine in 1991. "Eddie really gave me a tough time. If I touched him, he pulled away. He called me things like 'frog lips.' He had this real strong presence."[4] Finn snapped a Polaroid of Furlong and asked if he would like to come out and audition for a movie. He dropped his guard quickly after that. Furlong's auditions didn't go well at first—he was awkward, inexperienced, and intimidated by Hamilton, with whom he was asked to read. But Finn kept pulling for her boys' club find, and Cameron agreed that Furlong had some indefinable natural quality. The boy did with ease things that professional child actors struggled with, like crying convincingly. Though Cameron kept auditioning other actors, after watching Furlong, they all seemed phony to him. Finn assigned a dialogue coach to work with Furlong for a few weeks, and then Cameron saw him again and hired him. Casting an inexperienced actor like Furlong as the lead in what was about to become the most expensive movie to date was one of the bigger risks

Cameron took in his career, as nervy a move as depending on still-nascent CG technology to deliver his villain.

The John Connor part would have been demanding for any actor, much less a total newcomer. Furlong had to cry on cue with Hamilton in one scene and flee the T-1000 on the back of a dirt bike in another. He had to get used to the sound of gunfire around him and to filming grueling, sometimes frightening action sequences. For the dirt-bike scene, Furlong was hooked onto a moving camera car and pulled along as a tractor-trailer truck flipped over behind him. In a chase scene where he rides on Schwarzenegger's motorcycle, the action hero kept inadvertently clocking Furlong on the back of the head with his gun, once nearly knocking him out. The easiest part of Furlong's job turned out to be sharing scenes with his massive costar. The day he met Schwarzenegger, the twelve-year-old nervously extended his hand to shake. "Shake hah-der. Give me a real hahd one this time," Schwarzenegger said, immediately falling into his character as stand-in father figure and keeping it up for the duration of the shoot. The action hero and Furlong were "about the same age emotionally," Hamilton told Schwarzenegger biographer Nigel Andrews. As the three spent long stretches together in a car in the desert during filming, she said, "I would just sit there helpless while Arnold was giving Eddie tips on women. It was excruciating."[5] Over the course of the production, Furlong would grow up, not just as an actor but as a teenager. About halfway through filming, his voice changed, necessitating lots of extra work in the dubbing room to rerecord his early scenes. Furlong had begun the shoot as a small, frail child, but after eating from the catering truck for months, he had grown noticeably. Late in the production, when Cameron had to return for a pickup shot of Hamilton and Furlong standing on either side of a car, their height ratio didn't match the scene as filmed months earlier. For continuity, the crew had to dig a hole for Furlong to stand in.

The T-1000

Cameron spent a lot of time working out the rules that would govern his villain, which he envisioned as a metal liquid that could rapidly shift its shape and mimic almost anything—a person, a table, a knife blade. During the writing process, he was in his living room excitedly explaining the T-1000 to his friend and collaborator Stan Winston when Winston raised a concern. "I don't know who the bad guy is," Winston said. "I need a specific character, a specific image." To Winston, what Cameron was describing sounded like a blob of goo, not an iconic evildoer. "From a story standpoint, I thought it was a problem," Winston later recalled in an interview for the picture-book history of his studio, *The Winston Effect*.[6] Cameron respected Winston's instincts for creating memorable characters, and he started reconsidering how he would shape this one. Later that same night, the effects artist got a phone call from his friend. "I've got it!" Cameron said. "He's a cop!" The form the T-1000 would take for most of the movie was a Los Angeles police officer. This solved the storytelling dilemma Winston had raised and also gave Cameron an opportunity to underline a central theme in both of the *Terminator* movies—how people, especially those in violent jobs, like soldiers and cops, can become barbarized. "The *Terminator* films are not really about the human race getting killed off by future machines. They're about us losing touch with our own humanity and becoming machines, which allows us to kill and brutalize each other," he says. "Cops think of all noncops as less than they are, stupid, weak, and evil. They dehumanize the people they are sworn to protect and desensitize themselves in order to do that job." Cameron's creation of an LAPD villain in his 1990 script eerily predates and is strangely linked to one of the darker moments in the department's history. One of the locations in *T2* is the very spot in the

San Fernando Valley where police pulled over Rodney King in March of 1991. The famous amateur video has two chunks of footage on it, the first of the *T2* crew driving around on an insert car shooting Schwarzenegger and Furlong on a motorcycle, and the second of King being beaten in the same location just weeks later.

One of the rules the T-1000 had to play by was that it could turn into a knife but not a gun, a limitation revealed when the character passes through the bars of a mental institution, but its pistol gets caught. As Cameron saw it, the T-1000 could harden portions of its mass to form edge weapons and stabbing weapons, but it couldn't convert part of its mass into a complex machine involving separate, detached pieces or make gunpowder to launch projectiles. It was important to Cameron to show the audience the character's restrictions. It also meant lots of work for Winston, who would create hundreds of blades, from spike fingers to knife arms, for the T-1000's effects. "In science fiction you have to have rules and you have to state them, and you have to play by them," Cameron says. "Somehow it makes the fantasy more real, by adding complexity."

The director was looking for a lean, agile actor to play his villain this time around, someone more in line with his original vision of the Terminator as an infiltrator. "I wanted to find someone who would be a good contrast to Arnold," he says. "If the 800 series is a kind of human Panzer tank, then the 1000 series had to be a Porsche."[7] Early concept art for the film shows Billy Idol's sneering visage in the cop uniform. At one point, Cameron was considering the rock singer for the role, until Idol broke his leg in a motorcycle accident that would prevent him from getting into running shape in time. A much less familiar face, a Georgia-born actor named Robert Patrick who had played a string of bad guys in Roger Corman movies and a terrorist in *Die Hard 2,* ultimately won the T-1000 part. A college athlete in football and track, Patrick had just the kind of athleticism Cameron was seeking and an intensity that could sell the audience on this unusual villain with little dialogue. Patrick threw himself into the unique physical demands of playing a liquid character, hiring a trainer and focusing on flexibility that would allow him to make his body look more fluid on camera. He practiced sprinting while breathing only through his nose to appear robotically smooth as he ran. The actor's incredible speed actually created a problem for the production one day. The T-1000 was supposed to be on foot, chasing young John Connor on his dirt bike out of a parking garage. A camera car was towing Furlong on his bike, with Patrick in hot pursuit, delivering his best liquid-metal sprint. The scene calls for young John Connor to get away. But Patrick, running in heavy cop shoes, caught up with the camera car and tapped Furlong right on the shoulder. Cameron had definitely found that human Porsche he wanted.

The T-1000 fantasy was realized by blending Patrick's performance with nascent CG techniques and the highest art in makeup and puppets. Dennis Muren, who had supervised ILM's work on *The Abyss,* returned to shepherd the company's thirty-five CG artists through the process of delivering Cameron shots of this strange, intelligent liquid metal. Working from film and photos of Patrick, the ILM team built 3-D models in their computers, duplicating the actor's movements, right down to a barely perceptible limp from an old football injury. Cameron was taking an even bigger leap of faith this time than he had on *The Abyss.* If the pseudopod sequence hadn't worked, he could have cut it and still had a movie, but the T-1000 was central to the story. If it couldn't be done, *T2* wouldn't be made. For the scenes in which the T-1000 mutates from one form into another, ILM relied on a technique called morphing, which it had pioneered in the 1988 Ron Howard movie *Willow.* In *Willow,* a character smoothly transforms from a goat into several other animals before becoming a human. A flop at the box office, *Willow* didn't lead to the excitement about the digital breakthrough that ILM had thought it would. It wouldn't be until *T2* that the technique took off to the point of overkill, appearing in everything from movies like *The Mask* to Michael Jackson's "Black or White" video to TV commercials for hair-loss products.

Some of the things Cameron wanted the T-1000 to do were a stretch for ILM—literally. When the computerized character extended into certain poses, giant black gashes appeared in his shoulders. The movements were ripping up geometry. Scientists visited the company's San Rafael, California, offices to help the artists with the mathematical challenges the T-1000 posed. "I'd go by and there'd be somebody giving a lecture at a blackboard, and it was like something out of a joke science movie with the math on there," says Muren. Muren's team pulled it off, thanks in part to a cool new piece of software invented by a twenty-something ILMer named John Knoll and his brother Thomas, a grad student at the University of Michigan. That software happened to be the very first version of Photoshop, still a few years away from becoming the industry-standard graphics-editing program. Cameron breathed easier when he saw an early proof-of-concept shot of the T-1000 walking out of an explosion. With sparks reflected on his sleek, chrome body, the liquid-metal man looked just as Cameron had envisioned him. *This might actually work,* he thought. Each step the ILM team took built on the one before it, enabling them to achieve once-impossible shots like the T-1000 sliding through the bars of the mental hospital. "It wasn't like you couldn't have done this two years ago. It was more like you couldn't have done this a week ago," marvels Muren. Cameron's wild ideas gave the ILM artists opportunities to advance their craft in ways they wouldn't have if they had been creating something more mundane, like a CG bear. "The movie pushed us right to the very edge," Muren says.

The budget for the work ILM did on *T2* was more than $6 million, a sum considered astronomical at the time, although it would quickly be surpassed. One thing that helped sell the liquid-metal man to audiences was the considerably more low-rent sound effects that accompanied its movements. The noise of the T-1000 shape-shifting through the metal bars was actually dog food sliding out of a can. Other oozy sounds came from dipping a condom-covered microphone into a flour-and-water mixture and then shooting condensed air into the goop. "I like the fact that ILM had to spend millions of dollars on the visual effects and all we had to spend was thirty-five cents on a can of dog food," says the movie's sound designer, Gary Rydstrom. ILM's schedule for delivering the T-1000 images was so rigorous that the background plates had to be photographed before Cameron shot the scene in which they belonged. For the scene where the T-1000 is lying on the floor healing instantaneously from gunshot wounds, for instance, Cameron had to photograph the floor, committing to the lighting and camera angles in advance, and give the plates to ILM so it could begin working on the special-effects shots. Months later, he finally filmed the footage with Patrick that would lead up to the special-effects shot and follow it, hewing to the same lighting and angles he had originally promised.

Although *T2* is best remembered for the strides it led to in CG, of the fifteen minutes that the T-1000 displays its morphing and healing abilities only six were accomplished with pure computer graphics. The other nine were achieved with the use of puppets and prosthetics created by Winston's studio, the first time physical and digital effects were deployed so symbiotically. Typically, a T-1000 sequence would be divided between ILM and Winston—Winston's prosthetics would show a bullet hitting the T-1000's chest, for example, and ILM would close the wounds digitally. The effect was so smoothly executed that many of the shots later assumed by keen-eyed industry viewers to be CG are actually from Winston's crew. One of the most often misattributed is the moment when Schwarzenegger delivers his classic line, "Hasta la

vista, baby," and shoots the frozen T-1000, which shatters. For that sequence, Winston's studio built a fiberglass dummy of Patrick and filled
it with metallic flakes and Vacumetalized urethane foam shards. The
crew then blew the foam apart with Primacord. The first attempt at the
shot was underwhelming. The microscopic pieces blew out, as in an explosion, not down, as they would after gunfire, and the smoke
shrouded some of the effect. So Cameron added giant fans blowing
down on the dummy, dispersing the smoke and making the pieces flut-
ter magically to the ground. With the help of another simple sound
effect—a bunch of nails thrown on the floor—the sequence comes off
brilliantly.

As usual, Cameron threw himself into the design effort on *T2*, lean-
ing over Winston's concept artists at their drafting tables and weighing
in with sketches of his own. Winston artist Crash McCreery was laboring on a complicated design the team had nicknamed "pretzel man"
one day when the director was stalking the floor of the studio. "That's
cool, but it should be like this," Cameron said, as McCreery remembers, taking a napkin and in a few seconds drawing a perfect sketch of
the effect, the T-1000 splaying open after a shotgun blast. "As an artist,
you look at that and you just want to throw your pencil down and give
up," says McCreery.[8] From those designs, Winston's crew created several foam-rubber puppets of Patrick with a Vacumetalized inner portion to approximate the appearance of liquid metal. The puppets were
used to depict the T-1000 in its various stages of battle—in addition
to pretzel man, there was the "donut head" puppet for the T-1000 with
a gaping gunshot hole in his brain, "splash-head" for a shotgun blast
to the noggin, and "cleave man" to show Patrick being sliced through
with a steel rod.

One of the more ingenious effects the Winston crew devised were
appliances that would represent the impact of bullet hits on the liquid-
metal man. The artists spent weeks shooting pellets into mud and

studying the impressions they left to get the right look. They then sculpted those forms in several sizes and fitted them with a spring-loaded mechanism that would snap open the bullet wounds on cue. The wound rosettes attached to a fiberglass chest plate Patrick wore under a prescored costume. When a puppeteer released a radio-controlled pin, the chrome bullet wounds would bloom on the actor's body.

The Art of Making Mayhem

Film sets take on the personalities of their directors, and Cameron's sets are bustling and sometimes brutal. On *T2,* the accelerated production schedule meant Cameron's usual kineticism was ramped up even more. From shooting script to release date, the crew had just twelve months to deliver all of the movie's ambitious action sequences and special effects. Shooting began in the Palmdale desert in October 1990 and continued through April 1991 at locations all over California, from a dormant steel mill in Fontana to flood-control channels in the San Fernando Valley to a crowded shopping mall in Santa Monica to an office building in Silicon Valley.

The first-act chase sequence, which winds through the Valley flood channels, contains some of the film's trickiest action photography and most dangerous stunts. The T-1000 is driving a tractor-trailer truck chasing Schwarzenegger and Furlong on a motorcycle. Shortly before they filmed the sequence, the crew realized the truck was too tall for some of the bridges it had to pass under. Cameron decided to use the logistical problem to his storytelling advantage and make this semi a "convertible," prescoring the truck so the top would slice off cleanly when it went under the first overpass. Several cameras were used to shoot the sequence, including one held by Cameron from a motor-cycle sidecar, the tractor-trailer looming above the director while he bumped along four inches from the ground. At one point Cameron wanted a shot of the T-800 alone on his bike to look more intense. He radioed Schwarzenegger, who was not just his star but by now his good friend and frequent weekend motorcycling companion, and asked the actor if there was any way to take his Harley-Davidson Fat Boy around the corner faster. "Not with me on it," said Schwarzenegger, a man who knows his limits and is one of the few people who can say no to Cameron. The director switched to a longer lens and undercranked the camera slightly, and Schwarzenegger looks to be scooting along plenty fast in the final shot.

Perhaps the film's most troublesome location was the freeway. The production had arranged to close a five-mile stretch of highway in San Pedro, California, to shoot a night chase scene in which the T-1000 pursues the Connors and the T-800 via both semi and helicopter. (Bad guys always get to drive the semis in Cameron's films—good guys get stuck with station wagons, vans, pickups, and motorbikes, creating a kind of vehicular underdog effect.) The trouble started on this shoot when the production's cabling was stolen and *T2*'s beleaguered pro-ducers, B. J. Rack and Stephanie Austin, had less than twenty-four hours to find enough replacement gear to light five miles of road. After the cable was laid a second time, guards were hired to watch it for the duration of the shoot. Some nights rain prevented the crew from film-ing Schwarzenegger, Hamilton, and Furlong barreling down the high-way in a SWAT van, so the crew shot it "poor-man's process." They parked the van under an overpass, and a bunch of grips rocked it back and forth from the outside as lighting and effects crews swept spot-lights and squibs past the windows.

Despite the image suggested by publicity stills of men like Steven Spielberg and Martin Scorsese gazing sagely through lenses, it's rare for a director to hold his own camera in Hollywood. Cameron can, and often does, with great pride. A crew-tested diversion tactic when Cameron is in a foul mood is to ask him, "How'd you get that shot, anyway?" Inevitably, Cameron's spirits lift and he starts a long, detailed story by saying something like, "Well, the camera operator didn't have the guts to get on the dolly. . . ." Like asking Dad about his college football career, it works like a charm—by the time the story is over, the director has forgotten why he was mad. During *T2,* Cameron had a few chances to add to his lore. His Steadicam operator, Jimmy Muro, balked at what Cameron wanted him to do for one chunk of the freeway chase scene—follow the T-1000's helicopter as it flew under an overpass. Muro, a young, enthusiastic film school grad, had become a Cameron favorite on *The Abyss* for his determination to deliver smooth shots while running backward holding his eighty-pound Steadicam rig in the tight confines of the Deepcore set. But that night on *T2,* Muro recalls, "I said, 'Jim, I don't want to do this,' and he said, 'OK, I'll do it.'" Cameron had faith in Chuck Tamburro, the helicopter pilot, a Vietnam vet and masterful flier, who would make the dangerous maneuver twice so the director could get both the forward and rear angles. Cameron considers filming those shots—and all the fancy helicopter work in this sequence—some of the most exhilarating moments in his career. "I've always loved good action in movies," Cameron says. "I love how you can sit in the safety of a theater seat and still feel your heart pounding and a palpable sense of personal jeopardy. To get to do that, to cast that spell myself, over audiences worldwide, is one of the great thrills of my job which makes all the grueling hours and lost sleep worthwhile."

T2's compressed schedule had no effect on Cameron's usual maddening perfectionism. His take-ending catchphrases, "That's exactly what I didn't want!" and "Perfect! Let's do it again!" chafed the *T2* crew, some of whom took to wearing T-shirts that said "Terminator 3:

Not With Me." One chunk of the freeway sequence called for the T-1000 to be flying a helicopter and reloading a machine gun at the same time. But on the night of that shoot, the director realized he hadn't given the T-1000 enough arms for the two tasks. This is classic Cameron logic—he asks the audience to suspend disbelief enough to accept time travel and cyborgs, but he's not going to ask them to believe a character could load a gun and fly a chopper two-handed, even for a shot that flashes by at lightning speed. The T-1000 would have to grow two new arms—and fast. At 5:00 a.m. the freeway would reopen. A frantic effort ensued to rouse Winston's crew, asleep in their homes, to rush to their studio in the San Fernando Valley, pick up some supplies, and drive the forty miles to San Pedro to help improvise a new four-armed costume. It was the kind of middle-of-the-night call guys like Winston artist John Rosengrant grew accustomed to during the frenzied making of *T2*. "You'd be lying there, and you weren't supposed to shoot for three or four more days, and then that phone would go off and you'd pick it up and hear the crackling walkies and ADs talking in the background," Rosengrant recalls. "Somebody says, 'Can you be down here with the bullet-hole number five shirt?' Oh my God, what?!" Austin, who was producing her first Cameron film, was afraid Winston's fabulous bullet wounds wouldn't arrive in time, so she went down to the catering truck, found some tin foil and a Magic Marker, and sat on the side of the freeway creating makeshift ones. Winston's wounds made it at the last minute, but Cameron, amused by Austin's resourcefulness, used some of hers in the scene, too. One sign of just how much Cameron appreciated his scrappy producer on the movie is the name on the police uniform the T-1000 wears—"Austin."

One night while filming a scene from the future war sequence in the Fontana steelyard, the director was intent on getting a shot of a Terminator endoskeleton's foot stepping on a child's skull just right. It was a complicated shot that required several puppeteers to move the Terminator with precision and explosions in the distance to be timed correctly. Winston's crew had fashioned crushable wax skulls for the purpose. For any other director, they would have made ten skulls. This being their third film with Cameron, they knew enough to make twenty-eight. But by take twenty, at 3:00 a.m., Winston's guys were sweating it. No one wanted to tell Cameron he would eventually run out of skulls. At take twenty-six, the director finally decided to move on, reluctantly. Winston's crew went home disheartened, thinking they had failed. The next day when they arrived on set, Cameron beckoned them to his trailer and popped in a videotape from the previous night's shoot. "Watch this!" he said. "It's perfect!" It was the fifth take.[9]

A Violent Movie About Peace?

As usual, the editing room was just the next circle of hell for Cameron. As it had been on *The Abyss,* Cameron's biggest challenge was the ending. The ending isn't just where Cameron rolls out his most spectacular set pieces; it's also where he tries to drive home his larger message. And the director had a lofty goal for this action epic, with all its explosions, shoot-outs, clubbings, and poundings. "I think of *T2* as a violent movie about peace," he told *Newsweek* four months before the film's release. "And I'm perfectly comfortable with these ambiguities. It's an action film about the value of human life."[10] Cameron might have been fine with that dichotomy, but his backers were having some trouble. The first ending to *T2* cuts from the industrial inferno of the steel-mill battle to Hamilton in age makeup many years in the future, having averted a machine takeover and nuclear apocalypse. As bright sunlight streams down, she sits in a park watching an adult John Connor, now a U.S. senator, playing with his daughter. There are a lot of problems with this ending, some tonal and some logical. It seemed to be a scene from another film—our intense, athletic heroine had become a placid grandma. If Sarah prevented the future war, how did she ever meet the father of her son? And how did a delinquent like John Connor become a senator?

Carolco demanded a test screening, a process Cameron had felt burned by on *The Abyss*. The screening was held at George Lucas's Skywalker Ranch. There was a consensus among the crowd: they hated the ending. Initially reluctant to accept the results of the screening, Cameron eventually backed down and substituted a new final scene. "I began to think that the message of the film might be better served by not letting the audience off the hook so easily," Cameron explains in an introduction to a published version of the *T2* script. "We decided not to tie it all up with a bow, but to suggest that the struggle was ongoing, and in fact might even be an unending one for us flawed creatures trying to come to terms with technology and our own violent demons."[11] Cameron's final rewrite on *T2* came just a month before the film's release, when he cut the future park coda and replaced it with a shot traveling down a dark highway at night, with a voiceover from Sarah Connor: *"The unknown future rolls toward us. I face it for the first time with a sense of hope, because if a machine, a terminator, can learn the value of human life, maybe we can, too."*[12] It was a good compromise: Cameron got to keep his nonviolent message but packaged it in a way that was a lot less jarring to audiences.

With what Kassar had already spent to lock in the talent and what Cameron had ordered up in effects and action sequences, *T2*'s budget had ballooned, eventually making it the first movie ever to top $100 million in production costs. It was Cameron's first "most expensive movie in history," but it wouldn't be his last. The financial decision wasn't as risky as it sounds. Thanks to lucrative distribution deals, *T2* earned Carolco its money back before it played on a single screen. When it did hit theaters, on the July 4 weekend in 1991, *T2* accounted for more than half of all the movie tickets sold in North America. It would go on to earn more than $200 million domestically and more than $500 million worldwide, making it the highest-grossing film in the now-four-movie *Terminator* franchise. As he had with *Aliens,* Cameron delivered a sequel that expanded the audience for the original story without alienating its fans. *T2* garnered mainly positive reviews—the *New York Times* called it "a swift, exciting special effects epic that thoroughly justifies its vast expense,"[13] and *Newsweek* said, "For all its state-of-the-art pyrotechnics and breathtaking thrills, this bruisingly exciting movie never loses sight of its humanity."[14]

T2 earned four Academy Awards, for sound, makeup, visual effects, and sound-effects editing. The film's most enduring impact would be on the field of CG. The strides ILM made on *T2* enabled its next big project, *Jurassic Park.* "*T2* was the film that changed everything," says Muren. On the other side of the world, in New Zealand, a young horror director named Peter Jackson was taking note. "My God, I had no idea a computer could even do this," says Jackson, who was a decade away from releasing the first *Lord of the Rings* movie, and launching into the epic that would show just how lifelike a computer-generated character could become. "It was CGI, but it looked incredibly realistic. It was the genesis of the whole CGI movement."

For Cameron, everything about making *T2* had been thrilling, from the pioneering effects to the wild action sequences to falling in love with Hamilton. But after directing his fourth science-fiction movie in a row, Cameron was ready for a new challenge—maybe a character-driven drama or a comedy. Something small, for a change. Naturally, of course, his next movie would involve landing a Harrier jet on top of a skyscraper.

7.

MYTHS AND *LIES*

Little Movie, Big Deal

After the astounding success of *Terminator 2,* Cameron reached a pivotal moment in his career. The sequel had earned him heaps of Hollywood capital—every studio in town wanted to be in business with a filmmaker who both dreamed and earned on a spectacular scale. But Cameron had his eye on something more intimate, a nonfiction book by Daniel Keyes called *The Minds of Billy Milligan,* about a rapist in Ohio who suffers from multiple personality disorder and whose lawyers successfully use his mental illness as a defense for his crimes. "I was looking for a small drama after the 'most expensive movie in history,'" Cameron says. The director found Milligan's story and his long history of childhood abuse both moving and intriguing as a cinematic exercise. "To do all those characters and externalize the drama that was playing out in that guy's head would have been as big a challenge, in its own way, as making *The Abyss*." He optioned the rights to Keyes's book from Sandra Arcara, a New York–based restaurateur who was trying to establish herself as a producer, and he got to work on a script with Todd Graff, the actor and writer who had played Hippy in *The Abyss*. Cameron and Graff's script, "The Crowded Room," employs a lot of the same visual flourishes that mark the director's sci-fi writing, but this time the science and the set pieces take place inside the human mind. "The Crowded Room" uses a flashback structure like the one Cameron would employ on *Titanic* and reads as a great psychological thriller. But Cameron's little movie was about to hit a big wall.

In the spring of 1992, Cameron signed an unusual $500 million, multipicture domestic distribution deal with Fox that gave him power to put any movie he wanted into production without Fox's approval up to a budget of $70 million and retained for him ownership of the copyrights to his own films. In exchange, Cameron's Lightstorm Entertainment would have to shoulder its own overhead costs as well as take responsibility for any budget overages, which the company planned to do by selling the foreign distribution rights to its films itself. It was a remarkable deal for a filmmaker—typically, studios acquire the worldwide rights to a film, pay for the entire production, and own the movie outright. The deal gave Cameron both more control and more responsibility than a director typically enjoys or bears. "I'd just made *T2* for Carolco and I admired how they rolled, being their own bosses, mavericks, entrepreneurs," Cameron says. "I'd been fed up with the studio system after *Aliens* and *The Abyss,* both of which I felt were not released properly. So I figured coming off of *T2* I could set up a structure which would allow me to call the shots myself." The *Los Angeles Times* said the deal "may be a classic" and heralded the ingenuity of its architects, Lightstorm president Larry Kasanoff and Cameron's agent at ICM, Jeff Berg.[1]

"The Crowded Room" was not part of the new deal but was still in the works with a modest budget. But days after Cameron's gargantuan pact with the studio was announced, Arcara sued him. She alleged that she had been cut out of the preproduction process on "The Crowded Room" and refused to finalize the deal until she was given an increase in her fee, from $250,000 to $1.5 million. The director had become a victim of his own success. Arcara told *Daily Variety* that Cameron "is a much more powerful director and has a lot more clout now. . . . He's not the same person he was when I brought him the project."[2] Cameron was discovering the downside to being the biggest gorilla in the forest—a lot of little critters want to climb on your back. He dealt with Arcara's demands with his usual pragmatism. "I don't negotiate with terrorists or extortionists, so I told her to take a flying fuck and collapsed the project," Cameron says. "The Crowded Room" was dead, and with it any prospect of Cameron's departing from the big-budget event movies Hollywood expected from him. The director felt an obligation to make his first movie for Fox under the historic deal a highly commercial one. Arcara would later take "The Crowded Room" to other studios, where various director-actor combinations were floated, including David Fincher and Brad Pitt, Steven Soderbergh and Sean Penn, Danny DeVito and Leonardo DiCaprio, and Joel Schumacher and Colin Farrell, but the movie never got made.

Strange Days

The eighteen months after the release of *T2* was the busiest writing period for Cameron since his *Aliens* and *Rambo* marathon—in addition to "The Crowded Room," he was at work on a treatment for a Spider-Man movie and a futuristic film noir story that had been gestating in his brain since 1985 called *Strange Days*. *Strange Days* takes place on the last days of 1999, when Los Angeles is a smoking, rubble-strewn mess and there's a new kind of high-tech contraband on the streets called superconducting quantum interference devices, or SQUIDs. SQUIDs are a kind of virtual-reality headgear that taps into the brain and records every sensation a person experiences. People wear them to feel the thrills and terrors of others, from criminals to lovers. It's *Cops* on crack. *Cops* was the only reality show on the air when Cameron wrote *Strange Days,* but he clearly foresaw the camera culture that was coming. In the story, a grubby ex-cop named Lenny Nero traffics in the high-tech contraband and gets his hands on a disc of the police beating a rap star to death.

Cameron had sufficient motivation to stop putting off writing *Strange Days*—wait another seven years and it would actually *be* the eve of the millennium. But the director finally started tackling the story at the behest of Kathryn Bigelow. "I'd always liked it," Bigelow says. "It was a dark, edgy, gritty take on mediated reality and the perils of life lived on-screen." Cameron and Bigelow had divorced immediately after *T2,* and at some point he had stopped trying to hide his relationship with Linda Hamilton from her and the rest of the world. Despite Cameron's affair, he and Bigelow remained friends and would for years. It's a testament either to Cameron's decency in divorce proceedings or to his perceived power in Hollywood—or perhaps to a combination of the two—that his ex-wives stay on good terms with him. In the spring of 2009, seventeen years after they split, Cameron eagerly left the *Avatar* set on a Friday night to take in a screening of Bigelow's highly praised Iraq war thriller, *The Hurt Locker,* with his current wife, Suzy Amis.

Cameron's 1992 description of L.A.'s near future in *Strange Days* isn't a wild *Blade Runner* vision with flying cars and perfect blond cyborgs. It's grimly predictive—the future will be like today, he tells us, only worse. He's a better macro futurist than a micro one. His idea of

1999 fashion—an "Auschwitz meets *Metropolis* look" for women and kilts and bicycle shorts for men—didn't pan out, thankfully. But *Strange Days* is an amazingly accurate portrait of Los Angeles circa 2009, even more so than the year Cameron intended, 1999. Here's how he described the city:

> The economy is worse. The jobless rate is up. New housing is down. All the indicators are creeping steadily into the red. . . . California, the Shake 'n Bake state, is still mailing out IOUs and waiting for the Big One to make Barstow into beachfront property. The freeways are a nightmare of gridlock, with smaller cars parked closer and closer together. Gas is over three bucks a gallon. . . . There are security cameras in malls, cameras in office buildings, cameras in banks, cameras in schools, cameras in convenience stores. . . . Reality shows and amateur video dominate TV programming. It is the age of scopophilia, voyeurism, and vicarious living. . . . We like to watch.[3]

Cameron wrote his ideas for *Strange Days* in an eighty-page novella-like document that he called a scriptment. It's a term the director had coined as a joke back on *The Terminator* to describe the long, detailed story outlines he writes, a kind of hybrid of script and treatment that contains some dialogue and long chunks of narrative description. Most treatments are under twenty-five pages, but Cameron's scriptments run much longer—the one he wrote for *Avatar* is about one hundred pages. As a writer, Cameron's strengths are his savvy use of structure and his uncanny ability to paint vivid pictures that even Hollywood's most notoriously unimaginative species, the studio executive, can see in his head. But dialogue is Cameron's weak spot, and he knows it. His blood-and-thunder lines—"Come with me if you want to live," "Get away from her, you bitch," "I'll be back"—are memorable and oft quoted, but everyday banter stumps him. On *Strange Days,* Cameron made an extra effort to capture realism in his characters' speech. "I'm proud of that piece of writing more than the others for the sound of the dialogue," Cameron says. "I was trying to channel Elmore Leonard. Didn't quite succeed, but it is still my best dialogue."

Bigelow would direct *Strange Days,* the first time since *Rambo* that someone else had made one of Cameron's scripts and the only time he has ever trusted another filmmaker with one of his original ideas. When Cameron's other projects prevented him from turning his novella into a shooting script himself, *Age of Innocence* screenwriter and frequent Martin Scorsese collaborator Jay Cocks took over the writing. "I think he felt in good hands with Jay," says Bigelow. "Jim pretty much let the project go at that point from a creative standpoint." Cameron relinquished the writing but played a crucial role as a producer, mediating between Bigelow and the studio. "He kept us well insulated from studio turf battles and executive politics," Bigelow says. The resulting movie is unsettling and indeed a bit strange. Upon its release, some critics praised Bigelow's daring direction. She relied on handheld and point-of-view camera work to suggest the experience of wearing SQUIDs—a technique she applied more skillfully fourteen years later on *The Hurt Locker*—and made an unlikely casting choice for the sleazy ex-cop Lenny, Ralph Fiennes, engaging in a bit of genre slumming between *Schindler's List* and *The English Patient.* Audiences didn't connect with the movie's bleak future vision: on a $42 million production budget, *Strange Days* grossed less than $8 million.

What if James Bond Had to Answer to His Wife?

Back before Schwarzenegger had a state to run and Cameron had five kids, they often got together to ride their motorcycles through the canyons of the Santa Monica Mountains, Schwarzenegger in front, leader-of-the-pack style. "Jim doesn't have to be the lead guy," explains Tom Arnold, their mutual friend and sometime biking companion. "Arnold does. Everyone is in Arnold's wake." The subtle variations in machismo expressed by the director and his leading man are best illustrated by their choices of driveway art—Cameron buys new Corvettes, while Schwarzenegger prizes his Austrian army tank. One guy likes speed, the other strength, but they're both playing at superherodom in their own ways. On their Sunday rides, Cameron and Schwarzenegger would often stop at the Rock Store, a mom-and-pop shack on a twisty stretch of Mulholland Highway that has been a gearhead mecca since Steve McQueen rumbled through in the sixties. "When we get together, we have great conversations about things you wouldn't expect—education, the environment, relationships with women," Schwarzenegger says. Occasionally, they met without their hogs, sharing breakfast at Schatzi, Schwarzenegger's now-closed Santa Monica restaurant, known in the 1990s for its excellent *Wiener schnitzel* and the German-language lessons piped into the restrooms. It was at Schatzi one morning in early 1993, with the action hero bent over his usual vat of oatmeal, that Schwarzenegger announced to Cameron what their next movie would be. It was just the two of them. They hadn't met Tom Arnold yet, but would very shortly.

Both men had reason to be hungry for a sure thing that morning. Schwarzenegger was fresh off filming *Last Action Hero,* an action-comedy that was plagued by bad buzz and would go on to become the summer of 1993's biggest flop. Cameron had signed his massive deal with Twentieth Century Fox the previous spring and had yet to put a movie into production. Joe Roth, the filmmaker-friendly chairman who had approved Cameron's deal, had moved on to Disney, and now the man running Fox was a relative unknown named Peter Chernin, an executive whose background was mostly in TV. Cameron wanted to come out swinging with his first film under the deal, to cement his relationship with the studio as well as with Lightstorm's new foreign partners.

Schwarzenegger's brother-in-law Bobby Shriver had shown him a French movie called *La Totale!*, a farce about a secret agent whose family thinks he's just a boring civil servant. *La Totale!* doesn't have any big action set pieces, just a couple of short chases. It was the potential of the character—a man who is a hero at work but flummoxed by domestic life—that appealed to Schwarzenegger. He brought a copy of *La Totale!* for Cameron to watch, which the director did that night, immediately becoming intrigued. "I saw the film as an anti–James Bond, a reality check on the uber–male fantasy," Cameron says. "You might be able to travel the globe and kill all the bad guys in clever ways and save the world from time to time, but as a man you still had to answer to a woman when you came home. Bond himself is a pathetic eternal bachelor who will never know the truth of what it is to be a man, to be a husband and father, which is why that fantasy works, especially for married men. Because Bond has nobody to answer to." The joke of this movie would be "What if James Bond had to come home and answer to his wife?" At the time, Cameron was in a relationship with Linda Hamilton, unmarried and expecting his first child, and Schwarzenegger was married to Maria Shriver and a father of two. "Arnold and I both were drawing on our experiences as husbands— the good, the bad, and the ugly," Cameron says. He saw the movie as a broad action comedy on a giant scale—a crowd-pleasing vehicle for Schwarzenegger and for him. Cameron would call his domestic epic *True Lies.*

The sci-fi auteur was a little daunted by the prospect of writing comedy. "I had done funny moments in movies that were otherwise as serious as a coronary," he says. "But I'd never done a film that needed comedy in order to work on a fundamental level." Schwarzenegger's representatives were anxious to get his next movie in the works to resuscitate his image. By the time Cameron finished his *Strange Days* scriptment, he had just weeks to write *True Lies* before the actor's camp said he would have to move on to something else. In a time crunch as usual, Cameron enlisted Randall Frakes, whose floor Cameron had slept on while writing *The Terminator*, to share the writing duties. After Cameron and Frakes finished their draft, the director didn't think it was funny enough. The situations were inherently humorous, but the script lacked laugh lines and sight gags. Cameron brought in a team of comedy writers to punch up the jokes. Unimpressed, he kept only a few of their lines, including one uttered by Schwarzenegger when he detonates a missile with a terrorist attached: "You're fired."

Cameron's commitment to realism in his writing can create some strange juxtapositions. In 1993, with the cold war over, Hollywood was on the hunt for new villains to replace the Russians. For *True Lies*, Cameron picked a Middle Eastern terror cell operating in Florida. When Cameron and Frakes started researching the subject, they grew concerned about real life imitating their fiction. "We realized how easy it would be to smuggle the weapons in, how difficult it would be to detect them," Frakes recalls. "We discovered how committed and serious religious fanatics and political fanatics were in the Middle East and how anti-American they were. We got nervous. We didn't want to give anyone any ideas." On a crash run to deliver the script, they decided the answer was to make *True Lies* as silly as possible, which they did with its bombastic set pieces. But nestled in the middle of this action comedy is an eerie monologue delivered by Aziz, the head terrorist, to a henchman holding a camcorder:

> You have killed our women and our children, bombed our cities full of fire like cowards, and you dare to call us terrorists. But now the oppressed have been given a mighty sword to strike back at their enemies. Unless the U.S. pulls all military

forces out of the Persian Gulf immediately and forever, Crimson Jihad will rain fire on one major U.S. city each week until our demands are met.[4]

The script was written eight years before 9/11. Al Qaeda was just a start-up in Sudan, and the idea of a terrorist delivering threats via grainy black-and-white video was still something audiences could laugh at. Today, Aziz's speech sounds like something heard on CNN. After the 2001 terror attacks, Cameron abandoned the idea of a *True Lies* sequel. "Somehow, having fun with nuke-toting terrorists just didn't sit as well as it had," he says.

Master of His Domain

Cameron had been involved in two CG milestones at this point in his career, the pseudopod on *The Abyss* and the T-1000 on *T2,* both accomplished at George Lucas's Industrial Light & Magic in northern California. After making *T2,* he believed the visual-effects business was at an important crossroads, converting from optical compositing to digital. Historically, special-effects photography had meant layering each element of a shot—a painted background, an actor's performance, a model—on separate pieces of film and running them through an optical printer. It was a painstaking process and when done incorrectly revealed telltale matte lines and variations in color and film quality where the separate elements met. If you've ever seen an actor in an older movie who appears edged in a spooky halo when he's supposed to be sitting on a sandy beach, he's probably the victim of a poorly executed composite. But in the 1980s, it became possible to combine the various elements of a shot digitally and therefore seamlessly. One of the reasons ILM was able to deliver the T-1000 shots so precisely was its early use of digital compositing. Cameron wanted to be part of the digital revolution in special effects. "I wanted to make sure that as a filmmaker I was always ahead of the wave, not behind it," he says. To do so, he felt he would need a lab of his own.

About the time he was thinking of founding his own special-effects company, Cameron visited Stan Winston's shop. The director was amazed to see that Winston, a master of old-school effects, had installed about ten workstations with CG modeling software and had artists creating CG creatures for him. Winston had also stood at a milestone in effects evolution, while working on *Jurassic Park* for Steven Spielberg. Clearly, Winston felt, in the future creatures would be done as much with CG as with prosthetics and animatronics. It even seemed possible that CG would replace those arts at which he was a world leader. "So typical of Stan to attack rather than entrench, by getting out ahead of the pack and incorporating CG into his stock-in-trade," Cameron says. The director pitched his friend the idea that instead of ten workstations he could have two hundred, staffed by the best animators and artists in the world. Winston bought that pitch and joined Cameron as a cofounder of the effects company Digital Domain.

There were two other important pieces of the Digital Domain puzzle to be solved—the money and the person to run it. Rae Sanchini first met Cameron when the director boarded Carolco Pictures' 1990 flight to Cannes. Then an executive at the company, Sanchini was charged with the ostensibly simple task of escorting Cameron after the festival from France to Carolco's North Carolina studio, which the director was to scout as a possible site for filming *T2*. When their flight from the Orly airport was delayed, setting off a chain reaction of missed connections, Sanchini and Cameron ended up living out an upscale version of *Planes, Trains & Automobiles*. By the end of the trip it had taken five flights—one on the Concorde—and two long cab rides to deliver Cameron to the studio. He confessed to Sanchini an hour into their journey that he had no intention of filming there, having hated his experience shooting in the South on *The Abyss*. "He was just being nice," Sanchini says. "He carried my bag from gate to gate to gate. But it was a nonstarter." The trip wasn't a complete bust, however. Cameron and Sanchini hit it off. Her father had worked in the space program, and she was a huge sci-fi literature fan, so they had plenty to talk about on their three-hour layovers. Sanchini was also whip smart, had just earned her J.D./M.B.A. at UCLA, and was playing a key role in Carolco's aggressive growth. When their long journey finally ended, she remembers, "I said, 'I've failed horribly. I'm probably gonna get fired tomorrow.' And Jim said, 'Well, I'll hire you.'" Sanchini wasn't fired when she got back to L.A., but two years later Cameron did hire her, to help him put the financing together on Digital Domain. She ultimately raised fifteen million dollars from IBM, which took a 50 percent stake in the company and provided much of the hardware to get it started. Digital Domain wasn't a hard sell—the guys behind *T2* and *Jurassic Park* were as promising a team to back in the nascent digital-effects industry as existed. The person to run Digital Domain day to day would be Scott Ross, who had overseen ILM during *T2*. Cameron knew Ross as a sharp manager and a hard charger and asked him to join them as a third founder. The company's first bold move would be to wholly embrace digital compositing and not even bother to open an optical department. It was a risky decision at the time—most of Hollywood was still relying on opticals. But setting up Digital Domain that way gave the company an almost instantaneous advantage over all the established effects houses.

Cameron learned a lot from Digital Domain about business and about managing people. Strategy and boardroom politics were an alien world to him, but he got the hang of it, the lingo and the jockeying for power. He watched closely how Winston ran his shop of artists and took notes on his friend's motivating leadership style. Mostly, he was excited about being a pioneer. Thanks to its early adoption of digital compositing, Digital Domain quickly became the number-two visual-effects house in the world, behind ILM. Where the company was never able to lead, however, was in the main area that interested Cameron and Winston: CG creature and character animation. In the mid-1990s, Cameron would write a movie to give the company something to set its sights on—*Avatar.* But Digital Domain's first picture would be *True Lies.*

Funny People

When Cameron wrote the character of Schwarzenegger's wife in *True Lies,* Helen Tasker, he already had Jamie Lee Curtis in mind. He had met Curtis through Bigelow during the filming of *Blue Steel.* "Jamie struck me as kooky, wicked smart, sexy, and cool. We got to be friends, the three of us," he says. Curtis, the daughter of Janet Leigh and Tony Curtis, had broken out in John Carpenter's *Halloween* in 1978, playing the kind of capable heroine that inspired some of Cameron's own female characters. She'd gone on to make some B horror movies before landing a choice comic role opposite Dan Aykroyd and Eddie Murphy in *Trading Places* in 1983. Curtis loved the notion of playing a dowdy wife desperate for a little adventure in her life in *True Lies.* This was one casting decision that should have been easy. There was only one problem: Schwarzenegger didn't like the idea. "He didn't see what I saw," Cameron says. "And Arnold was, of course, accustomed to getting his way." Schwarzenegger didn't like to confront or question Cameron creatively, so he gave word via his agent at the time, Lou Pitt, that Curtis was a no-go. "I thought, Oh, too bad. She would have been great. But this thing is Arnold's baby, so I have to honor his choice," Cameron says.

So began a three-month search to find the perfect Helen. Cameron met with lots of actresses, and screen-tested one with Schwarzenegger, who seemed like a strong choice. Then one night, after a long day of location scouting in Washington, D.C., the director returned to his hotel room to find a videotape on the table. It was *A Fish Called Wanda*, the John Cleese comedy, which Cameron had asked his office to get months earlier so he could check out Curtis's recent work. He popped it in, planning to wind down for ten minutes with a glass of wine, and ended up staying up till 2:00 a.m. watching the movie. "Jamie was pitch perfect in her dual role and was sexy and charming and fun," Cameron says. "She had to play Helen." But how to deal with Schwarzenegger? The director returned to L.A. and called his friend, who dropped what he was doing—whatever it was, it involved wearing purple board shorts—and came over to Cameron's office immediately. "I said, 'How much do you trust me?'" Cameron recalls. "And Arnold said, 'Of course, I trust you completely.' 'No, really, no bullshit. How much do you trust me?'" Schwarzenegger made it clear he was being sincere. "Then it's going to be Jamie Lee," Cameron told him. Schwarzenegger froze. "I can only guess what he was thinking, but his jaw clenched for a long time and then he relaxed and said OK." Schwarzenegger would throw himself into the film, never showing a hint of resisting the casting choice once it had been made. In the end, he happily agreed to share with Curtis something rarely surrendered willingly in Hollywood—his above-the-title credit. "Even though he can believe he is utterly correct and is accustomed to acting on his instincts and being in charge, Arnold listens to the others he trusts, like Maria Shriver, and even sometimes me," Cameron says.

The script called for Helen Tasker to strip for her husband, Harry, thinking she was stripping for an arms dealer. The scene proved to be one of the more controversial of Cameron's career, with some critics accusing him of misogyny. "A strain of crudeness and mean-spirited humiliation, especially toward women, runs through the film like a nasty virus," wrote the *Los Angeles Times*'s Kenneth Turan,[5] while Roger Ebert called the dance "cruel and not funny."[6] Curtis had heavy input into how the scene was filmed. As Cameron had originally written the sequence, she would be naked but shot in silhouette. One day during preproduction, the actress blazed into Cameron's office, lobbying to play the scene differently. She wanted to undress only to her bra and panties and deliver an awkward striptease fully lit. To make her case, Curtis peeled off her clothes and started performing a klutzy burlesque in her underwear in front of the director's desk. "It was that day that I realized how cool my job really was," Cameron says. "I stammered out, 'Yeah, sure, Jamie, that's a good idea.'" Curtis's suggestion allowed Cameron to play the scene with a bigger wink, adding a pratfall where Helen slips in the middle of her amateur pole dance. The director and his actress blocked out the dance while Schwarzenegger was in his trailer, and he wasn't in on the gag. Watch the scene closely—as many Curtis fans have—and you'll see that when the actress falls, a concerned Schwarzenegger jumps up to help her and then sits back down in the shadows, realizing he's breaking character. "It plays because Harry realizes he's breaking character from the shady arms dealer he's posing as," Cameron says. "We did a second take, but it wasn't as funny."

Interestingly, some of the scene's biggest champions were women, who seemed to pick up on the fun Curtis was having when she filmed it. Caryn James of the *New York Times* called Curtis's evolution in the film from a mousy legal secretary to a tangoing superspy "witty and liberating" and praised Cameron for charting "the comic course of a female stereotype falling to pieces."[7] While male critics interpreted the striptease as demeaning, many female critics saw it as freeing— perhaps they noticed the twinkle in Curtis's eye, while the men were distracted by her other assets. "Jamie Lee's character was empowered by tapping into her sexuality in a way that she hadn't been doing in her marriage," says Hollywood blogger Anne Thompson, who was writing for *Entertainment Weekly* at the time. "She managed to pull it off in a way that was not at all icky for me." The performance would win Curtis her first Golden Globe. And *True Lies,* with its husband-and-wife spy fantasy, paved the way for Brad Pitt and Angelina Jolie's married assassins in *Mr. and Mrs. Smith* eleven years later.

Because he was uncertain about his comedy script, Cameron wanted to hedge his bets by casting witty actors whom he could count on for some improvised laughs. Curtis was one. Now he'd need to find a really funny guy to play Gib, Schwarzenegger's sidekick. At the time, Tom Arnold was married to Roseanne Barr and was writing for her hit sitcom. Arnold's road to Hollywood had been a bizarre one—he worked in a meatpacking plant slicing up pigs in Ottumwa, Iowa, before embarking on a stand-up-comedy career in the eighties and developing a cult following for a routine in which he taped a live goldfish to a little motorcycle and shot it through a ring of fire. He'd played five scenes as a bartender in the Dustin Hoffman movie *Hero* but was otherwise a stranger to the big screen. Mostly, Hollywood knew him as a human punch line, Barr's opportunistic husband. But somehow, Arnold's agent got him a reading with Cameron. "I was the last person in town to audition for *True Lies,*" Arnold recalls. "I was like, there's no way I'm gonna get this. This is too big of a part. I just wanted to tell people I met Jim Cameron." The director brought in Schwarzenegger to read with him, and the preening action hero and excited comic were both jostling for the camera. "Tom was fun in the reading, completely manic, an opposite to Arnold's solid, brooding determination," Cameron recalls. After Schwarzenegger left the room, the chubby comedian took Cameron aside. "He's not that big," he said. "I think I could take him." The line cracked the director up and sealed the deal.

Cameron knows a lot about a lot of subjects—he can talk energy policy with a think-tank researcher, helicopter engines with an engineer, and the Punic Wars with a classical historian. But one of his rare blind spots is Hollywood gossip. This is not a man who watches E! So he gave Arnold the gig and called Fox to let them know, never expecting a problem. "I had never seen Tom on *Roseanne,* and I'd never particularly taken into account actors' television baggage," Cameron says. "I just saw a guy that could play the character as I imagined him." Fox, as Arnold later learned, was mystified by the casting choice. "They go, 'Don't you read the papers? Don't you watch TV?'" Arnold says. Cameron confessed that he didn't really. The studio said it wouldn't approve Arnold, and Cameron threatened to take his picture elsewhere. Ultimately, the director got his way, as he had with Schwarzenegger on Curtis. He filled out his cast with old friend Bill Paxton as a con man, Art Malik as the terrorist Aziz, Eliza Dushku as the Taskers' daughter, and Tia Carrere as a female villain.

The Raw Deal

There was a fatal flaw in Lightstorm's bold new financial plan, which revealed itself quickly when Cameron's company started prepping *True Lies.* None of the funding from Fox or Lightstorm's patchwork of foreign partners kicked in until there was a completion bond in place, a written contract that guarantees a movie will be delivered on schedule and within budget. But no bond company would cover *True Lies* without a detailed budget, which meant that Cameron needed to be far down the road of preproduction—having bought the story and hired the actors—in order to have the bond issued. If the funding is based on the bond, and the bond is based on work that requires funding, "that big shiny dragster engine ain't gonna start," Cameron says. The director's team had assembled his deal backward—they should have locked in equity financing first, before selling off distribution rights. Now he was committed to making a movie with Hollywood's biggest action star, and he had no money to do it and nothing to sell to raise the money.

Cameron fired Kasanoff, the architect of the plan, and asked Sanchini, who had arranged the IBM financing for Digital Domain, to sort the mess out for him. The first person she turned to was Fox's new head, Peter Chernin. Originally, Fox was committed to providing only a portion of the funding on *True Lies,* but Sanchini and Cameron convinced Chernin to make Fox the movie's primary financier, insuring any cost overruns and removing the need for a completion bond. In exchange, the studio took over worldwide distribution rights to *True Lies* and two of Cameron's future films. "Peter really stretched to help us out," Sanchini says. This was the beginning of a lucrative long-term relationship between filmmaker and executive that would endure the crucible of making *Titanic.* Chernin and Cameron have some important qualities in common. They're both well-read men—Chernin was an English literature major at UC Berkeley—and both straight shooters, neither of which are terribly common traits in show business. "I like Jim 'cause he's smart and he's not full of shit," says Chernin. In terms of its budget and logistical problems, *True Lies* would prove to be merely "the kindergarten version of *Titanic,*" Chernin says. Not that anyone knew that at the time.

After the financing crisis on the movie was solved, Sanchini, who Cameron says "basically saved my bacon," stepped in as president of Lightstorm. And the director got back to the business of making his movie. Lightstorm reverted to a more traditional model, a filmmaker-led company that relied on a studio to finance its pictures. "It's a comfortable arrangement that works like this," Cameron says. "I propose a movie which they know will cost a lot, they whinge and cry that it costs too much, but they say yes because we made money all the previous times. Then I make the film and they whinge and cry and say it's never going to make money, then it does, then we start the process all over again. If one of these things ever doesn't make money it will break the loop, and all bets are off. So my boss is really the audience, not the studio."

"Nobody Would Do That. Not Spielberg. Nobody."

Production on *True Lies* started in August 1993 in Santa Clarita, California, during a heat wave. By the time principal photography wrapped more than six months later, Cameron would have pushed his crew through six cities and the 6.7-magnitude Northridge earthquake. A bathroom shoot-out was the first action sequence on the schedule. The scene took up less than half a script page and was budgeted to take a day to shoot. Peter Lamont, the British production designer who had built Cameron's spaceships in *Aliens,* was on board to help create the sets. Two days before the crew was set to film the washroom sequence, Cameron surveyed the space and deemed it insufficient. He wanted the bathroom three times as big and rigged so there could be water spraying and lights strobing—which would look fabulous, but this was the first anyone was hearing of it and it required a total redesign of the set. "The washroom started out quite small and gradually grew in stature," says Lamont. "The whole thing got better and better, with real tiles, real mosaic on the floor." But the shoot dragged on and on—by halfway through day one, they hadn't even gotten through the first line of dialogue. Stephanie Austin, Cameron's producer on *T2,* was back working with the director and in charge of communicating with Fox. By day three, the crew was still in the bath-room. "Everybody's in a panic, and the studio is calling to see how we're doing," says Austin. "I said, 'Jim, where are we going with this?' He was completely oblivious as to why we would be worked up about it." In the end, the bathroom sequence took five days. It would prove to be among the easiest parts of the shoot.

Jon Landau, Fox's vice president of production at the time, visited the set during the washroom marathon and scratched his chin. It was plain to see that Cameron was a man on his own mission. Call sheets—the stated plan for the day's shoot—didn't seem to affect the director's process at all. Fresh off supervising another talented obsessive, Michael Mann, on *The Last of the Mohicans,* Landau, a New York native and USC grad, knew production inside and out. And the executive's per-sonality, an unlikely combination of boyish enthusiasm and preter-natural calm, suited the organized chaos of a Cameron set perfectly. "I liked Jon, and when you like the guy who's the studio executive on your film, there's something there," Cameron says. After *True Lies,* Cameron would bring Landau on as Lightstorm's resident producer.

Cameron was also getting to know a new cinematographer on *True Lies,* Russell Carpenter, whom he had originally interviewed for "The Crowded Room" when he was looking for a nonunion DP to make a low-budget film. Casting the right director of photography is as im-portant as casting the right leading man, and it's a matter of finding a DP with both technical ability and chemistry with the director. *True Lies* was a huge step up for Carpenter professionally. His biggest prior credit was *Pet Sematary II.* But he was talented and had two qualities that suited a firebrand like Cameron well—a hunger for the gig and an agreeable temperament. During preproduction and the first few weeks of shooting, Carpenter enjoyed a honeymoon period with Cameron. But eventually, he became part of the crew family and therefore sub-ject to the director's merciless management style. "I went through days where I felt, 'I'm just this far from a nervous breakdown,'" Carpenter recalls. One of those days occurred while screening dailies at Lightstorm. Cameron and his department heads were there, about twenty-five people in all, watching a scene where Schwarzenegger returns home late at night and looks in the mirror. When the shot came up on the screen, Schwarzenegger's reflection was dark. Carpenter made a note to himself to ask the photo lab to lighten it and glanced over at Cameron, who was looking down at his lap and shaking his head. "Jim said, 'I've got the highest-paid actor in this or any parallel universe, and I cannot see his eyes,'" Carpenter says. "I'm starting to freak out." A few more shots went by, and Cameron was getting angrier and louder. "He said, 'Where did you learn to read a light meter?!'" Carpenter wanted to turn into liquid mercury and melt under the crack of the door. When the lights came up, the DP stalked to the parking lot, called his wife, and told her he had given it his best shot but was sure he was going to be fired. As he paced on his cell phone, apoplectic, some other Cameron regulars were watching and laughing. Carpenter glared at them. "He does that to everybody," they told him. "Every cinematographer who has ever worked with him." Carpenter didn't believe it, so he called Mikael Salomon, Cameron's DP on *The Abyss*. "Did he use the line, 'Where did you learn to read a light meter?'" Salomon asked. Carpenter exhaled. "I just realized, 'OK, this is just gonna be an endurance test. It becomes a game of last man standing.'" The truth is, Cameron doesn't fire people that often. His phrase is "Firing would just be too merciful." And not only did he not fire Carpenter, he hired him on two subsequent projects.

While filming in Washington, D.C., Schwarzenegger got in the habit of taking impromptu field trips from the set with other cast members, much to Cameron's consternation. On one occasion, the production had traffic blocked on Constitution Avenue. When a light went out on the set, Schwarzenegger figured it would take twenty minutes to fix and roped Tom Arnold into a tour of the capital. Snagging the van he drives in the scene, the action hero cruised his sidekick past the Lincoln Memorial, the Capitol Building, several Smithsonian museums. But while they were gone, instead of taking twenty minutes to fix the light, it took twenty seconds, and Cameron, with one of the capital's busiest streets closed, couldn't find his actors. "We come back around and Jim is standing in the middle of the road, arms crossed," recalls Tom Arnold. "I'm like, 'Oh, fuck.'" Cameron lunged in the passenger door to get into Schwarzenegger's face. "He's like, 'Do you want Paul Verhoeven to direct the rest of this motherfucker? You do that shit again and that's what's gonna happen,'" Arnold remembers. Schwarzenegger was contrite. "I said, 'Why'd you take that from him?'" Arnold says. "''Cause I was wrong," Schwarzenegger told him. "He was blowing up, accusing us of holding up the production," Schwarzenegger recalls. "But by the time lunch came around, it was all forgotten."

Cameron applied his usual aggressive directing style to the new milieu of comedy and tested Arnold's improv chops. During one scene, Schwarzenegger and Arnold pull up in a car and Schwarzenegger stops it and comes around to the passenger side to grab some surveillance documents about his wife. Arnold didn't say Cameron's line the first time. Or the second. "He said, 'Can you say my line once? Can you just one fucking time do it?'" Arnold recalls. "So I said it. He goes, 'OK now, guess what, smart-ass, we're gonna do seventeen more takes and I want seventeen different lines.'" The comic had to think of seventeen ways to ask why Schwarzenegger had stopped the car. The winner was "My turn to drive?"

He already had a reputation for action excess before *True Lies,* but the lengths Cameron went to for the movie's third-act set pieces sealed it. For one formidable sequence to work, he had to establish convincingly that Schwarzenegger was flying a Harrier jet. The jet is supposed to hover near a Miami high-rise while Schwarzenegger's teenage daughter clings to its nose and a terrorist dangles from a missile on the wing. To help him accomplish the task, Cameron called John Bruno, the effects supervisor who had won an Oscar for his work on *The Abyss.* Austin had managed to secure from the U.S. military the use of some Harrier jump jets, from which a full-size mock-up was made. Cameron and Bruno knew they would have to mount their jet on some kind of a motion base to move the plane safely with Schwarzenegger in it and Dushku strapped onto it. They assumed they would accomplish the shot using a green-screen background in the safety of a studio, and they were filming some test footage with a model when Bruno made a suggestion: why not put the plane and its base on the roof of a real skyscraper? This is, plainly, insane. It would involve placing the world's biggest action star and his adolescent costar on a fiberglass model on an aviation gimbal three hundred feet up in the sky in the middle of a major city. "Nobody would do that," Bruno says. "Not Spielberg. Nobody. Especially with Arnold in it." But the more Cameron thought about it, the more it made sense to him. There would be no need for a green screen, because the sunlight and the background would all be there in the shot. It would lend some needed realism to the fantastical sequence. And it would be really, really fun to do. To pull it off, however, he needed to have camera positions. So he and Bruno came up with the idea of using a building that was under construction and had a giant crane next to it. They built a rig to hang a camera crane under the construction crane—a crane on a crane. It was a gonzo piece of rigging, but once they got the hang of using it, they could position the camera anywhere in space around the plane. And they could allow the crane to be in the shots, because it was part of the story that the building was under construction. At the end of the day, they had believable shots of their action hero flying his jet around a skyscraper in Miami.

The only thing Cameron didn't think of was lightning. There are a lot of thunderstorms in Miami, and the crane was a giant lightning rod. One day the production broke for lunch and the crew traveled down to street level to eat. Clouds starting rolling in, and there was a tremendous crash of thunder. The rig had been hit. Nobody was hurt, and after lunch they all went back to work, a little nervously. For the rest of the shoot, they learned to keep a careful eye on the Miami sky. When they finished with the jet mock-up, the crew took it off the base and used the crane to lift it down to the street. Cameron was watching as they did it and got an idea. "I figured we could strap the stunt doubles onto the mock-up of the Harrier and dangle it off the side of the building and spin it with tag lines, while shooting it from the helicopter," he says. Just another day on the set of a James Cameron movie. He canceled the shooting he had planned for that afternoon and ran to the helicopter while the stunt guys got their safety rigging on. Within an hour, the lead terrorist's stunt double was crawling around on the Harrier thirty stories above the street. And Chuck Tamburro, the same helicopter pilot who had dived under a freeway overpass for Cameron on *T2*, flew the director around the dangling jet in tight circles while he shot the stuntmen on a long lens. Once the cables were digitally painted out later, the ad hoc maneuver yielded some of the most dynamic and real-looking shots in the sequence.

By this point, however, the shoot was behind schedule and over budget. For the second time in a row, a Cameron film looked sure to bear the "most expensive movie ever made" title. Paxton had enough time to film some of his scenes, go off and shoot an entire other movie, and return to the *True Lies* set for more work. Roseanne Barr would call the director periodically demanding that her husband be freed up from this endless shoot to return to his TV gig. But on it went. After Miami, the crew moved on to the Florida Keys for its most challenging sequence—a massive helicopter and car chase on the Seven Mile Bridge in which Curtis's character was to be plucked from the roof of a speeding limo and dangled over the water. The helicopters had to fly low and close, which was deafening and made communication difficult. Cameron was coordinating crane movement, actors, stunt drivers, and pensile stunt doubles. "It was exactly the kind of big, crazy, hardware-intensive scenario I love," he says. He wanted two cameras on one helicopter. Tamburro, the aerial coordinator, needed a copilot in order to fly the precise path Cameron wanted, which included yanking a stunt-woman through the roof of the limo an instant before it plunges off the bridge at seventy miles per hour. With two camera operators and two pilots, that left no room for Cameron in the helicopter. "There was no way I was going to sit on the ground while they had all the fun," he says. So he paid one cameraman to sit at a picnic table on the ground while he operated the crewman's mount.

Seeing her double swinging around under the helicopter, Curtis thought this all looked like a good time, and she asked to fly for her close-up. Cameron had planned to shoot that angle in front of a green screen. "But I said, 'All right, I'll do it if you will,'" he says. So while Curtis was rigged with a body harness, Cameron was cabled to the airframe of the helicopter. He stood on the skids and leaned outward at a fifty-degree angle so he could shoot at Curtis downward, handheld, as they flew, with Tamburro keeping the helicopter in a low hover. "Once she was hooked up, we took off and flew over the bridge at sunset, with me gunning down and Jamie screaming her lungs out," Cameron says. "I'm not sure how much of that was acting."

When *True Lies* finally wrapped in March 1994, it was indeed another "most expensive movie ever made," costing $120 million. It would earn that back and then some, opening at number one and making $379 million worldwide—an impressive haul and a strong comeback for Schwarzenegger but $140 million below the steep bar Cameron and the action hero had set with *T2*. Critical reaction to the movie was decidedly mixed. *Variety* dismissed *True Lies* as "141 minutes of extravagant fodder for an enticing three-minute trailer"[8] while the *New York Times* praised the movie as "the first successful romantic comedy in which trucks, as well as heartstrings, are blown to bits."[9] In addition to the charges of sexism leveled against the film, the National Council on Islamic Affairs boycotted *True Lies* for its portrayal of Islam, and Muslims picketed theaters carrying signs that read "Open Your Eyes and Terminate the Lies" and "Hasta La Vista Fairness." There is a heroic Middle Eastern character in *True Lies,* a double agent named Faisil, played by Grant Heslov, who wipes out most of the Miami terror cell in a hail of gunfire in the third act. But that didn't provide enough balance for critics who found the Aziz character cartoonish and racist and likened the portrayal to the worst of Hollywood's old cowboy-and-Indian movies. In response, Fox added a disclaimer to the credits: "The film is a work of fiction and does not represent the actions or beliefs of a particular culture or religion."[10]

Pow!

Ultimately, Cameron accomplished three important tasks with *True Lies:* he tackled a new genre, solidified his relationship with Fox, and, perhaps most important, got his special-effects house off the ground. Digital Domain swapped in backgrounds where green screens were used—including some of the shots on the Harrier that were too dangerous for the rooftop rig—and rotoscoped out the stunt wires. On its first film, the company earned an Oscar nomination for its visual effects.

After *True Lies,* Cameron's next project could have been based on a character he'd been dreaming about since he was a ninth grader in Chippawa: Spider-Man. He had lobbied Carolco, the independent studio behind *T2,* to purchase the rights to the Spider-Man comics, which they did in 1990. Carolco's executives had a habit of seat-of-the-pants deal making that endeared the company to Cameron, who had made his $100 million *Terminator* sequel with it based on terms laid out in a simple half-page memo. But in this instance, a hasty contract would come back to haunt all the parties involved. Cameron wrote a Spider-Man scriptment for Carolco that was widely admired in Hollywood. The comic's creator, Stan Lee, adored it and gave a Cameron-directed Spider-Man movie his hearty endorsement. "It was the Spider-Man we all know and love," Lee said of the treatment. "Yet it all somehow seemed fresh and new."[11] When Lee's Spider-Man series appeared in the early 1960s, it broke ground by featuring a high-school-age hero who was lonely, misunderstood, and, above all, relatable. Cameron's treatment showed that he hadn't forgotten what it was like to be a defiantly unhip teenager. He opted to make his Spider-Man movie an origins story, explaining how Peter Parker developed his web-slinging powers. But he made some thoughtful changes to the iconic character, starting with Spider-Man's wrist shooters. Lee's comic called for Peter Parker to build them himself, but Cameron thought a biological explanation was more plausible. "I had this problem that Peter Parker, boy genius, goes home and creates these wrist shooters that the DARPA labs would be happy to have created on a twenty-year program," says Cameron. "I said, 'Wait a minute, he's been bitten by a radioactive spider. It should change him fundamentally in a way that he can't go back.'" In Cameron's treatment, the wrist shooters simply grow as Peter becomes spiderlike. Here's how he described the character waking up the morning after he was bitten:

> He notices his wrists. They are oozing a pearlescent white fluid from almost invisible slits about a quarter of an inch long. He pushes on the skin next to one of the slits and a dark shape, the size and color of a rose thorn, emerges from beneath the skin.

It shoots a jet of liquid silk into his face. . . . He gets out of bed
and pulls the silky webbing off himself, realizing how strong
the stuff is. He looks again at the horrifying "spinnerets" on his
wrists. He is hyperventilating, freaking out. Like the guy in
Kafka's "Metamorphosis," he has woken up to find out he is a
bug.[12]

Cameron also updated the comic's supervillain, Electro, for the information age in a character he called Carlton Strand. Electro was a
robot that functioned on pure electric power, while Cameron's Strand
could touch a computer or a cable and absorb the data flowing through
it—an acknowledgment that information itself is real power.
Cameron's scriptment is darker and more adult than anyone expected
from a comic-book movie in the 1990s—Peter Parker says "motherfucker," and Spider-Man and Mary Jane have sex atop the Brooklyn
Bridge. Adult-oriented comic-book adaptations like *The Dark Knight*
and *300* found huge audiences more than a decade later, but Cameron's
writing was a dramatic departure from the accepted wisdom about the
genre at the time, namely that it should be nearly as family-friendly as
a Disney movie. It would have been fascinating to see what the creator
of the rough-edged characters of the Terminator franchise did with the
adolescent superhero. But the James Cameron version of Spider-Man
never happened, because Hollywood's real-life supervillains descended—lawyers. When Carolco filed for Chapter 11 in 1995, it became clear the company's claim to the Spider-Man rights had been
tenuous all along. "Here I am working on Spider-Man, and it turns out
that there's a lien against the rights and Sony's got a piece of it, and
Carolco doesn't really own it even though they think they own it,"
Cameron says. With Carolco down, Cameron tried to get Fox to go
after Spider-Man. The studio would have been happy to buy its top-
earning director his pet project if it had just been a matter of rights, but

procuring Spider-Man now meant entering a nasty legal fight and potentially a bidding war involving multiple other studios and producers with overlapping claims on the project dating back to when Marvel had first put the film rights up for sale in 1985. "They're so risk-averse," Cameron says. "For a couple hundred thousand dollars in legal fees they could have had a two-billion-dollar franchise. They blew it."

At a certain point, Cameron's heart wasn't in it either. He had another myth occupying his mind—*Titanic.* And by the time Sony finally emerged with the rights in 1999, Cameron was no longer interested in telling a story that wasn't wholly his own. Nonetheless, his early-nineties treatment served as an important source for the Sam Raimi–directed *Spider-Man* movie that was released in 2002 and the franchise that has gone on to earn $2.5 billion so far. The most notable similarity is the origin story—Tobey Maguire's Peter Parker has organic wrist shooters, just like the ones Cameron detailed in his scriptment. Asked why he doesn't have a credit on the film, Cameron pauses for a beat. "I'd say that wasn't terribly polite of them." Disputes over screenwriting credit are common in Hollywood and tend to be resolved by the Writers Guild of America against writer-director hyphenates like Cameron in favor of those who earn their income solely through screenwriting. On a project like *Spider-Man,* which is based on existing characters and passed through the hands of multiple teams of writers over the years, the credit claims are potentially numerous. At the end of the day, the sole screenwriting credit for *Spider-Man* went to *Jurassic Park* and *Mission: Impossible* writer David Koepp. Unlike other Spider-Man writers who waged unsuccessful battles via the WGA over their contributions, Cameron never fought for his name to appear on the film. Thanks to *Titanic,* he was a very wealthy man who could afford to forgo the potential residuals. And there was, of course, always the possibility that the movie would be bad, which it wasn't. But the decision to let the issue drop was a classy one.

The Spider-Man story says as much about Cameron's business style as it does about his comic-book tastes. For much of the director's career he has had no agent or publicist, relying instead on a tight circle of colleagues like Lightstorm president Rae Sanchini and *Titanic* and *Avatar* producer Jon Landau to mediate between him and the outside world. Cameron is vehemently antilitigious. His lawyer, Bert Fields, and Fields's team at Greenberg Glusker review Cameron's contracts but rarely hear from him personally. "He's not a guy I would call and say, 'Let's do lunch,'" says Fields, who at various points has represented Steven Spielberg, Jeffrey Katzenberg, Tom Cruise, and Michael Jackson. "He would say, 'Why, what's wrong?'" Cameron rarely lunches or parties and applies none of his laser-beam focus to the Hollywood power struggles detailed in industry blogs or the pages of *Variety.* "He's not money motivated, which is unusual," says Fields. "Jim doesn't say, 'What does Spielberg make?' which some of my other clients do. I don't think he thinks in those terms." When it comes to his *Spider-Man* credit and any potential lost earnings, Cameron's inner circle seems more aggrieved than he does. "I didn't feel that injured." He shrugs. "Slighted, but not injured."

8.

THE UNSINKABLE

"Take Me to Russia"

Quentin Tarantino once told this joke on *The Howard Stern Show:*

> This Hollywood guy dies and goes to heaven. Peering through
> the Pearly Gates, he glimpses someone riding overhead in a
> crane with a movie camera and says, "I didn't know James
> Cameron was dead." Saint Peter replies, "No, that's God. He
> only thinks he's James Cameron."[1]

Before *Titanic,* Cameron already had a reputation in Hollywood for
on-set tyranny, profligate spending, egomania—pretty much everything
short of the wholesale slaughter of innocent extras. By the time he finished
Titanic, he would add to his notoriety by a factor of 1,000. But the grueling experience of filming this movie, possibly the most arduous shoot

in Hollywood history, would fundamentally change Cameron as a director and as a man.

As a teenager, Cameron discovered *A Night to Remember,* both the seminal 1955 nonfiction book by Walter Lord that detailed *Titanic's* final night and Roy Ward Baker's faithful 1958 film adaptation of the story. Like the rise and fall of the great civilizations he studied in history class, the story of the glittering steamship's sinking enthralled him. It was the end of the world—his abiding fascination—told within the microcosm of a 2,223-passenger ocean liner. But it wasn't until oceanographer Robert Ballard found *Titanic* more than two miles deep in the North Atlantic in 1985 and dived the wreck in 1986 that Cameron began to pay attention to the ship with the eyes of a storyteller. In a documentary about Ballard's sub dives, he saw his first glimpse of an ROV—a remotely operated vehicle—that Ballard had taken down to *Titanic* on his submersible to explore the wreck. Intuitively, Cameron understood how the ROV worked, the tethers, the thrusters, the lights. "I realized that robots were being used in the deep ocean," he says. "It was a science-fiction dream come true. Inner-space exploration with all the trappings of outer-space fiction."

Cameron largely forgot about *Titanic* for the next several years. Then in 1992, for no reason whatsoever, the director took a VHS copy of *A Night to Remember* off his shelf and watched it. "I realized by the end that it would be a fantastic movie to retell that story, probably with a love story added to the mix of real characters," he says. "And with the new robotics, you could do a wraparound present-day story of the real wreck and tie the two together. It all popped into my mind at once." After watching the tape, Cameron started sifting through a stack of new mail, stopping on a black card covered with rivets, meant to suggest the hull of *Titanic.* The card was an invitation from Al Giddings, his underwater cinematographer on *The Abyss,* to a screening of *Titanic: Treasure of the Deep,* a documentary Giddings had just directed about an expedition to the wreck. Coincidence or kismet, the documentary would stoke Cameron's growing interest in a fictional *Titanic* movie. At the screening, he was intrigued by footage that showed the filmmakers working with a team of Russian sub pilots on a research ship called the *Keldysh,* diving in their advanced Mir submersibles to the twelve-thousand-foot depths of the wreck. After the event, Cameron made his way through the crowd of more than eight hundred people to speak with Giddings. "He was so blown away he was kind of stuttering," Giddings recalls. The two filmmakers huddled in the theater that night, talking until the janitors kicked them out just before midnight. "Jim said, 'This is incredible. I want this to be my next movie. Take me to Russia.'"

Letters were exchanged and visas granted, and just weeks later, in August 1992, Cameron found himself in Moscow with Giddings, meeting Dr. Anatoly Sagalevitch and his team at the P. P. Shirshov Institute of Oceanology. From Moscow the filmmakers flew on an Aeroflot shuttle to Kaliningrad, the industrial home port of the *Keldysh,* where Cameron was given a tour of the research vessel and treated to Russian hospitality—lots of vodka and a few of the captain's heartfelt songs accompanied by his guitar. As he sat on the great Russian ship, Cameron had no idea that over the next eleven years he would spend ten months of his life there and dive in the Mirs more than fifty times, to depths as great as three miles. On the 1992 trip, Cameron, Giddings, and Sagalevitch discussed how they could mount a 35 mm movie camera in a titanium housing on the front of the sub, where it would go, and how the lights would work. They talked about how the expedition could be organized and financed. After the collapse of the Soviet Union in 1991, Sagalevitch's funding had been slashed to almost zero, and he was eager to dive again, even for something as unscientific as a feature film. After many vodka toasts, Sagalevitch and Cameron agreed to work together on something never done before, a Hollywood movie shot miles under the ocean, for real.

Cameron would make *True Lies* before revisiting the idea of diving

Titanic. At any given time, the director has multiple movie ideas, scripts, and treatments saved on his computer or tucked in his desk. Which movie he makes next is decided intuitively based on themes that interest him at the moment, what he needs financially to pull it off, and what new technical or dramatic territories he wants to explore. Often those closest to him, like Lightstorm president Rae Sanchini, simply wait for word of Cameron's choice. After *True Lies,* the director was weighing *Titanic* against another film. "I had a lot of doubts about *Titanic,*" he says. "Could it be done? Could the deep dive filming be done? Could we create the technology? Would anyone want to see it?" While he was ruminating, he received a fax from Sagalevitch that read, "It is sometimes necessary in life to do something extraordinary." In Cameron's mind the line seemed to glow on the page. "Yes, I realized, sometimes you have to do something extraordinary. Something crazy. I called Rae and told her we were doing *Titanic.* And that was that."

Love Stories

Cameron is fond of saying that all his movies are love stories, and it's true—the apocalypse-straddling romance of the *Terminator* films, Ripley's maternal love in *Aliens,* the stale marriages rekindled by potential nuclear annihilation in *The Abyss* and *True Lies.* But he had never made a movie in which the love story was the primary reason for the film. And nothing entices him so much as virgin territory. As he had after *T2,* Cameron began to contemplate a logistically simpler film after *True Lies.* He told his friend director Guillermo del Toro, "I want to do a small movie next, to prove to people I'm not just about giant movies, about spectacle. I'm gonna do a love story." Del Toro, believing his friend really was looking for an intimate-scale tale to tell, recommended Cameron read Carson McCullers's *The Heart Is a Lonely Hunter,* the poignant novel about a deaf-mute and a teenage tomboy living in a small Georgia town in the 1930s. Many months later, Cameron would go back to his friend. "Jim said, 'I'm writing my love story. Do you want to read it?'" del Toro recalls. "'It happens on the *Titanic.*'" So much for small.

To Cameron, diving the *Titanic* wreck was paramount, making a movie incidental. Wreck diving had been a passion of his for years—he loved the romance and the mystery of these human tragedies buried under the sea. And this was the chance to dive the Mount Everest of shipwrecks. "I'm an explorer at heart, a filmmaker by trade," he says. "There is nothing that Hollywood can offer more tantalizing or powerful than the chance to explore a place nobody has ever seen." Cameron found the class- and gender-driven math of survival on *Titanic* fascinating—a woman in first class had a 97 percent chance of living through that bitter-cold night in the North Atlantic in 1912, while a man in steerage had a 16 percent chance. To fund his adventure, Cameron would write a tale of a tragic, life-and-death romance. He would center his story on a first-class female and a third-class male. If great love stories are made of overcoming obstacles, death is surely the biggest obstacle of all. At this point, Cameron figured his love story would cost about $80 million to make, a modest budget by his own record-breaking standards and $40 million less than *True Lies* had cost. After all, he had to be realistic about the box-office potential of a long, period film where everybody knows the ending—1,500 people die—and there's no chance for a sequel. There would be no big stars, no car chases, no aliens, nothing audiences had come to expect from Cameron and nothing that obviously spelled success.

In March 1995, Cameron made a simple pitch in the office of Twentieth Century Fox president Peter Chernin. The director had nothing written down. Instead, he brought *Titanic: An Illustrated History*, a coffee-table book of paintings of the sinking ship by artist Ken Marschall with text by *Titanic* historian Don Lynch. Cameron flipped to the centerfold image of the ocean liner, lights blazing, bow underwater, lifeboats departing into the black night, and said, "Romeo and Juliet on the *Titanic*." That's all. *Titanic* was sold, essentially, with one sentence. "Making *Titanic* was hell," Chernin recalls, fourteen years after this meeting. "It was as difficult a production as ever happened in the history of Hollywood. Every day I thought I was going to get fired. But my private creative interactions on that film were hands down the best experience of my career, starting with that meeting." Cameron and Chernin would spend the next few hours discussing the dramatic potential of the *Titanic* story and the flashback structure Cameron planned to employ. But Cameron's real sales job would come on the issue of diving the wreck, his primary reason for wanting to make the film in the first place. Before he could climb into one of the Russian subs, the director had to convince Chernin the dives were a crucial part of making the movie. Cameron said he needed the underwater shots of the wreck regardless of whether he captured them for real or created them with CG special effects, and shooting for real would be, if not cheaper, at least not much more expensive than CG. Cameron proposed that the expedition be charged at least partly to the marketing budget, for it would attract more publicity than trotting the cast around the talk-show circuit. At $4 million, the dive budget was relatively minor compared to the kind of preproduction commitments studios make on other films on a regular basis to buy a script or commit an actor. Nevertheless, "there were a few eyebrows raised," concedes Sanchini. "They didn't even have a script at that time."

Planet Ice

Like *The Abyss,* making *Titanic* would be a feat of engineering as much as art. The first step in photographing the wreck would be building a 35 mm movie camera that could function at thirteen thousand feet underwater, where the pressure is about five thousand pounds per square inch, enough to crush a scuba tank like a beer can. Prior to Cameron's shoot, all film work at that depth had been accomplished via the crude method of poking a lens up to the view port of a submersible. Cameron wanted a camera outside the sub that he could pan and tilt and maneuver cinematically. In addition to the camera itself, he would need a remote device and a camera housing. For the task, the director recruited his engineer brother, Mike, who had built the SeaWasp diver-propulsion vehicle used on *The Abyss.* The *Titanic* shoot would also require an ROV like the kind Ballard had used in his 1986 dive of the wreck. Cameron conceived of his ROV, which he would name Snoop Dog, as a movie prop more than anything. The little robot would be a character in the present-day section of the film. He promised himself he wouldn't really go inside the wreck with it. But Snoop Dog would still need to function as a camera-carrying robot in the deep ocean. For that job, he hired Western Space and Marine, the Santa Barbara company that had manufactured the helmets on *The Abyss.* The race to get the equipment ready was on. The American engineers and the Russian scientists had strikingly different working styles, however. At one point, Mike Cameron faxed Sagalevitch a list of thirty questions about the electrical schematics of the subs. Sagalevitch returned it two days later, saying simply, "Mike, Mir has big power. No problem."[2]

In August, the *Keldysh* scientists and Cameron's crew began to arrive in Halifax, Nova Scotia, the port from which they would depart on their journey to _Titanic_. At this point, the project was referred to as Planet Ice—except for a handful of executives at Fox, and the scientists, engineers, and crew involved with the expedition, no one knew a major Hollywood director was boarding a Russian research vessel en route to filming the real _Titanic_. The largest research ship in the world, the 422-foot-long _Keldysh_ could house a crew of 130 and boasted a pool, a basketball court, and multiple stills for making vodka.[3] Not many years before Cameron's journey, the KGB had bugged the ship. In the new era of openness, the sound system was used for broadcasting music at parties. Cameron wasn't much interested in the _Keldysh_'s recreational options. He had a conference room converted into a projection suite where he could examine test footage from shallow dives. His crew had brought on board detailed models of the shipwreck and the Mirs, and Cameron and the Russian pilots spent hours practicing maneuvers around the model _Titanic_, Cameron operating a lipstick-sized camera and the Russians steering their tiny subs. The model sessions weren't just child's play—it could take ten hours to get down in the sub to the shooting location, and Cameron would only have twelve minutes of film once he got there. Preparation was crucial, or precious time and costly dives would be wasted.

On the morning of September 8, 1995, Cameron folded his long limbs into the seven-foot-wide cockpit of Mir 1, next to Sagalevitch and a Russian engineer. The three men would share the claustrophobic quarters for the next fourteen hours on their journey to _Titanic_ and back. About the length of a flight from New York to Tokyo, this trip would include no cocktail service or reclining seats, and the bathroom was a plastic bag, which the Russians took pride in never needing. Cameron conserved his energy on the ride to the bottom, napping, reading, and gazing out the small view-port window as the water outside darkened from green to blue. By nine hundred feet, it was completely black. . . . Just 11,600 more to go. At the surface, the air in the sub had been hot and humid, but as they descended, it grew colder, eventually reaching just above freezing. The men layered on extra clothes they had packed, drank some tea, and began to prepare for their landing. Once they reached the bottom, they located the wreck using sonar, a new type the Russian pilot was still learning to use. Sitting in the pitch darkness, they knew *Titanic* was ahead of them . . . somewhere. The Mir was roughly the size of a cement mixer, and Sagalevitch was piloting it by looking out a window six inches in diameter. There was no way to see behind them, to the sides, or above. And they were maneuvering near an enormous wreck—a mass of twisted, jagged steel and draped cables, traps that could snag the sub and pin them to the bottom of the ocean until they suffered a lingering demise by hypothermia. The constant threat of imminent death, incidentally, made the dive terribly fun for Cameron.

First they came upon a mound of clay taller than the sub. Sagalevitch rose up to climb over the mound, and the silt from the thrusters swirled around the ports, blocking their view. When the silt cleared, Cameron got his first look at her—*Titanic*—a black wall of steel, covered in rivets, coming straight at him about ten feet ahead. They were too close, moving too fast. Sagalevitch hit full thrust back and up, and sediment again swirled in front of the view port. Cameron braced himself for a crash. But instead, the Mir sailed over a guardrail right onto the deck of the ship. The pilot set the sub down, gingerly, and everyone froze. They looked at one another, stunned. They were sitting on top of *Titanic*. They had seen the ship just in time to avert a head-on collision. "This is when I realized that deep-ocean wreck diving was not a precise science," Cameron says. His memorization of the wreck, from studying diagrams, deck plans, and the practice model, came in handy immediately. "I was like an astronaut landing on the moon," he says. "I had prepared and trained myself for the moment so rigorously that I knew the layout of the wreck cold." When the silt cleared, he was able to discern that they were on the port aft end of the forecastle, looking out over the forward well deck, facing aft on the port side. Sagalevitch lifted up, and they started to explore. In the Mir's lights, Cameron looked out the view port at the very spot on the deck where the band had played "Nearer My God to Thee" as the water rose over the rails. "It was like a dream," he says. "I was so pumped and adrenalized and goal oriented that I immediately turned to filming the wreck." He was working from a shot list that required the other sub, Mir 2, to get in precise positions and rake its lights over the decks or the hull. So they went to work. No time for sightseeing. It wasn't until Cameron was back on the *Keldysh,* safe in his cabin that night, that he began to grasp that he had just sailed through the coffin of 1,517 people. He started to shake, and tears came to his eyes. "The enormity of the tragedy, the loss of life, the horror of what it must have been like hit me," Cameron says. "It was a deeply emotional place, but my reaction was delayed. I made a vow to myself at that moment to stop being an astronaut and to honor the place, and the event, by making time on every dive to take the wreck in."

There would be eleven more dives before the expedition was finished. Eventually, Cameron couldn't resist the opportunity to take Snoop Dog inside the wreck. Roving around inside the bones of the great ship, he saw once-luxurious suites overgrown with deep-sea animals, a woodwork fireplace with a crab crawling over the hearth, silt streaming through intricate bronze-grille doors. The footage would be used not only for the present-day re-creation of the *Titanic* wreck, but also for the period *Titanic.* "It set a level of excellence for the rest of the movie," Cameron says. "Sets and costumes had to live up to the example set by visiting the real wreck."

The worst of the dives came to be known as "the bottom storm." On Cameron's third trip down to *Titanic,* an unusually rapid current swirled the sediment, dropping visibility to less than ten feet and shoving the Mir around like a pebble at the beach. Sea stars bounced across the ocean floor like tumbleweeds. The veteran Mir pilot had never seen the odd and dangerous conditions before—it was like a sandstorm at the bottom of the ocean. But Cameron still wanted to shoot. At forty thousand dollars per dive, he couldn't conceive of wasting the trip. The poor visibility prevented him from filming any wide shots, but he could capture close-ups of anchors and portholes. At one point the turbulence kicked up so strongly that it blew the nickel-steel sub right off the wreck and set it down more than a hundred yards from the ship. The sub had landed in the lee of *Titanic,* which shielded it from the current so the Mir 1 crew could idle on the bottom and ponder what to do next while Sagalevitch held them in place with the thrusters. They had been utterly focused on jockeying around the wreck in the storm and not watching their power levels, which had been drained due to the extreme conditions. "Anatoly said, 'Oh, no,' something you never want to hear a pilot say, and we locked eyes for a second," Cameron recalls. Then each began shutting down power to his respective systems. They needed to abort the dive immediately, and the pilot started pumping ballast with what remained of the power. As the sub lightened, it rose sluggishly, the *wheeee-chung, wheeee-chung* noise of its power winding down. Finally, Mir 1 gave a last feeble cough and stopped. They were rising at only a few feet per minute and dead out of power. Cameron saw the bottom falling away with agonizing slowness. At this speed, Mir 1 might need ten hours to ascend. But at least they were going up. When they reached eighty feet from the bottom, however, the sub stopped and started to descend again. "I thought, 'What the fuck? That's not supposed to happen,'" Cameron says. They bumped back down on the ocean floor.

Stuck two miles from the surface in a storm, the Mir crew thought the battery might get enough of a bounce to run the ballast pump a little if it was given a break. So they sat in the dark, waiting, no one saying a word for half an hour. It seemed entirely possible *Titanic* was about to claim another three victims. Eventually, the pilot tested the pump. It groaned a few weak strokes and then quit, but they started to rise again. Curiously, at eighty feet, again they stopped, falling back to the bottom with a clunk. They sat for another half hour and tried again. What the Mir 1 crew didn't know was that they were in a kind of downdraft caused by the current blowing over the huge shipwreck. Each time they rose, they would hit the downdraft and get thrown back to the bottom. But each time they were blown a little farther from the wreck. On the third try, Cameron held his breath as they got to eighty feet and slowed . . . and then kept rising. Soon their rate sped up a bit, though they were still traveling at snail's pace. A normal ascent would have taken them two and a half hours from that depth. At this rate, they would reach the surface in about ten hours. It was going to be a long, cold, dark return. Sagalevitch started pulling up the floor of the sub. He reached his arm down in the darkness and grabbed a handle. "Maybe we should release some emergency ballast," Cameron recalls the pilot saying. "What? We have emergency ballast? And we'd had it all along!? I said, 'Yes, by all means, let's drop some emergency ballast.'" They began to rise a little faster. It would be only five hours to the surface.

Jack and Rose

Cameron's script called for the two leads to be quite young—Rose De-Witt Bukater is seventeen and Jack Dawson twenty. For the director, it was important that *Titanic* be a story of first love. "There is no purer, more consuming love than first love," Cameron explains. "For many of us, it is the most heightened experience we will have." But as written, Jack and Rose would pose perhaps the biggest challenge a young actor could face in 1995—a traditional character. They were retrograde roles, the kind that would have been played by Audrey Hepburn or Jimmy Stewart, actors who didn't need to chew scenery or suffer inner torment to transfix audiences. They could dazzle without appearing to do a thing.

Having discovered Edward Furlong for Cameron on *True Lies, Titanic* casting director Mali Finn had a nose for young talent. The first part she tackled was Rose. It was through Rose's eyes that the audience would be experiencing *Titanic,* and the actress who played her would need to be elegant, spunky, and strong. Finn was pushing for twenty-one-year-old rising star Kate Winslet. After her screen debut as a murderous schoolgirl in Peter Jackson's creepy *Heavenly Creatures,* Winslet had played a number of notable roles, including in an adaptation of *Sense and Sensibility* that had earned her an Academy Award nomination at the tender age of twenty. An abundance of period work had earned Winslet the nickname Corset Kate, a major deterrent for Cameron. He likes to discover things, including actors, and lacing Corset Kate up again in period costume struck him as lazy, unoriginal casting. But at Finn's urging, he met Winslet and filmed a screen test in a small period set the crew had hastily knocked together for the purpose. He was immediately bewitched by the graceful, unaffected young woman. "She was amazing to watch," Cameron says. "Poised, imperious, vulnerable, raw, tragic, and with the inner steel she would need to convince us all that she could survive that night, in both body and spirit." Cameron felt quite confident he had found his Rose, but he needed to be sure she had chemistry with the actor who would play Jack.

The search for Jack led the production to all the young heartthrobs of the moment, including studio suggestions like Matthew

McConaughey and Chris O'Donnell. Cameron didn't see twenty-two-year-old Leonardo DiCaprio as manly enough for the role. "He seemed scrawny and lightweight, not a leading man and not that attractive," Cameron says. But based on the strength of DiCaprio's performances as Johnny Depp's mentally handicapped brother in *What's Eating Gilbert Grape* and a heroin-addicted high-school athlete in *The Basketball Diaries,* the director invited him to a meeting at Lightstorm. Curiously, Cameron noticed that all of his female office staff chose to attend the meeting, even the accountant and the secretaries. He seated the actor next to the window so he could study how the sunlight played on DiCaprio's face. As the young man quickly charmed the room, especially the females, "I started to get a glimmer that he might be something," Cameron says.

After the meeting, Cameron flew Winslet in from the set of Kenneth Branagh's *Hamlet* in England, where she was playing Ophelia, and arranged for her and DiCaprio to read together. DiCaprio had earned his first Oscar nomination at nineteen for *Gilbert Grape* and had just been cast in Baz Luhrmann's *Romeo + Juliet.* He was starting to get some serious heat in Hollywood and wasn't especially interested in what looked to him to be a conventional romance. He was also a bit of a punk. When the actor showed up and Cameron handed him the script pages, DiCaprio declared, "I don't read." Cameron shook the young actor's hand, thanked him for coming, and walked away. "Wait," DiCaprio said. "You mean if I don't read I'm not even being considered?" Cameron made his policy clear—he doesn't cast anyone without seeing him work.

Reluctantly, DiCaprio agreed to play a scene with Winslet. He slouched into the rehearsal room, lit up a cigarette, and glanced at the script pages disdainfully. Sprawling on a couch, the actor turned to face Winslet. Cameron called action, and DiCaprio became Jack. "He transformed in a split second to the guy you see in the movie,"

Cameron says. "He was riveting. He was the guy I wrote. And you could see Kate respond, how it sparked her performance. It was instant chemistry and instant character creation." Just as abruptly, it ended, and DiCaprio slumped back onto the couch. After the scene, Winslet whispered to Cameron, "Even if you don't hire me, you have to hire him." The director let Winslet know she had the part. On her way back to England, she sent Cameron a single red rose and signed the card, "Your Rose."

DiCaprio had spent fifteen minutes auditioning for Cameron. For the next three months, the director would be auditioning for him. Jack was a role most actors in Hollywood would have been dying to play. Tom Cruise's agent had even inquired about it. But DiCaprio didn't really want it. He didn't like the character or Cameron's script. "I just wasn't used to playing an openhearted, free-spirited guy," he told the *Los Angeles Times*. "I've played more tortured roles in the past. It was difficult to be someone closer to me than anyone else."[4] Fox, meanwhile, didn't want to pay the actor the four million dollars his agent was demanding and was interested in then-bigger stars O'Donnell and Mc-Conaughey. And since DiCaprio hadn't allowed Cameron to tape his reading with Winslet, there were no witnesses to the miracle of the young actor's creation of Jack. Now Cameron was running out of time. He needed to set his leads, get the green light from the studio, and start building that boat. He met with DiCaprio once more. "I don't think you're right for this," Cameron told him. "You keep looking for a problem, an addiction, a limp. You're doing what you know, what you've gotten acclaim for, playing a retard, an addict. You're looking for an acting crutch." Cameron wanted DiCaprio to see Jack as a character who in the past would have been played by Jimmy Stewart or Gary Cooper, an actor who could make a plain old decent guy so compelling that he owned the screen. "When you can do that, then you are a man, my son. You want to do something more challenging? Believe me, this is the hardest part you will ever play." Only when he thought of the role as difficult in its own right did DiCaprio decide to take it. There were no real stars in Cameron's cast by design. The only diva would be the ship herself. And he wanted every penny up on-screen. Winslet earned under $1 million for her role, DiCaprio $2.5 million for his. Cameron's biggest name was Kathy Bates as the unsinkable Molly Brown. For Bates to get her $500,000 fee on the film, Cameron would have to kick in $150,000 of his own.

The Hundred-Day Studio

Although Twentieth Century Fox had helped fund the dives, by the spring of 1996 Chernin had yet to green-light the film formally. It was already becoming clear that Cameron's initial estimate of $80 million for *Titanic*'s budget was too conservative. Feeling they didn't have a very commercial movie on their hands, Cameron and Sanchini went to the studio with an unusual proposal. *Titanic* would be a labor of love for Cameron, not a chance for a big payday. He would take a cut both to his front-end fee and to his share of the movie's gross box-office receipts. Under the deal, if *Titanic* grossed progressively higher levels, Cameron could catch up. But he would get his full back end only if the movie performed at a very high level of profitability for Fox. On May 28, Chernin green-lighted *Titanic* at $110 million, provided the director agree to a few things—a PG-13 rating, another studio partner to share the risk, and a summer 1997 release date. The first two would be relatively easy to honor—the raciest moment in the movie would be Kate Winslet posing for a tasteful nude sketch. And Paramount Pictures would eagerly sign on as *Titanic*'s domestic distributor, leaving Fox with the international rights. But the very ambitious release date, just over a year away, would be a tricky commitment to keep.

Cameron had already begun to scout shooting locations with Jon Landau, whom he had hired as a producer after *True Lies*. They first discussed building the set at a shipyard in Poland, where marine fabrication was cheap, craning it in pieces onto a container ship, and then cruising around in the Baltic while they filmed. The director was taken with the light at that northern latitude—the same light deployed so gorgeously by Sven Nyquist, Ingmar Bergman's longtime cinematographer. But he wasn't just going to be sailing *Titanic*; he would be sinking her, which would require a tank. By building the tank set on a seashore, they could rely on distant ocean, sky, and natural sunlight to make the deck scenes look real and camera panning to create the appearance of movement. Cameron and Landau started to hunt for a low bluff within a hundred feet of the ocean with a clear horizon and no islands or busy shipping lanes. The director had long been interested in exploring shooting in Mexico. His theory was that you could use the cheaper labor available there for construction and film crews but get the advantages of being close to L.A. So he brought a model of *Titanic* and some key members of his production team down to a cliff near the rundown resort town of Rosarito, Mexico, just half an hour south of the U.S. border. Landau was there, along with a half dozen others, including Cameron's new assistant director, Josh McLaglen, and Peter Lamont, the British production designer on *Aliens* and *True Lies,* who had just put off retirement for a chance to build the grandest set of his career. Cameron set the model ship up on a table to see how the light and shadows moved across it at different times of day. He made smoke and watched how the wind took it, studying it for hours, videoing the deck and superstructure from different angles to make sure all the shots he needed would be possible. It was a long day that would determine just where Fox would invest a huge sum of money—and where Cameron and the construction and film crews would spend several taxing months of their lives. His production team waited expectantly to learn what their mercurial director would decide. "We got down to Rosarito in the morning, and Jim hated the site," Lamont recalls. "By the time we left in the evening, he loved it. He's a very strange cat." At one point, Cameron didn't like the background view, so he dragged the table about a hundred feet north, to the top of a low rise. Someone informed him that he had moved onto a different parcel of land. "Then we need to buy this one, too," he said.

Less than two weeks after Chernin's green light, thousands of Mexican and American construction workers descended on that patch of dirt on the Baja peninsula to build the first major Hollywood studio constructed since the 1930s. Fox had decided to make the beachfront tanks and stages a permanent asset of the studio, a site to be known as Fox Studios Baja. Crews had only one hundred days to hammer together a forty-acre facility with five soundstages, the world's largest outdoor filming tank, the world's largest indoor filming tank, the world's tallest soundstage, a wardrobe building, an actor's building, offices, and mills. And in not much longer than that brief window of time, the crews were building a facsimile of *Titanic* that was nearly as big and grand as the original ship, a monument to Gilded Age excess that had taken fourteen thousand men more than three years to construct. Cameron and Lamont had designed a ten-story, 775-foot version of *Titanic*. The set was 100 percent to scale but shortened by about ninety feet by removing some small, repetitive sections in the middle so the ship would fit on the land Fox owned. The height of the decks and the size of the doors, portholes, and boat davits were all accurate. This *Titanic* was finished on one side only—to convey the illusion of the other side, Cameron would flip the film picture, requiring every sign, uniform, and logo to be created in mirror image. The construction schedule was so tight that the sets were often being built concurrently with the soundstages that housed them—Lamont's crews hammered away on the dining room and grand staircase while workers finished the roof over their heads. Every weekend a new building went up, like a gold-rush town.

The sets themselves were exquisite and authentic right down to the sconces and the carpets. The china and furniture in the first-class dining room were faithfully reproduced, with enough settings for five hundred people. There was a degree of obsession in Cameron's dedication to the details, from the ship's stationery to its White Star Line–stamped ashtrays. He had always been a stickler for the little things, but diving the *Titanic* wreck had infused him with a messianic meticulousness. The end result was grand-scale craftsmanship of the kind Hollywood hadn't seen since Vivian Leigh swept down Tara's staircase in *Gone with the Wind.* Because there were very few existing photos of the actual *Titanic* interior, the sets were mostly based on its sister ship, *Olympic.* At one point, Lamont had four art departments working on the film, one in England, one in Mexico City, one in Rosarito, and one at Lightstorm in Santa Monica. The book by Ken Marschall and Don Lynch that Cameron had used to sell the movie to Chernin became the set bible, and its authors were invited aboard to walk the decks and survey the construction. The grand staircase was made with real oak columns and paneling, its carved balustrades molded from pieces of the *Olympic* that Marschall had collected over decades and loaned to the production. When the artist stood at the foot of the staircase he had studied as a painter, so faithfully and beautifully reproduced, he nearly wept.

Who Ate the Chowder?

While construction continued in Rosarito, the contemporary *Titanic* scenes would be shot back on the *Keldysh* off the coast of Halifax. Cameron had some old friends aboard, including Bill Paxton playing the treasure hunter, Brock; his dive buddy Lewis Abernathy as Brock's sidekick; and his trusted Steadicam operator, Jimmy Muro. He also had some new colleagues to get to know, including cinematographer Caleb Deschanel, whose idyllic lighting on *The Natural* and *The Right Stuff* made him seem a perfect hire for Cameron's first period film. Deschanel had begun to direct himself, however, and as a DP was accustomed to working with filmmakers who left him alone with his light meter while they worried about the actors. The partnership wasn't a natural fit for a photographically hands-on director like Cameron. Another feisty newcomer to Cameron's circle was Gloria Stuart, there to play the character of Old Rose, Kate Winslet's hundred-year-old counterpart. A once-glamorous blonde who had been a favorite of classic horror director James Whale, appearing for him in *The Invisible Man* and *The Old Dark House,* Stuart had been off the Hollywood radar for decades. Acerbic and prickly at times, the eighty-six-year-old would be one of the few people on the set who successfully pushed back at Cameron. One night, the director wasn't ready to shoot her close-up until 3:00 a.m. When Landau knocked on Stuart's trailer door, Paxton recalls, "she said, 'How dare you?' She read Jim and Jon the riot act. They were cowed by her." Producer and director decided to let Stuart have her beauty sleep and film the close-up another night.

On what was supposed to be their last day of shooting in Nova Scotia, Cameron enjoyed a big bowl of the caterer's mussel chowder. After the meal break, the director was back on set with his AD, Josh McLaglen, lining up a shot of Stuart, when a female stand-in's eyes rolled back and she fell to the floor. Suddenly, Cameron also began to feel woozy. He immediately flashed on the bowl of chowder he'd just eaten and asked the set medic for some ipecac, so he could induce vomiting. "I'm figuring maybe I can chuck this out and not have to lose the day," Cameron says. The medic didn't have any, so Cameron stalked off to the men's room upstairs, bottle of water in hand, to induce vomiting the hard way. He succeeded, but the violent purging left his eyes as red as a Terminator's. When Cameron returned to the set, no one was there. And the director was starting to feel very odd. "It was like the Twilight Zone," he says. "And I'm processing information very slowly now. I know I need to get out of the set, but I can't seem to remember how." Finally, a grip walked in and led Cameron to the dining area, where the whole crew was gathered. McLaglen was dividing them into two groups—"Good crew over here!" he said, waving to one side. "Bad crew over here!" At this point, bad crew—those feeling nauseous, dizzy, and disoriented, as Cameron was—consisted of about seventy-five people, 90 percent of the unit. When Cameron staggered in with his blood-red eyes, the crew really started to worry. He had been the first in the chow line. "They figured I was what they were all going to look like soon, like it was some kind of zombie virus," he says.

The teamsters—who must have skipped the chowder—started whisking the crew to the nearby hospital in vans. Cameron and his sickly party of seventy-five descended on a Canadian emergency room with one nurse and one doctor. And then things got really strange. People began moaning, crying, wailing, and collapsing on tables and gurneys. Deschanel, the DP, was leading a number of crew members down the hall in a highly vocal conga line. Muro, the Steadicam operator, was demanding to speak to a priest. Cameron was beginning to suspect a street drug was to blame and told Landau his theory. The producer, who hadn't had the chowder, patted Cameron on the knee, humoring him, thinking he was out of it. At this point, doctors were suspecting shellfish poisoning. Cameron looked up to see his second AD, Kristie Sills, talking to the doctors, giving them the names of various crew members. Realizing that she was also sick but was acting as the point person instead of getting treated herself, Cameron reached for his walkie-talkie. "Kristie, what's your twenty?" he said. Sills pulled her walkie from her hip and crisply replied, "I'm at the hospital, talking to the doctors." She was ten feet away, looking right at Cameron. "And what are you telling them?" he asked. Still staring right at her boss's face, she responded that she was giving them the names of the crew. "Kristie, you know you're talking to me on your walkie," Cameron said. "And I'm standing right in front of you. You're just as fucked up as we are." At that point, Sills leaped across the gap between them and stabbed Cameron in the face with her pen. The hospital staff tackled her and dragged her off, and Cameron sat, bleeding and laughing. Sills's drug-induced stabbing didn't stop Cameron from hiring her on his next Halifax-based film, *Ghosts of the Abyss*.

The doctor wanted the sick crew to drink boxes of liquid charcoal, saying it would absorb the poison, whatever it was, from their digestive tracts. Cameron stood up in front of the group with a box of the black sludge and told them they had to drink it. His crew all grudgingly started glugging the charcoal cocktail. "Even when he was completely stoned," Paxton says, "Jim was still the captain of the ship." Feeling better and seeing there wasn't much more he could do at the hospital, Cameron slipped out and headed back to the set. He and Paxton stayed up till dawn, talking about the bizarre night and sharing a six-pack of Budweiser. The workday had been ruined, but nobody had died. The next morning, Landau and Cameron started planning to finish shooting Stuart's scene. Fortunately, the actress had eaten in a restaurant, so she hadn't gotten dosed. A toxicology report came in, revealing that a pound of PCP had been dumped in the caterer's soup. Conjecture swirled that it was a disgruntled worker's revenge against the despotic director. Cameron's theory, pieced together weeks later, is that a fired crew member had a beef with the caterer and had dumped PCP into the chowder to get the caterer fired, too. An investigation was inconclusive. No one knows who spiked the soup. It remains an unsolved mystery of *Titanic*.

Smells Right

When Cameron returned from Halifax, one of the first things he did was replace Deschanel, his director of photography. The two strong personalities had clashed, and Cameron wanted to switch to a DP with whom he felt more comfortable. He hired Russell Carpenter, who had taken his licks as the new kid on *True Lies* and then shot *T2 3-D,* a film that accompanies a Universal Studios ride, with Cameron. His first day on *Titanic,* Carpenter asked Cameron what the film should look like. "He looked at me and he said, 'Everybody knows what these films look like.'" Not much had changed since the endless bathroom shoot-out scene on *True Lies.* Cameron still kept his cards close to his vest. The DP galloped off to the art department and scoured the artists' renderings. Ironically, he also ended up screening Deschanel's film *The Natural* for reference.

Construction crews in Mexico had been working around the clock, and Cameron inspected the sets with pride. Everything was spanking new, just as it had been when *Titanic* sailed. Cameron stepped into a stateroom belonging to Rose and her imperious fiancé, Cal (played by Billy Zane), a gilded mahogany chamber that Lamont and his crew had labored to reproduce in all its opulence. "Smells right," Cameron said approvingly. "I can shoot this." It was as ringing an endorsement as one was going to get from this director. Lamont was thrilled. Of course, all his hard worked would eventually have to be sunk, but he could enjoy it now.

The sets were so vast that the crew would often get lost in them and holler SOS calls over their walkie-talkies. "You'd say, 'Uh, guys, I have no idea where I am. Somebody please come find me,'" Carpenter recalls. Eventually, the production created a zone system to minimize the disorientation. There were days, such as the filming of *Titanic*'s triumphant departure from its Southampton, England, port, when up to two thousand extras swarmed the set, some speaking English, some Spanish. Another scene called for nearly 1,500 people to run toward the aft portion of the tilted set at once, just as passengers had done on the sinking ship.

The mechanics of the sinking itself were a technical marvel that Cameron accomplished with the help of Tommy Fisher, the physical effects supervisor who had been helping the director toss semis and blow up buildings since *T2*. The *Titanic* set, stood on its end, would be nearly as tall as New York City's Woolworth Building. Cameron came up with the idea of lowering it on cables into a deep pit in the tank. At a meeting at Lightstorm, he sketched his idea on a napkin—cables would support a long platform with the set on it. The cables would run over pulleys connected to large hydraulic rams around the perimeter of the tank. By linking a computer to the rams, they could not only sink the set vertically but program the rams to tilt it at two different angles as it sank.

Some of the most harrowing nights of shooting surrounded the tilting poop deck, an eighty-foot chunk of the set that would swing from horizontal to completely vertical, like a teeter-totter. It's the poop deck to which DiCaprio and Winslet are clinging as they ride the ship down into the ocean. Once the poop deck was in its vertical position, one hundred stunt performers would be dangling and jumping from it. It was a massive undertaking that the stunt crew rehearsed six days a week for several weeks. The risks of messing up were grave—a performer could fall to an impact below or fall on another performer, or a piece of the set could break loose and fall on someone. Much of the set, such as the huge brass bollards and the intake ducts, were made from foam rubber or coated with a thin layer of foam neoprene—it was, Cameron said, a Nerf set. Most of the stunt players were locked in by cables connected to body harnesses. Some had to fall down the set into a bag. It wasn't just the stunt performers who were tumbling down that deck. When Cameron and Muro were planning how they would shoot it, Muro recalls, "I said, 'Jim, let's grab the camera and slide down on our butts and fall into a pad down there.' Then I thought about it and I got a little nervous. He says, 'I'll do it.' He goes and puts on his knee pads. And he does it."

The tilting poop deck was, like so many Cameron action shoots, more organized than it looked. But one night, two falls went wrong. "Somebody zigged when they should have zagged," says Cameron. A stuntman broke his leg and a stuntwoman missed her landing and hit a set piece, breaking a rib. Cameron began to feel that there was too much risk in what they were doing. He called Rob Legato, who was supervising the visual effects on the film at Digital Domain. Legato had told Cameron he was just on the verge of creating realistic CG people with motion capture, a technique in which the actions of human actors are recorded and used to animate digital character models. Before that, the technique had never been used to show a human looking like a human in a movie—it had been used to create a skeleton, a robot, or a knight in armor. "He called me up and said, 'Can you really pull this off?'" Legato remembers. "He couldn't do the stunts he wanted to do. He just couldn't put anybody through that. He couldn't get the scene. Now this portion of the movie he thought he could get in camera, he has to do CG." Even though it would be months before he could prove it, Legato said, "Yeah, we can pull it off." Cameron deleted a number of shots he had planned and shifted them to the as-yet-unproven technique of motion-capture digital stunt shots. It was another of his digital leaps of faith. "With what we can do now, there is absolutely no excuse for a stunt person to be injured making a movie," Cameron says. "But at the time, we were still on the cusp of a lot of these techniques."

At the top of the tilting poop deck shot were Winslet and DiCaprio.

Above them, Cameron was in a basket hanging from a construction crane with Muro, his Steadicam operator, both of them tied in by safety harnesses. The crane operator raised them on the cable at the speed *Titanic* was supposed to be sinking—fairly fast at that point—and they climbed past Winslet and DiCaprio, very close, and then rose up and up, making the actors appear to go down and down until the cameras were forty feet above them. That put Cameron and Muro more than a hundred feet up, swaying in the crane basket. "When the poop deck went to its peak, the guys jumped off and started bouncing off each other, bouncing off girders," DiCaprio recalled. "Then you looked and saw, like, eighteen cranes with huge lights shining on you, and Jim Cameron coming from a little spot in the sky, zooming in past your close-up to the people diving below you. Kate and I looked at each other. Our eyes just bugged out and we said, 'How did we get here? How did we get to this moment in time?'"[5]

The Eighth Sunset

After years of designing bleak future landscapes and grim alien planets, for the first time in his career Cameron was trying to create beauty. For his part, Carpenter was obsessing over the painterly lighting. He was particularly pleased by a scene in which Rose's mother, played by Frances Fisher, adjusts Winslet's corset, the warm light dancing on the actresses' faces. But the DP held his breath while Cameron reviewed the scene in dailies. "Mmmhmm, mmhmm," the inscrutable director said, pausing. "Well, Merchant Ivory can just kiss my ass." It was a compliment, Jim Cameron style. They were getting there.

Cameron was determined to capture the shot of Winslet and Di-Caprio's sunset kiss on the bow of the ship with a real sunset, not a green screen. He had eight days of shooting daylight scenes on the deck in which to accomplish it. An hour before dusk each night, Cameron would glance up at the dipping sun and decide whether to move the crew to the bow for the kiss, based on how promising the sky looked. But day after day ended with the sun dropping into the Pacific with no poetry to it at all. On one of the early, ugly days the crew walked through a full rehearsal anyway. Cameron told the actors how he wanted them to kiss, with DiCaprio standing behind Winslet, the actress turning toward him over her shoulder. They got the timing down, the hesitation, the surrender. Her hand went to his hair. It was beautiful—all except the bald sky.

On the last possible day they could shoot the kiss, it had been mostly overcast all afternoon. An hour before sunset, dark clouds filled the sky, with a little, silvery opening at the horizon. It looked like another bust. But based on either hope or instinct, Cameron moved the crew to the bow. After a couple of false alarms earlier in the week, no one was moving very fast. They positioned the camera crane and placed some lights, added an orange gel to fake a sunset glow. "It all felt fairly cheesy and compromised, but I had to shoot something, and Fox was already coming unglued at how much time the shooting was taking," Cameron says. Winslet went to change her wardrobe, typically a two-hour process due to her elaborate corset, makeup, and hair needs, but the beauty departments had been warned to make it fast tonight.

Suddenly, as everyone was trudging along, the sun started to peek out. Cameron yelled for Winslet—now! Minutes later, she bustled out, her pit crew running alongside, pinning her dress and powdering her nose. The actors were lifted to the bow set on a platform, and Winslet climbed over the railing. Just then, the golden sun burst through the dark purple gray clouds and Winslet screamed, "Shoot! Shoot!" as she and DiCaprio leaped into their rehearsed positions. The focus puller hadn't had a rehearsal. He was going to be winging it. Carpenter yelled for an adjustment to match the artificial light to the golden orange of the sun. There was no time for the wind machine, but a nice breeze was blowing, and from the right direction. Cameron, who was operating a camera by remote, cued the crane that carried it and yelled "action." The camera closed in, and Winslet dropped her hands to DiCaprio's at her waist and turned slightly toward him. DiCaprio leaned in, they hesitated a beat as rehearsed, and then closed for the kiss as the camera arced around them. "I could almost hear the score," says Cameron. "My heart was pounding and I was trying not to blow the framing." Just as the scene finished, the sun ducked behind a cloud. The sky stayed red, and they shot another take, but it lacked the magic of the first. The next day in dailies they learned that take one was "a little buzzed." The focus was soft. But Cameron liked it. And that's the take that's in the movie. The image, the most remembered in Cameron's career and one of the most iconic in cinema history, is actually a bit blurry. Later, they would return to shoot close-ups and add some visual effects for certain portions of the scene—to the point where the actors were sick to death of it. Winslet in particular had good reason to be. "Leo and I had this agreement where, if ever we had to do any kissing, we would say, 'OK, we won't smoke, no onions, no garlic, no coffee, OK? Deal.'"[6] DiCaprio would then engage in all the forbidden activities right before the kiss scene. He became known as "stinky Leo."

Despite the brushing up that was done through special effects, in the end the memorable image was accomplished with the very low-tech combination of planning, teamwork, and luck. Reflecting on the serendipity of the shot, even Cameron, the industry's biggest advocate for CG, wonders if something is lost in the perfectly controllable environment that computers now afford filmmakers. "We could do that sunset now easily as green screen," he says, "and schedule it for Tuesday morning. But would I imagine that sunset? Those particular colors? Now we can create whatever we can imagine. But is our imagination up to the task? I don't know."

Money Money Money

The hundred-day Baja studio had been the beginning of *Titanic*'s budget spinning out of control. Initially, Fox had planned to lease the land and slap up temporary structures, but when the studio attempted to finalize the lease terms, the landowner demanded that the studio buy it. Forced into purchasing the land, Fox had shifted quickly to building a permitted facility. That meant heavier construction costs and a change to many of the sets. At the same time, Cameron's fixation on accuracy kept the art, prop, and costume departments churning through both time and money. Duplicating a model of Gilded Age excess turned out to be pretty excessive. "Some of it was Jim's appetite, which was boundless," Chernin says. Paramount, concerned about overages, had negotiated an agreement that capped its contribution at $65 million, leaving the heavy burden of the mounting budget on Fox's shoulders alone. "I was clearly considered the stupidest person in Hollywood," Chernin says.

Once construction began, there were constant attempts to rein in spending. The elegant first-class lounge, where a sullen Rose was to take tea with her mother, would have cost $250,000 to reproduce with accuracy. Instead the short scene was filmed against a green screen, saving a six-digit sum. Great care had been taken to build the hydraulic set so it could change angles twice to represent two stages in the sinking. Cameron eliminated the middle jacking position and went only from level to six degrees—saving costly production days they would have lost waiting for the change in position. To approximate the other angle, he dutched the camera and had actors lean as they walked. "We did nothing but pare down," says Sanchini. "Jim took a lot of heat for the overages on that film, but actually he did nothing but compromise."

There were some places where it was impossible to economize, like the lighting order, which was staggering. The ship had more than six hundred portholes, each requiring a light. Then there were the practical lights that were a part of the set—lamps on tables, sconces. Certain lights had to work above water, others below, and they all had to be safe and equipped with ground fault interrupters. The production placed an order for more than forty miles of cable, more than one thousand movie lights, and more than one thousand practical lights. "Fox sent us back a letter that said you're ordering too much, you really don't know how to manage your resources correctly, we're going to send down experts," Carpenter recalls. The studio dispatched two lighting veterans, who walked the ship and came back to Carpenter at the end of the day. "Their conclusion was, you don't have enough lights," the DP says.

Media buzz on the movie began to swirl around Cameron's apparent ravenousness with money. *Variety* launched a regular "*Titanic* Watch" column to detail the set's excesses, and *Time* ran a piece headlined "Glub, Glub, Glub . . . Can James Cameron's Extravagant *Titanic* Avoid Disaster?" It didn't help that *Waterworld,* Kevin Costner's $170 million high-seas adventure released in July 1995, was widely regarded as a costly misfire. Early efforts to market *Titanic* were challenging, too, including finding enough material to present at ShoWest, the Las Vegas convention of theater exhibitors, in March 1997. Almost none of the special-effects shots were done. It was decided to use a long, linear trailer instead of a bunch of quick-cut scenes. On a Sunday night, before she was to view the material, Sanchini got a call from a studio executive at Paramount. "I just saw the trailer, and I'm throwing up on my shoes," he told her. Paramount was expecting something Cameron-esque—chases, explosions—not a little old lady narrating a story about a necklace. Meanwhile, the production was dragging way behind schedule. Meant to take 135 days to shoot, *Titanic* would actually require 165 days of production. *Titanic* the movie appeared to be mirroring *Titanic* the ship—a creation that was far too large, a product of man's hubris barreling toward an iceberg.

Cameron tuned out the media hum, but the budget pressures weighed on him. "I felt very strongly that I had let these guys down," Cameron says of Fox. "I had told them I would do it for a certain amount of money, and I'd failed to deliver on that." In a series of exchanges during the making of the movie, Cameron kept offering to give Fox back money, first his front-end fee, then his entire share of the back end. Twentieth Century Fox president Bill Mechanic, the unfortunate Fox executive charged with reining the production in, told Cameron the back-end offer was a noble but ultimately hollow gesture, because the film would never see a dime of profit. He countered by suggesting that Cameron should not only surrender all his points on *Titanic* but give back half his points on the next film he did for Fox. This conversation happened in Cameron's living room. Mechanic's counteroffer didn't go over well. "Get the fuck out of my house," Cameron replied. The director rescinded his offer of the back-end points. "Nobody ever gives back money in Hollywood," says Chernin, Mechanic's boss at the time. "On the one hand, Jim was killing us. On the other hand, here was a man of great conscience." In the end, the filmmaker and his studio agreed on one thing. "We kept saying, 'Our only hope is to make a great movie,'" Chernin says.

Killing Off the Captain

As the shoot ground into months five, six, and seven, everyone was exhausted. The sinking sequences, wet and dangerous, were particularly taxing. Cameron was taking vitamin B_{12} shots and drinking wheatgrass to keep up his strength—he had sworn off caffeine on an earlier film, finding it just exaggerated his already intense personality. At first, the crew had staggered around the tanks in hip waders, but they had soon realized that if they tripped on a cable or a sandbag and their waders filled with water, they were doomed, so many had switched to wet suits.

The actors faced their own challenges in their own ways. "Leo was such a pussy he wanted heated water," says Muro. "And Kate needed the cold water for her performance. So there was a big difference." In the six-foot pool, where DiCaprio and Winslet were to be desperately scrambling for their lives, DiCaprio, who is about six feet tall, would stand. Winslet, breathless, never let her feet touch the ground. "He was such a little funny kid punk," recalls Muro. "And she was so mature. He would draw the youth out of her and she would bring some maturity to him." DiCaprio made such a production about getting into the water that Cameron called him a Persian cat. "He'd put one foot in, then pull it out and complain about the temperature, then slowly, over a minute or so, slip down into the water, whinging the entire time," Cameron says. "It was ridiculously dramatic. I just figured he hated water." Actually, DiCaprio turned out to be an accomplished scuba diver who didn't bat an eye at a treacherous underwater sequence where he had a rope around his waist pulling him into the depths. He would later say that filming *Titanic* "made a man out of me."[7]

Winslet, more stoic during the shoot, may have felt its rigors more acutely. During one sequence where she and DiCaprio were to be rushing along the flooding ship, blocked by a closed gate, the actress's long coat snagged the gate, submerging her and keeping her under. "I had to sort of shimmy out of the coat to get free," she said. "I had no breath left. I thought I'd burst. And Jim just said, 'OK, let's go again.' That was his attitude. I didn't want to be a wimp so I didn't complain." Though Winslet was not in physical danger—there were safety divers to swim to her rescue—she was badly shaken. "For the first time in my life on a film set I was thinking, 'I wish I wasn't here.' Some days I'd wake up and think, 'Please, God, let me die.'"[8]

By the end, Cameron felt the same way. He shot through the 164th day of production, that night, and into the following day, his last. By 10:00 a.m. he and his crew had worked around the clock and he was left with one task—to kill off Captain Smith. The crew had built a "caisson set" of the captain's bridge, an air-filled set that is below water level that you access through the top. The set was placed deep enough that the bridge windows were fifteen feet down, which pushed a ton and a half of force against each of the several windows. Electrically fired squibs would shatter the tempered glass of the windows.

The Polish stuntman doubling as the captain was named Pavel Cajzl. They called him Plastic Pavel because apparently he would bend but not break. Cajzl was rigged with two separate air supplies, a "hookah" regulator, which was plumbed up the inside of his leg, and a spare-air tank under his coat. Cameron's experience with a similar set on *The Abyss* was that the second the water rushed in, it would pick up dirt, rust, and debris and suspend it in a filthy broth that was impossible to see through. If Cajzl didn't have his own air source, he would drown, because the safety crew wouldn't be able to see anything in the murk. The only other person in the set was Cameron, who was going to operate the only manned camera. He had a bail-out hatch right above him and was standing with his back against the wall of the set, wearing scuba gear and hockey pads on his legs, over his wet suit, in case the water forced the window glass into the set hard enough to slash his shins.

Cajzl signaled that he was ready for the shot. Cameron rolled his camera. On the director's cue, the glass would be blown from the far side of the bridge to the near side, creating a wave effect and sending thirty tons of water into the set in seconds. It was the last shot. Cameron was done. He was exhausted and drained. Postproduction looked like it was going to be a living hell, with an impossible deadline and difficult visual effects that had barely been started. He had enough footage for a four-hour movie, was wildly over budget, and had been told there was zero possibility that the film could make money. His movie was the laughingstock of Hollywood, and the media was pillorying him daily. "I thought to myself, 'Lord, take me now. It's a really good time,'" Cameron says. He cued the squibs, which released the avalanche of water. First Cajzl disappeared, and a split second later Cameron was slammed against the wall. His world turned dark brown. When the watery fury subsided, Cameron slowly surfaced and saw that Cajzl was at the top and OK. The director himself was unharmed, and the shot looked good. Postproduction yawned before him. He had finished one impossible task only to face another, but that was tomorrow.

He dried off, feeling utterly depleted, and had a few toasts with the remaining crew. Someone produced a bottle of tequila, which Cameron promptly confiscated. He walked to the edge of the tank, where the set of the ship sat angled into the water, frozen in the act of sinking. It would be torn down as soon as his taillights faded out of sight heading north. Cameron sat and drank about half the bottle, saying his good-byes to the set, the tank, the entire adventure. Then he got up and went to the van that would drive him back to L.A. He was asleep before they pulled out of the studio.

Better Than Good

With each of his movies, Cameron has edged closer to the editor's chair. He's gone from standing back entirely on *The Terminator* to making some of his own splices on *Aliens* to learning how to use an Avid, the then-new digital editing system, on *True Lies*. On *Titanic* he was a full-fledged part of the editing team, which was rounded out by Richard Harris, who had schooled Cameron on the Avid on *True Lies*, and Conrad Buff, who had worked with the director since *The Abyss*. Cameron had the Avids set up at his Malibu home, which had become a kind of postproduction compound. He would deal with visual effects and other issues during the day and at night, alone, start cutting. Sometimes he recut the other guys' work; sometimes they recut his. Cameron made the final decisions, but it was a collaborative process. All three bodies would be needed for the workload: On a typical three-hour drama, editors have between six hundred and eight hundred thousand feet of film from which to cut. Cameron had shot well over twice that.[9]

The special effects were also overwhelming. Digital Domain couldn't handle the massive workload. *Titanic* ramped up from one special-effects house to seventeen to try to speed the process along. Cameron was trying to use the technology in a new way. *Titanic* wasn't *T2*, where the stunning special effects drew attention to themselves. This time his goal was to create a time and place in absolutely unassailable realistic detail, to have the effects go undetected by an audience immersed in the story. Digital Domain pushed the envelope of motion capture for the film's digital crowds, but there were hitches. The clothing never looked real, with rubbery folds at the knees and elbows. Faces looked like masks. Cameron used the shots wisely and didn't overplay his hand.

By May, it was becoming clear that the July release date was going to be a serious problem. Cameron still had to deal with looping the actors' dialogue, the musical score, the final sound mix, color timing, and hundreds more unfinished effects shots. He called Chernin and told the executive a summer release would mean a compromised film. Chernin asked for a day to think about what to do. Fox bit the bullet. The studio pushed the release date from July 2 to December 19. The change bought Cameron some breathing room, but not without new pressures. In the middle of the turmoil, the director ran into News Corporation chairman and CEO Rupert Murdoch at the studio. "I guess I'm not your favorite person," Cameron said to the media baron. "But the movie is going to be good," he promised. "It better be a damn sight better than good," Murdoch told him.

This was a period of some change in Cameron's personal life. Linda Hamilton, whom the director had dated on and off since *T2* in 1991, had struggled with mood disorders for years. After the birth of their daughter in 1993, she had suffered severe postpartum depression. "I think Jim said to me once, 'I like who I leave in the morning, but I don't always know who I'm going to come home to at night,'" Hamilton told Larry King in 2005.[10] During the making of *Titanic,* Hamilton had been diagnosed with bipolar disorder, had begun treatment, and was seeing improvement. Cameron saw an opportunity for a fresh start for the couple, and they married in July 1997. It was his fourth marriage, and like the others, it wouldn't last.

The Secret Song

Cameron's composer on the film was James Horner, with whom he had shared the miserably rushed postproduction experience on *Aliens.* When Horner met with him about the *Titanic* job, they devoted less than five minutes to addressing their respective disappointments about that score. "I apologized and he apologized," Horner says. "He said, 'Don't worry about it, man. It's history. It's gone. Let's talk about this movie.'" They discussed what Cameron wanted on *Titanic*—a score with a tremendous amount of heart. And what he didn't want. "There was gonna be no song, dammit, in my movie," Horner says, recalling Cameron's certitude. "That was a closed issue." Cameron had snuck one song into *T2*—"Bad to the Bone," played when Schwarzenegger enters the biker bar—over his editor's protestations. But the director rarely uses songs in his films. "They never seem to fit tonally," he says.

On *Titanic*, Horner never gave it another thought. He had his marching orders. But as he grew close to finishing the score, Horner was stumped about how to end the movie musically. "The score is such an emotional roller coaster architecturally, compositionally," Horner says. "How am I gonna write another piece when the end credits roll that means anything?" The composer decided the way to solve his dilemma was with intimacy—a solo voice. And then he wrote a melody and quietly enlisted lyricist Will Jennings to collaborate on it. "And within two days it spun out of my control into a song," Horner says. He had an idea who might be right to sing it, an old friend whom he tracked down where she was performing in Las Vegas—Celine Dion. Horner flew to Vegas and sang his song for Dion, who loved it and was eager to record a demo. "I explained to her that I was in verboten territory here, that if Jim ever found out he'd have my head," Horner recalls.

Secretly, Horner flew to New York to meet Dion in the studio. There were supposed to be just four people there, but all of Sony's top brass showed up, nearly twenty people in all, including the record label's chief, Tommy Mottola. Dion sang a complete take of the song, "My Heart Will Go On." When she finished, the room was hushed. Some of the executives were dabbing their eyes. "She came out and said, 'Well, so what does everybody think?'" Horner recalls. There was universal approval from the Sony entourage, who disappeared in their limos while Horner made four copies of the recording. He brought it back to L.A. but felt he couldn't play it yet for Cameron. He was waiting for the right time to explain this concept of a song. Every few days, Horner saw Cameron to go over some aspect of the score, and the time never seemed right. Dion's camp anxiously checked in. Had Jim heard the song? Did he love it?

One day, Cameron seemed a little happy—or at least not gruff. Some special-effects sequence had come back and it hadn't been screwed up. Horner seized the moment. "He asked me if I was in a good mood, and I said, 'Of course not. What's the question?'" Cameron recalls. With some trepidation, the composer played his song for Cameron. "I thought, 'Oh, no, he's pushing a song,'" says Cameron. "A song! Would you put a song at the end of *Schindler's List*? There's not going to be a song at the end of *Titanic*. This is a serious historical drama." But as the song progressed, Cameron noticed how cleverly Horner had reorchestrated the main romantic theme of the score and how emotionally affecting the lyrics were. The song embodied the dramatic themes of the movie perfectly. He was won over within the length of one playback. Horner asked if Cameron recognized the singer, and the director said no. Told it was Celine Dion, Cameron said, "Oh, she's big, right?"

A Hat on a Hat

The first test screening for *Titanic* was at the Mall of America in Minneapolis. Cameron flew there ahead, alone, ostensibly to test the audio systems, while Landau, Sanchini, and eight or nine Fox executives rode in on the corporate plane. Cameron had roped off seats for himself at the theater. He likes to sit in the middle of the audience, but not next to an audience member who might recognize him and definitely not next to an executive, so Sanchini was his buffer. Cameron almost always projects an image of complete confidence around studio brass. Some of the time, he's faking. That day, he was terrified. His reputation, Fox's and Paramount's money, people's jobs were all riding on *Titanic*'s being better than good. "He said, 'Someday I'm going to die at a preview screening of one of my films. I'm just going to have a heart attack and die. I know it. This is where it's gonna end for me,'" recalls Sanchini. Cameron had rigged the audio so he could ride the volume the whole time—to focus on anything but the anxiety. When the lights went down, he whispered to Sanchini, "We'll know in the first few minutes if this has all been worth it." The movie started, with its sepia-treated titles and the deep dive footage of the wreck, and the audience was wooden. No reaction. "We're fucked," Cameron whispered to Sanchini. "It's all over. There's no point." But by ten or fifteen minutes in, the crowd started responding—a special-effects transition from the wrecked *Titanic* to the ship in its pristine period drew a "wow," and DiCaprio earned some chuckles. The film seemed to get over some kind of a hump with the audience, and Cameron exhaled.

When the focus-group leader interviewed the crowd after the film, it came out that the audience thought they were going to be seeing *Great Expectations*. That's what they had been told, for reasons of security. They thought the first few minutes were a trailer for *Titanic*. Aside from the source of the confusion, Cameron learned something else from the audience. The reaction cards were off-the-charts good, except for one scene. "We thought people wouldn't like all the slow, mushy stuff in the beginning, but they did," says Sanchini. "They thought the movie was too long in the sinking." Originally, Cameron had larded the film with plenty of action he thought audiences and studios expected from him. He had spent three days and well over a million dollars on a soggy, angled set shooting a virtuoso chase scene and gunfight in the middle of the sinking. But the preview audiences felt a gunfight in the middle of the sinking of *Titanic* was wrong. "It was supposed to be a Jim Cameron moment," Sanchini says, "but they didn't want it."

To the shock of almost everyone who had worked on it, Cameron cut the chase scene. "I liked it," he says. "It was a technical marvel." But he realized he had successfully created a strong enough sense of jeopardy from the sinking ship that the idea of additional peril from a guy with a gun was superfluous—"a hat on a hat." To close a gap created by the cut scene, Cameron filmed a quick pickup shot with Winslet and DiCaprio running downstairs from the dining room to the corridor. He locked the picture at three hours and fourteen minutes.

King of the World

Cameron had indeed made another "most expensive movie ever," this time with a budget topping $200 million. But at the moment before *Titanic*'s release, he also knew he had made a good movie. Cameron's fingerprints were all over *Titanic,* right down to Jack's sketches, which he had drawn himself. He was satisfied as a filmmaker and proud of the accomplishment, not just for himself but for the huge team who had helped him. *Titanic*'s biggest surprise, however, was yet to come, as the movie exploded at the box office, and in the strangest way possible.

Titanic's reviews were mostly positive. Roger Ebert called it "flawlessly crafted,"[11] and the *New York Times'* Janet Maslin said *Titanic* was "the first spectacle in decades that honestly invites comparison to *Gone with the Wind.*"[12] But some critics felt the spectacle had come at the expense of the script. The *Los Angeles Times*'s Kenneth Turan was particularly scathing, writing, "What really brings on the tears is Cameron's insistence that writing this kind of movie is within his abilities. Not only is it not, it is not even close."[13]

On its opening weekend, *Titanic* took in $28.6 million, beating the James Bond film it was up against by a hair. But then it began to build from weekend to weekend, seemingly defying gravity. It just wouldn't come down. *Titanic*'s box office peaked on Valentine's Day 1998, when it earned $13 million in a single day, seven weeks into its release. Teenage girls, in particular, were driving the box-office numbers and embracing *Titanic* with Beatlemania levels of fervor, going to see the movie over and over again in packs. Within two months of *Titanic*'s release, 45 percent of women under twenty-five who had seen the movie had seen it twice. Some held *Titanic* parties, where they convened to listen to the soundtrack—and cry. But it wasn't just young women propelling the movie's success. Young men, the traditional box-office drivers, still showed up for the action. And older audiences of both genders represented an unusually large number of ticket buyers. In the middle of a decade culturally marked by cynicism and irony, an utterly earnest movie was drawing audiences in droves. What people around the world really needed, it seemed, was a good old-fashioned wallow. Laughter is regional, but audiences from Tokyo to Rome to Mexico City were all crying in the same places. A graduate student in Cairo named Rania al-Razaz told the *New York Times* that she had waited more than a week to get a ticket to *Titanic* in April. "It is not an American movie," al-Razaz said. "It's a human movie."[14] Former *New Yorker* film critic Pauline Kael sniffed to *Newsweek* that *Titanic* was "square in ways people seem to have been longing for."[15]

The movie's cultural influence spread far beyond the multiplex. Libraries couldn't keep *Titanic* titles on their shelves, and Walter Lord's 1955 book *A Night to Remember* and the 1912 Senate inquiry into the sinking were both reissued. The J. Peterman catalog sold hundreds of thousands of dollars' worth of replica *Titanic* paraphernalia, including life jackets, blueprints for the ship, and a fifteen-foot anchor with a $25,000 price tag. Restaurant chefs promoted *Titanic* menus, and cruise lines, curiously, reported a surge in ticket sales. *Titanic,* once a symbol of man-made tragedy, was now synonymous with romance. Cruise-ship passengers kept trying to ride the bow as Jack and Rose had, before learning, sadly, that this was prohibited on most vessels. Many did, however, inquire about the number of lifeboats aboard.

The film finally started to come back down to Earth after Valentine's Day, but it did so slowly. *Titanic* was number one for sixteen weeks— a record—ultimately grossing $1.8 billion worldwide—another record. Once the money started to pour in, there was some drama about whether Fox would pay Cameron's back end, now that there was actually going to be one. In truth, they had no choice legally. They had turned down Cameron's offer to surrender it a year earlier. "I liked that it was a lot of money," says Cameron, who declines to say just what he made from *Titanic.* "But I liked it best of all that they had screwed themselves by being greedy, like the dog that drops the bone into the pool to get the one in the reflection."

Titanic was nominated for a record fourteen Academy Awards, and it won eleven, including Best Director, Best Editing, and Best Picture, tying the record set by *Ben-Hur.* Cameron's films had won many Oscars over the years, but this was the first time the director would get statues for his own mantel. By the end of the night he would also have to make three speeches. Cameron attended the ceremony with Linda Hamilton. "It was nerve-racking," he says. "And the strap on Linda's gown had broken, so it had somehow become all about the gown. I was just happy when it was all over." In his first speech, for his editing Oscar, Cameron kept his cool, letting the other editors speak first, and mentioned his daughter. In his second, for directing, he raised his trophy aloft and shouted, "I'm king of the world!" just as DiCaprio had when he clung to the tip of *Titanic*'s bow. It didn't go over quite as Cameron intended—many interpreted his demeanor as cocky rather than jubilant. "The funniest moment of the whole thing, in retrospect, was the quizzical expression on Warren Beatty's face when I greeted him backstage," Cameron says. "His expression was like, 'What the fuck were you thinking?'" Cameron toned it down for his last speech, for Best Picture—a moment of silence for the victims of *Titanic*. Though eclipsed in most people's memories by the "king of the world" sound bite, what Cameron chose to say in that last speech reveals how *Titanic*, the ship and the movie, had impacted him personally: "The message of *Titanic*, of course, is that if that great ship can sink, the unthinkable can happen, the future's unknowable. The only thing we truly own is today. Life is precious. So for these few seconds, I'd like you to also listen to the beating of your own heart, which is the most precious thing in the world."

Cameron was forty-three when *Titanic* was released. However immodest it may have seemed to say so at the Oscars, he really was king of the world. For him, the movie was a career height he never expected to reach again. And for the next several years, he wouldn't even bother to try. Upon finishing *Titanic*, he told a Canadian journalist he planned to spend the next year with his daughter building sand castles in their backyard. "I just want my heart rate to beat like a quiet, flat line for a while," he said.[16] He was about to enter a new phase in his life, one of family and exploration. At what would be the apex of his powers as a director, Cameron would step away from feature filmmaking altogether.

9.

A MODERN-DAY MAGELLAN

Toys and Adventures

After *Titanic*, Cameron took to calling himself "the world's busiest un-employed filmmaker." While various possible feature projects crossed his desk—a *Planet of the Apes* remake, *Terminator 3*, a *True Lies* sequel, a comet script he wrote called *Bright Angel Falling*, *Spider-Man*—he didn't commit to any of them. He had already conquered Hollywood and, frankly, wasn't all that interested in it. Instead, he set his sights on uncharted territories—the deep sea, space, and new technologies. "He wanted to live," says Cameron's friend Guillermo del Toro. "And he lived to an extent that most of us just dream about. After the Oscars, Jim went to *his* Disneyland. It was a time for him to have toys and adventures." Cameron had come of age in an era of exploration. The space race, Jacques Cousteau's underwater expeditions—in the 1960s, the spirit of discovery was robust around the world. For Cameron, that love of adventure never flagged. "He'd have been one of the ones that would have crossed the country in a covered wagon," says the director's mother, Shirley. "Anything new that he could get into." After *Titanic,* Cameron had both the means and the time to indulge his wanderlust. "I did feel like I was in a position where I could do other things that didn't make sense before," Cameron says. "It's like that moment in *Serpico* where he says, 'You know ballet? From this position I can do anything.' I've got my fuck-you money and I can kind of step away for a while. My career's not gonna go anywhere. I can do all the cool stuff that I've always wanted to do." Cameron thought he might take two or three years for deep-ocean expeditions and produce and develop some projects to work on later. "It wasn't full stop, just leave Hollywood like J. D. Salinger or something." But the director's break from feature filmmaking would last much longer than he anticipated.

Breakups

When Cameron founded Digital Domain in 1993 with Stan Winston and Scott Ross, his goal was to influence CG research and development and then utilize the company's advancements to make his own movies better, as George Lucas had done with Industrial Light & Magic in the 1980s. Cameron was Digital Domain's CEO, chairman of its board, and also the company's biggest client. It seemed to make sense going in that his films would supply Digital Domain with lots of opportunities to do pioneering, lucrative work in the field. But the director's personal creative path and the company's business plan began to diverge, ultimately breaking apart entirely at a tense board meeting at Digital Domain's Venice, California, offices in 1998. The board had become concerned about conflicts of interest between Cameron, CEO, and Cameron, filmmaker. As a CEO, Cameron's responsibility was to push for Digital Domain's growth as a business. As a filmmaker, his motive was to get the most CG bang for his buck. On *Titanic,* the company had earned its first Oscar but also been overwhelmed by the volume of the work, which Cameron received at a discount. "I always felt that I did both what was best for Digital Domain and best for my films, but the board had issues," Cameron says. "I had begun to dislike the dynamic. When it was clear that the very controls I needed fell mostly into a conflict-of-interest category, it obviated the upside to me."

Cameron couldn't realistically ask other companies to bid on his effects movies. But what he wanted from Digital Domain—cutting-edge work, particularly in the area of creature design—was beginning to seem impossible in the increasingly corporatized structure of a company backed by IBM and media group Cox Communications. "As a business, 'no' comes up more often than 'yes,'" says Rob Legato, who created *Titanic's* digital stunt doubles while supervising the movie's visual effects at Digital Domain in the 1990s. "It was a struggle for Jim. Digital Domain came into being because of him, and then all of a sudden there's a board of directors and you're no longer taking risks, you're no longer trying things." At the same time that Cameron was growing frustrated by his company's risk-averse strategies, the board was discovering the ugly truth about the special-effects business—it's just not all that great. A good year for the company was a 5 percent margin. Digital Domain's president, Scott Ross, wanted to expand, to turn the effects house into a production company, following the model that had grown Pixar from an animation R & D shop to a major Hollywood studio. But Cameron already had a production company—Lightstorm—and he didn't want another one. Ross was trying to set up an IPO to fund the expansion, and a Goldman Sachs banker was about to deliver a report on the progress of the public-offering plan when Cameron interrupted her, stood up, and read a handwritten note to the board. "I basically thanked them for the honor of serving with men of their excellent caliber and gave my formal resignation as both CEO and chairman of the board," Cameron recalls. As the director turned to leave, Winston, his creative partner and friend since *The Terminator*, stood up, echoed Cameron's remarks, and walked out with him. Publicly, Ross issued a statement thanking Cameron and Winston for their contributions and explaining that "as Digital Domain has matured, the company has attained an increasing degree of self sufficiency."[1] But privately, the board was furious. The names Cameron and Winston were the strength of its brand, and Wall Street wouldn't be bullish on an IPO without them.

When Cameron finally got around to making his next effects movie, *Avatar,* seven years later, he would turn not to Digital Domain but to Weta Digital, Peter Jackson's award-winning effects house, for most of the CG work. Weta's filmmaker-centric structure was what Cameron had been hoping to create in his own company. Digital Domain survived without Cameron. Though it never went public or became the next Pixar, in 2006 *Armageddon* and *Transformers* director Michael Bay bought the company. In 2009, Digital Domain earned its first Oscar since *Titanic* for reverse-aging Brad Pitt in *The Curious Case of Benjamin Button*. "I was proud of what we created at Digital Domain," Cameron says. "Almost overnight we created a world-class powerhouse for visual effects, which is still—seventeen years later—one of the top houses. But now it's Michael Bay's problem."

Cameron would be ending another, much more personally meaningful partnership that year, with Linda Hamilton. After an up-and-down relationship that started during the filming of *T2* in 1991, they had married in July 1997 but were already separated by the summer of 1998. In the mid-nineties, Hamilton had begun treatment for the mood disorder that had plagued her for years, and she and Cameron had hoped to find some stability as a family with their daughter,

Josephine, then five. But Cameron had just spent three years of his life immersed in making *Titanic*. When he finally emerged from his single-minded focus on work, his home was far from peaceful. It was clear even at the Oscars in March that the couple was troubled. They bickered on the red carpet, in full view of cameras. Asked by a reporter if *Titanic*'s eleven Oscars had changed her husband, Hamilton sounded like anything but a proud wife, replying sharply, "He was always a jerk, so there's no way to really measure."[2] In December, Hamilton would file for divorce, citing irreconcilable differences. Years later, she would talk openly about her struggle with mental illness and how it affected her marriages. "By the time Jim and I were together, I was really spiraling out of control," Hamilton told Oprah Winfrey in 2005. "I fought him. I fought everything about his life. I really said a lot of cruel, aggressive things to him. You know, words that should never be spoken to one that you love."[3] It would be Cameron's fourth divorce.

Going Deep

For Cameron, peace is found under the ocean. After finishing a movie, he says, "I usually go diving first, to decompress by literally decompressing. I find the underwater world to be a great antidote to Hollywood. Nobody down there knows who you are. You're just part of the food chain." Cameron wanted to get back into the sea as soon as possible after *Titanic*, not just as a scuba-diving tourist but as a deep-ocean explorer. He figured his best shot would be selling a documentary about revisiting the wreck—this time with new technology that would allow him to take audiences deeper inside it—and packaging it with a trip to the sunken German warship the *Bismarck*. He also saw the expedition as an opportunity to test some new 3-D cameras he had been developing with Vince Pace, a technician and cameraman who had helped build the underwater lighting system that had won a technical Oscar on *The Abyss*.

When Cameron first contacted Pace about building 3-D cameras together in 2000, most of Hollywood still considered the format a fad best forgotten. After a brief golden era that began with *Bwana Devil,* a 1952 drama about man-eating lions, and peaked that same decade with a string of Vincent Price horror films including *House of Wax* and *The Mad Magician,* 3-D languished, only to be revived every decade or so as a gimmick and then abandoned again. With traditional movie cameras and projectors, 3-D was cumbersome for filmmakers and exhibitors and sometimes dizzying for audiences. Making a 3-D movie involves filming an image with two cameras: one representing the left eye, the other the right. When synchronized and watched through glasses that allow each eye to see only its own movie, the two films create an illusion of depth. But with traditional movie cameras, perfect synchronization is nearly impossible, and the imperfections lead to ghosting images, sometimes even making audiences nauseated and giving them headaches. Cameron had experimented with 3-D for *T2 3-D: Battle Across Time,* a twelve-minute, $60 million movie made to accompany a Universal Studios theme-park ride in 1996. Despite relying on two heavy film cameras mounted together—an unwieldy package the size of a 450-pound washing machine—his team was able to achieve some revolutionary dynamic shots by relying on a system of cables. The project excited Cameron about the prospects for 3-D in the digital era. As he had done so many times before in his career, the director ignored the prevailing wisdom and set about finding out for himself what the real potential of 3-D was. If he liked what he saw, he vowed to film his next feature using 3-D cameras.

Cameron was also working with his brother Mike on building miniature robotic cameras he could send in to explore the nooks and crannies of the *Titanic* wreck. Snoop Dog, the ROV he had used in 1995, was too big to sneak into portholes, and it relied on a cable connected to the Mir submersibles for its power source. If the cable got snagged, the robot was lost. Cameron funded the research for his own mini ROVs starting in 1998. It took three years and one million dollars each to engineer the Cameron brothers' two bots, which were given the names Jake and Elwood in a nod to the Blues Brothers. More than anything, Jake and Elwood were a triumph of miniaturization. Most robots that could operate at the two-and-a-half-mile depths of the *Titanic* wreck were the size of refrigerators. Jake and Elwood are closer to the size of microwaves. Unlike Snoop Dog with its cable, Jake and Elwood relied on an internal battery and sent data back to monitors through a fiber-optic cable the width of a human hair, which spooled out from the bot. It was two thousand feet long and could get caught or broken without the ROV's being lost.

In September 2001, Cameron found himself back aboard a Russian sub, making his way to the *Titanic* site, this time with considerably more technological firepower. He also brought Bill Paxton along on the expedition to provide a layman's view of the dives for the documentary cameras, as well as scientists and historians, including his consultants on *Titanic*, Ken Marschall and Don Lynch, and his friends John Bruno and Lewis Abernathy. With Jake and Elwood, the expedition crew was able to see sights no one had seen since the night the *Titanic* went down—leaded-glass windows, wrought-iron gates, a mahogany sideboard that, remarkably, was still neatly stacked with White Star china dishes despite the violence of the ship's breakup and sinking. Jake and Elwood were a huge success. But on the second dive, Elwood abruptly began to lose power. The ROV's battery exploded and it drifted to the ceiling of D deck and stuck there. Now Cameron had his own wreck within the wreck. The expedition took on a new purpose. "I wasn't gonna leave a million-dollar vehicle inside the *Titanic*,"

Cameron says, "but to get it back I had to risk another million-dollar vehicle, the only other one in existence." The bots had been designed to be able to rescue each other. They were lined with Velcro, and one could attach to the other and pull it. But a first attempt didn't work, nor did a second on the following dive. The crew was determined not to leave Elwood behind. "The one Blues Brother doesn't desert the other Blues Brother!" Abernathy roared. It was he who suggested a very low-tech tool that was employed on the final rescue attempt.

Cameron and his crew departed in a calm sea on the morning of September 11, 2001, determined to bring Elwood home. They were going to try to retrieve a cutting-edge piece of technology using a coat hanger as a harpoon. About an hour into their descent, Cameron's youngest brother, John David, who was manning communications aboard the *Keldysh,* sent a message down to the director in Mir 1: "Terrorist activity. World Trade Center. Air travel stopped." The crew in the sub wasn't sure what to make of the information. "Do not understand," Jim Cameron said. "Are you recommending we abort the dive? Over." "Do not, I say again, do not abort dive," John David responded.[4] Both sub crews had heard the message. They could only wonder what was going on in the world above them. But soon they were back on the ocean floor, immersed in bot rescue. Cameron was operating Jake, trying to spear the mesh around Elwood's propellers with the hanger. After a few attempts, he snagged him, but the robots weren't moving. Now Elwood was hanging on to Jake. Cameron was ready to give up on Elwood and cut the connection between the two ROVs, but that didn't work either. He couldn't sever them. So he tried one last time to tow Elwood in, giving Jake all his power. Suddenly the tug on the line changed. "Hey, we're going!" he yelled.[5] Both bots were coming home.

The crew members in the Mirs were ebullient when they emerged at the surface and boarded the *Keldysh* to share the good news. But the mood on the Russian ship was grim. They were surfacing to a changed world. The crew in the subs learned what they had missed—a terrorist attack had toppled the World Trade Center and hit the Pentagon, and a hijacked plane was down in Pennsylvania. Three thousand people were dead. "All of a sudden everything we're doing means nothing," says Cameron. "It felt like it was so trivial. You're invested in your own fantasy, feeling like it's life or death, and then you realize it's stupid, it's juvenile." But after absorbing the initial shock of the news, the expedition crew began to see the parallels between the tragedies. *Titanic* was the defining disaster of a new century, and so was 9/11. The *Titanic* was a "safe tragedy," Cameron says, a metaphor from another era that helped them talk about loss and grief and shock.

After a few days, they resumed diving *Titanic*. In light of the terror attacks, Cameron put on hold his initial plan to travel to the *Bismarck* next. By the time the 2001 expedition was over, he had spent 330 hours of his life down at *Titanic,* more time, even, than the ship's captain had before the liner went down.

Jim the Guy

Cameron's friends talk about "Jim the Guy" as if he is a whole other man from "James Cameron the Director." "It's wild," says Schwarzenegger. "He literally becomes a different person." Some people who know them both call his intense on-set alter ego "MIJ" (Jim backward). They try to read Cameron's face like storm clouds. "I much prefer Jim the Guy," says John Bruno, who has known the director in both capacities since the mid-1980s. "I can judge him by the way he answers questions, the way he's talking to people. It's just a tone. He'll be sharp with somebody. If he turns around and says, 'This is fucked,' then that's not the day to ask him something." At work, his friend Guillermo del Toro says, Cameron has a laserlike focus, "and everyone knows what happens with lasers."

Del Toro may have the best story about Jim the Guy. The two directors met at Ron Perlman's Fourth of July barbecue in the early nineties, years before del Toro directed *Hellboy* or the Oscar-winning *Pan's Labyrinth* and became an industry darling for his darkly poetic fantasies. The day they met, del Toro was trying to raise money to finish his first movie to be released in the United States, *Cronos,* which starred Perlman. Cameron had just finished the $100 million *T2* and was attending the party with Linda Hamilton, Perlman's costar from the TV show *Beauty and the Beast. Cronos* had cost $1.7 million to make in Mexico—at the time, it was one of the country's most expensive films. "I hear you and I made the most expensive movies in our respective countries," Cameron said to del Toro. "When can I see yours?" A few months later, Cameron would be the first person in the United States to see *Cronos* projected, in the Charlie Chaplin Theater at Raleigh Studios in Hollywood. Cameron watched the whole movie with Guillermo Navarro, del Toro's cinematographer, by his side translating it, because the filmmakers had no money left for subtitling. Cameron loved *Cronos* and found in del Toro a kindred spirit. Like Cameron, the jovial Mexican director had worked his way up on the technical side of filmmaking—he learned makeup and special effects under the master Dick Smith and had done every job on a film set, from operating the sound boom to assistant directing.

Financing *Cronos* required del Toro to choose between eating and postproducing his movie. "I lived like a hobo," he says. But when he was in L.A. he stayed at Cameron's guesthouse in Malibu, often for months at a time. Cameron and del Toro, both bachelors then, would order takeout together, watch movies, and run errands in Cameron's sports cars. "He's an astonishingly scary driver," del Toro says. "We were very happy to go shopping for laser discs together. I would buy three. He would buy one hundred. He would love for me to suggest weird stuff." They watched Cameron's favorite movie, *The Wizard of Oz* ("because it's perfect," Cameron explains, tellingly), anime, and bad Italian horror movies that del Toro picked out. They went to see *2001: A Space Odyssey* at the Cinerama Dome in Hollywood. They also critiqued each other's rough cuts, sometimes spending days in the editing room together to chew over problematic sequences in their movies. Del Toro helped Cameron avoid being taken advantage of when building the studio for *Titanic* in Baja.

But it was when his father was kidnapped in Guadalajara, Mexico, in 1998 that del Toro realized just how much he could count on Jim the Guy. Miramax had recently released del Toro's biggest budget movie, *Mimic,* a $30 million production, and in his hometown the director was now believed to be a Hollywood high roller. Criminals captured Federico del Toro and demanded a ransom from his son. Then they doubled it. Over the course of the seventy-two-day ordeal, Cameron called and e-mailed del Toro constantly, counseling his friend on hiring the right people to perform the ransom negotiations based on his own experience with personal security. He reviewed the references from the negotiators. It was Cameron who loaned del Toro the ransom negotiator's salary, a sum big enough to alleviate the family's financial burden. "Of all my friends, Jim was the Gibraltar stone," del Toro recalls. He would pay Cameron back immediately upon his father's release, and move his whole family from Mexico to the United States. "It's easier to talk about the legend of the artistic dictator," del Toro says. "Few people know Jim's other side." But after *Titanic,* as Cameron threw himself into endeavors far afield from traditional moviemaking, Jim the Guy would start rearing his head more often.

In June 2000, Cameron married Suzy Amis, the shy, willowy actress, then thirty-eight, who had caught his eye while playing Rose's granddaughter in *Titanic*. The daughter of an air force pilot and a homemaker in Oklahoma, Amis had been recruited as a model at sixteen and soon began living in Paris and appearing on magazine covers as one of the Ford Agency's "faces of the '80s." In 1986, Amis made her stage debut as a teenage temptress in an off-Broadway play called *Fresh Horses*—she was the only thing critics liked about it. By the time she was cast in *Titanic*, Amis had turned in strong performances in movies better known by reviewers than by audiences, like *The Ballad of Little Jo*, a revisionist Western in which she played a frontier woman who passes as a man in order to get by in a rough mining town. Her son, Jasper, from her marriage to her ex-husband, actor Sam Robards, accompanied Amis on every shoot. During the filming in 1996, Cameron had a three-year-old daughter of his own, Josephine, and a complicated on-again, off-again relationship with her mother, Linda Hamilton. Amis had the spirit of adventure that Cameron found irresistible in a woman—she could fly a Cessna, shoot a rifle, ride a horse. But there was something unusual about her—for an actress, she didn't seem all that interested in being famous. It was clear to the cast and crew around them that Amis and Cameron had some kind of spark. "I could tell Jim was sweet on her," Paxton says.

Cameron and Amis would go on to have three children together, Claire, Quinn, and Rose, and raise them in Malibu with Josephine and Jasper. For the first time, Cameron's friends and family didn't hold their breath for signs of trouble. He seemed to have found a partner who balanced, rather than heightened, his intensity. "Suzy is a peaceful, earth-mother type who really brings out the best in him and lets him be him," says Tom Arnold. "He really respects her. He's always really respected women. You can tell that in his characters, and if you know him personally, he's very introspective about his life and mistakes he's made." Cameron's films that deal with marriage have shown a very traditional view—in the end, the warring Brigmans of

The Abyss and the Taskers of *True Lies* reconcile. It's a happy ending he had never managed to accomplish in his own life. When he made *True Lies* in 1994, Cameron wanted the poster to be a picture of a hand grenade with a wedding ring for the pin pull. "I had not met Suzy yet, so to me marriage was still a grenade range," he says. But *True Lies* ends with the family intact, with everyone in on secrets and acting as a team of spies. "You can see from the way the film resolves that I was a big fan of marriage, fatherhood, and true love," Cameron says. "And I still am."

"Why the Hell Do You Wackos Want to Go to Mars?"

In August 1999 at the University of Colorado at Boulder, Cameron addressed a group of about seven hundred would-be Martians. They were mostly members of the nonprofit Mars Society—scientists, engineers, students, and red-planet fans with earthbound day jobs like teaching and hotel management who advocate Mars's exploration and settlement. "You people are all out of your minds, you know that?" Cameron taunted them. "You do understand that Mars is really, really far away, and it's really, really cold? And if you did go there, you couldn't come back for years? Why the hell do you wackos want to go to Mars?" Cameron, as he would then confess, is one of the wackos. At the time he addressed the convention, he was planning a fictional 3-D IMAX film and a five-hour TV miniseries meant to depict as accurately as possible the first human journey to Mars. Earlier that year, NASA had launched two probes to Mars, stoking interest in and enthusiasm about the planet, and Cameron had begun to see the human colonization of Mars as our species' best plan B should Earth become uninhabitable. He had read astronautical engineer Robert Zubrin's

1996 pro-terraforming tract, *The Case for Mars: The Plan to Settle the Red Planet and Why We Must,* and hired Zubrin as a consultant on his Mars movie.

Cameron's picture was about a group of explorers who travel to the red planet, establish a settlement there, get in a jam, and use their wits and grit to get out of it. Though he was writing a fictional piece, Cameron was interested in making the story as credible as possible. As he had with *Titanic* in hewing to the history and time line of the sinking, Cameron worked within a rule set, in this case the rules of physics, and drilled down to the finest details. As far as Cameron was concerned, fantastical science fiction like *Star Trek* and *Star Wars* made space travel look too easy and leaped over the true challenge and adventure of exploring other planets. "My Mars project was true science fiction, where it's extrapolation from present-day reality to a very specific future reality," says Cameron. "That's different from sci-fi fantasy, which is really what *Avatar* is, 'cause in *Avatar* we go to another world and make up our own rules when we're there."

Cameron got his hands on an unofficial NASA study document called the Design Reference Mission 2.0 (DRM) that laid out different concepts for traveling to Mars, and he began analyzing the math. What Cameron discovered was that the DRM math didn't really add up. When he asked NASA engineers about it, they sheepishly agreed, saying the DRM was "notional," meant to be a thought exercise. "And I had taken it seriously, for months," Cameron says. But he had also been embellishing and improving on the DRM, and had even designed his own Mars lander and rover, combining them into one, which he called a "lander rover." It was a design that had not previously appeared in NASA literature. But when Cameron brought his drawings and spreadsheets to the Johnson Space Center in Houston to show the engineers there, they conceded that his unorthodox idea could actually work. This was a functional spaceship design by a man who had just a few junior-college physics classes under his belt. "If Jim Cameron had been a trained engineer, he would have been a remarkable one," says Zubrin. "As it is, he comes up with a lot of creative ideas. Some of them are a little off, but the ones that are good, more conventionally trained engineers would never have come up with." In 2011, NASA will be sending a $4 billion ship to Mars—a lander rover. It's not Cameron's design, but it's similar.

Cameron had hoped his Mars movie, which would have been the first fictional 3-D IMAX movie, would boost the 3-D format. But a number of things happened to dampen interest in the red planet and the perceived potential of the movie commercially. The two Mars probes launched in 1999 failed, to the great disappointment of Mars watchers. And two other Mars films opened in 2000, Brian De Palma's *Mission to Mars* and a Val Kilmer movie called *Red Planet,* both of them critical and commercial disappointments. If he was going to inspire the industry to embrace 3-D, Cameron felt he had to turn to a potentially more widely appealing movie. "He said, 'Look, I know the fact that those movies didn't do well doesn't mean a Mars movie won't do well,'" Zubrin recounts. "'But there's that impression. And if I'm going to take this 3-D IMAX technology and make it universal, I have to have a movie that's so successful that no theater will turn it down.'" So Cameron decided to make what he thought would be a more commercially viable sci-fi movie his first fictional 3-D effort—*Avatar.* "I figure I just need to make the Mars film before we really go to Mars, and that gives me another twenty-five years or so," Cameron says.

Although Cameron temporarily shelved his Mars project, his real-life space-travel ambitions only grew. In 2000, he approached Energya, a privately run Russian space program, about going up to the Mir space station and filming a documentary there with his 3-D cameras. He underwent exhaustive medical tests—eye exams, tooth exams, treadmill tests, a colonoscopy—and passed the rigorous training in

Moscow. But by the time Cameron returned to the United States, the Mir space station was being shut down due to lack of funding. Energya called Cameron and proposed that he go to the International Space Station instead, which sounded great to him but meant involving NASA, a cautious bureaucracy that had just been embarrassed by the first space tourist, Dennis Tito, arriving on a Russian ship without NASA's blessing. "I said that I didn't just want to be a space tourist," Cameron recalls. "I wanted to stay on the ISS for a month and make a 3-D film about living and working in space." Cameron's filming mission was gaining momentum. He got commitments for nearly $30 million in funding, but he needed more, for insurance. He learned that training for the project, in which he intended to perform a space walk, would mean spending eighteen months abroad. At this point Cameron had a young and growing family. He asked NASA to give him six months to think over the project. In that time, the Space Shuttle *Columbia* disintegrated over Texas, killing all seven crew members, and NASA became a very different place. "There was no way my mission made sense in a post-*Columbia* environment," Cameron says. "They weren't even flying their own people, let alone pushy filmmakers." Cameron shelved the project, but his relationship with NASA continued.

In 2002, the director became a member of the NASA Advisory Council, an independent civilian board that offers input to the NASA administrator. This put him at a table beside men such as astronauts Buzz Aldrin and John Glenn, and a cadre of renowned scientists and engineers. He also helped design a 3-D HD camera to go on future Mars missions. Cameron's main function at NASA has been to guide the agency in telling its own story better and to serve as a kind of motivational speaker for its scientists and engineers. In a 2005 speech to aerospace professionals in Orlando, Florida, Cameron entreated NASA to showcase the passion of its scientists and to let ordinary people get to know them, identify with them, and experience space travel

vicariously through them. "There are six billion of us here on the ground who are not gonna get to go and a handful of us who will," he said. "Those who go become the avatars for the rest, the eyes and ears, the hearts and spirits for the rest of humanity." The rapt crowd in Orlando greeted the speech with thunderous applause. Cameron is a science groupie. His ultimate dream is to get to space, but hanging out with astronauts and becoming a part of their world is a nice consolation prize.

Experimental Girl

Cameron keeps a running ideas list on his computer. In his own cryptic shorthand, he sketches out possible characters and scenarios—concepts inspired by an article he just read in *Scientific American* or a person he met. There are dozens of them, some just a few words long, others a descriptive page or two. "I'll run out of time before I run out of ideas," he says. One of the concepts on Cameron's list in the late 1990s was the phrase "experimental girl." It was that idea that would evolve into the director's first foray into network TV and would launch the career of an unknown teenage actress named Jessica Alba.

Cameron had been looking for a project to do with an old friend from his Roger Corman days, Charles ("Chick") Eglee. Eglee wrote Cameron's first film—*Piranha II*, a creative experience they would both rather forget, except for the friendship—and went on to become an executive at Steven Bochco Productions, producing dramas like *Murder One* and *NYPD Blue*. Twentieth Century Fox was encouraging Cameron to try creating a TV show, and Lightstorm president Rae Sanchini supported the notion. "TV just seemed like a good avenue for some of Jim's ideas," Sanchini says. "The stakes aren't so great. You can experiment, try things, you can respond to things happening in society. There's a lot of fun stuff about TV and the immediacy of it." In the fall of 2000, Cameron's "experimental girl" would become the new Fox show *Dark Angel.* Max Guevara, a genetically engineered female supersoldier, lived in a dystopian future society—Seattle, Washington, in the year 2019, after an "infocalypse." Terrorists had detonated an electromagnetic pulse weapon in the atmosphere over the United States, destroying most computer and communications systems and plunging the country into an era of economic depression, rampant crime, and authoritarian government. Sanchini looked at hundreds of actresses for the role of Max, including Rosario Dawson and Jacinda Barrett. Alba had been a working actor since the age of thirteen, appearing in a Nickelodeon show, a few episodes of *Beverly Hills, 90210* and the Drew Barrymore comedy *Never Been Kissed.* But she was finding that her exotic looks—she's Mexican, Danish, and French Canadian—were preventing her from getting lead parts or the kind of regular work she could make a living from as an adult. "If I didn't get *Dark Angel,* I was just gonna go to college and figure something else out," Alba says. She had been warned about Cameron—that he was fiery, a little scary. So she was shocked to arrive for her audition at Lightstorm to find him holding the camera and lighting the room himself, without the usual phalanx of casting assistants and producers. "He said he wanted to write the script around whoever was gonna play Max," Alba recalls. "We talked about Max's backstory. How does she deal with emotions? I was kind of taken aback. Here was this hugely powerful man, and he was interested in what an eighteen-year-old thought." Cameron specifically did not want a blonde-haired, blue-eyed supergirl. "He said he believed the future of the world would be biracial," Alba recalls. "At the time that was taboo a little bit. But he really wanted me to own it."

Dark Angel's two-hour pilot was an accomplishment in a variety of ways. It was one of Cameron's first projects to come in at budget, for one thing. At $10 million, the show was extravagant by TV norms, costing nearly twice as much as a typical two-hour pilot. But by Cameron standards, it was delightfully low rent. "It was fun to be working down and dirty and fast instead of these movies that take forever," he says. When *Dark Angel* premiered in October 2000, *Time* praised the show's dark vision and Alba's athletic performance. "We have seen the Woman of the Future, and she kicks butt," the magazine said.[6] Other critics agreed, and even *New York Times* political columnist Maureen Dowd weighed in, confessing that she was more interested in watching *Dark Angel*'s "snappy dialogue, captivating style and gripping fight scenes"[7] than the leaden 2000 presidential debate the pilot aired against. Apparently, many viewers felt the same way, as more than seventeen million people tuned in.

In its first season, *Dark Angel* held on to a considerable audience with the help of its lead-in, *That '70s Show.* But by its second season the futuristic drama would become a victim of time-slot shuffling, ending up in the dead zone of Friday nights, airing after a slate of comedy reruns. Cameron was stunned by his impotence in the world of network TV. This was a man who could call a studio chairman and buy himself six more months to finish a movie, but he couldn't rescue *Dark Angel* from network programming hell. Nevertheless, the show was profitable, so its creators were shocked by what happened on the eve of their third season. Cameron, Sanchini, Alba, and Eglee were about to fly to New York City for Fox's upfronts—the meetings where networks announce their new seasons to advertisers and press—when Cameron got word that *Dark Angel* had been canceled and replaced at the eleventh hour by *Firefly,* a space Western from *Buffy the Vampire Slayer* creator Joss Whedon. *Firefly* ended up averaging just 4.7 million viewers per show and was canceled after one season. "So that was my ten-minute adventure into network TV land," Cameron says. "Which was despicable."

Thematically, *Dark Angel* had a lot of Cameron touchstones: a strong heroine, a massive technological failure, characters soldiering through a gritty, realistic future world. But the show's most lasting impact was the launching of Alba as a genuine phenomenon. She would go on to appear in movies like *Sin City* and *Fantastic Four,* becoming a kind of postracial sex symbol and heroine. As Cameron had predicted, Alba's enigmatic beauty turned out not to be a problem at all.

See You in the Sunshine

On May 27, 2002, fifty-one years to the day after the feared German battleship sank off the coast of France, Cameron made his postponed expedition to the *Bismarck* for a Discovery Channel special. He brought with him two German survivors of the battle that had sent the Nazi superweapon three miles down in the Atlantic with 90 percent of her crew, 1,995 men with an average age of twenty. This was a very different wreck from *Titanic.* As the Mirs approached the warship, which Cameron called the Death Star, they came upon a giant, faded swastika painted on the side. There was no beauty to the *Bismarck.* It was a tool of war and a grim grave site. The stoic battle survivors, now in their seventies, were brought to tears by Cameron's underwater images of the ship.

There was some controversy about how exactly the *Bismarck* had gone down, and for Cameron, this expedition would turn into a detective story. During World War II, the Nazis wanted to use the *Bismarck* to cut off the convoy that was Britain's lifeline. After the Nazi warship destroyed the *Hood,* one of Britain's best ships, and killed all but three of its 1,415 men, "Sink the *Bismarck!*" became the country's rallying cry. And on the eighth day of the Nazi warship's first mission, a fleet of British ships and aircraft delivered a steady pounding, sending the feared German vessel down. The victory became a point of British pride, even spawning a movie and a song. But some German survivors had claimed that it wasn't the Brits' shelling that brought down the *Bismarck* but the Germans themselves, who sank the ship to avoid its being boarded.

With his ROVs, Cameron was able to take images and see parts of the warship not viewed since its sinking. He found that none of the torpedoes or shells had penetrated the second layer of the *Bismarck's* inner hull, that British torpedoes hadn't in fact caused any significant flooding. Cameron put forward a theory to explain large gashes observed by a prior expedition: he suggested that the *Bismarck* had suffered a "hydraulic outburst" when it hit the bottom, causing the sides to bulge out and break in places. It was an important idea in shipwreck forensics, to look not only at what had brought a vessel down but also at what had happened once it hit the bottom. Based on Cameron's findings, the wounded *Bismarck* would have sunk without the scuttling, but it might have taken half a day, enough time for many more German sailors to be rescued. The director's theories weren't well received by proud British historians, but they were by the scientists who specialize in maritime forensics.

In 2005, Cameron would get involved in another controversial piece of detective work for the Discovery Channel, *The Lost Tomb of Jesus,* a documentary asserting that Jesus' tomb may have been found in Jerusalem in 1980, during an apartment construction project. The documentary challenges the notion of the resurrection as a physical act and suggests that Jesus and Mary Magdalene were buried together as husband and wife and that they had a son. Charlie Pellegrino, Cameron's friend from diving *Titanic,* was writing an accompanying book and brought the project to the director to executive produce. "I pursue film projects where I think I'm going to learn something, where I believe my curiosity is going to be satisfied in some way," Cameron said while promoting the documentary in 2007.[8] "I was fascinated by early Christianity and how it all began. We now know more about Jesus than we've known for literally thousands of years."

By this point, Cameron was getting very far from the business of being a filmmaker, but he was so engaged intellectually and emotionally by his expeditions and discoveries that he almost didn't notice. Between 2001 and 2004 he spent seven months at sea and went on forty-one deep-submersible dives. He was beginning to experience a shift in his priorities. "Previously, everything had been about the film," Cameron says. "Do whatever, sacrifice whatever, move to England, give up your salary, whatever it takes to make the film, put on the show." But on the expeditions, for the first time in Cameron's career, the film wasn't as important as the moment he was living. Before he closed the hatch on his sub on every dive, Cameron would call out, "See you in the sunshine," keenly aware that there was a chance he wouldn't. The expeditions began to change Cameron's notion of leadership. He was responsible for people's lives, for deciding whether or not to dive when a hurricane was making its way closer. "It's not about the movie and the artistic temper tantrums," he says. "Those are completely out of place." He also began to see that his critical management style could use some tweaking. "You learn to deal with people from a place of respect," he says. "Before you open your mouth, if there's an assumption that you respect that person, you're gonna deal with them differently."

After the *Bismarck* trip, Cameron even bought his own subs, detouring his family trip to Paris to pick them up in Toulon. Cameron's wife and children would often see him off and welcome him back from his voyages in port. In 2003, he would film *Aliens of the Deep,* a hybrid of a Jacques Cousteau documentary and an outer-space fantasy. Cameron teamed up with NASA and Jet Propulsion Laboratory scientists to investigate the ocean's hydrothermal vents, the site of a unique ecosystem of organisms that don't require any sunlight to live.

The shrimp, crabs, and worms that thrive there derive all their energy from the heat of the vents. Though scientists have known about the ecosystems for years, it was a revelation to most of the film's audience that life can exist without the sun. In the documentary Cameron posits the theory, supported by astrobiologists, that the vents provide a plausible idea of what life beyond Earth might look like, perhaps on Europa, a moon of Jupiter believed to have liquid water oceans underneath its icy surface. The expedition would fire up Cameron's imagination to tell his own science-fiction story. The strange bioluminescent flora and fauna he saw informed his creature and plant design on *Avatar.*

In exploration, Cameron had found his passion, and in movies, he had a way to fund it. But beyond his own enjoyment, Cameron was beginning to see exploration as a cultural value that needed boosting. Where were the twenty-first century's Magellans and da Gamas? More important, where was the spirit of discovery in the regular citizen, who had once watched the moon landing and been filled with wonder and a sense of possibility? "Exploration is not a luxury," Cameron wrote in a 2004 issue of *Wired.* "It defines us as a civilization. It directly or indirectly benefits every member of society. It yields an inspirational dividend whose impact on our self-image, confidence and economic and geopolitical stature is immeasurable."[9]

By 2005, Cameron had devoted seven of his midlife years, potentially a director's most productive, to the discovery of new places and new technologies rather than to making movies. He was ready now to bring what he had learned about life and work and science back with him to Hollywood.

10.

PROJECT 880

avatar *n. 1. The descent to earth of a Hindu deity, esp. Vishnu, in human or animal form. 2. An embodiment, as of a quality or concept: an archetype. 3. A temporary manifestation or aspect of a continuing entity.*[1]

In the Monster's Head

In April 2008, in a windowless Los Angeles warehouse where Howard Hughes had built his airplanes some seventy years earlier, another secretive and occasionally mad genius was at work. Cameron, in a hockey jersey and jeans, was doing something elite directors do not do—holding a camera. "Why can't I see anything?!" he yelled from an apparently empty warehouse floor to a small crew huddled over computer monitors in the corner. "Oh, oh, oh, I'm in the monster's head!" Cameron backed up, and a peek in his camera lens revealed blackness giving way to a thick and vivid rain forest where a tall, blue, alien version of Sigourney Weaver was battling the monster whose head had just blocked the director's view. On the warehouse floor there was no rain forest, no monster, no Weaver. Just a bunch of guys and their computers. But Cameron's camera was allowing him to shoot inside a virtual universe of his own creation. He swooped in over the monster's shoulder and entered the world of *Avatar*.

At this point, Cameron hadn't released a feature film in over a decade. Except for a brief stint playing himself on the HBO show *Entourage* in 2005, he had been largely absent from the Hollywood scene, riding in his subs, filming his documentaries, tinkering and building new filmmaking toys. But now the director was back on a set, telling a story that had been knocking around in his brain for years, about an ex-marine's struggle for survival on an alien planet called Pandora. Pandora's floating mountains and bioluminescent jungle are home to a tall, blue humanoid species called the Na'vi and a number of exotic creatures—six-legged horses, glowing wood sprites, winged banshees. A mysterious resource called unobtainium is plentiful there, drawing humans in a future century to colonize Pandora. Because the planet's air is toxic for humans, a group of genetically engineered human-alien hybrids, or avatars, are sent in, including wounded former marine Jake Sully.

Avatar would not be based upon a comic book, novel, or video game, making it unique for a big-budget film in its time. This would be a wholly original piece of work from one man's brain, meant to entertain and—as the best futuristic fiction does—raise timely questions about the present. The director wrote his first treatment for *Avatar* twelve years before he ended up inside the monster's head. The only problem with making the movie in 1996 was that it was impossible. The technology did not exist.

The Digital Manifesto

Cameron jokes that he is like a Plains Indian who wastes no piece of the buffalo; in his case, it is ideas that are made use of down to the marrow, sometimes decades later. He started creating some of the images in *Avatar* in the 1970s. While driving a truck for the Brea Unified School District, Cameron began to paint some fanciful scenes that would linger in his mind—flying jellyfish, wood sprites (which he called "dandelion things"), blazingly colorful bioluminescent forests and rivers, fan lizards, and big-eyed cats. In 1978, when he wrote the sci-fi spec script with his friend Randall Frakes called *Xenogenesis,* they had to create a number of planetary environments to tell the story of a woman and a man looking for a place to start a new Earth. Cameron painted cloud-wreathed mesas, luminous forests, and multicolored flying creatures for the unproduced feature, which ended with the voyagers ultimately finding the planet that would become their new home but discovering that its air was toxic. The human children who inhabited the world would have to be genetically modified in the womb to survive there. These hybrids would grow up tall and lean, with robin's-egg-blue skin and golden eyes. One of Cameron's late-seventies paintings was of a tall, slender, blue girl standing in a field of magenta grass. There were flying creatures he called air sharks that had rows of glassy teeth that jutted forward like snake fangs. In 1996, when he wrote the first treatment for *Avatar,* the air sharks became bansheerays because of their stingraylike silhouettes. In the design process for *Avatar* that began in 2005, they became less raylike, grew four wings, and were christened simply banshees. All of the ideas had been around for years in Cameron's mind, looking for an outlet. When he started to write the treatment for *Avatar,* the story gelled in three or four weeks, and the creatures and characters, as well as many new ones, quickly found homes. "It spilled out," he says. "But only because I had been processing it in my imagination for decades."

Cameron wrote the treatment in large part to inspire the artists at his special-effects house, Digital Domain. They had created digital composites on *True Lies* and would be kept busy on *Titanic* for at least the next eighteen months, but neither movie involved much CG animation, nor any creature or character animation at all—Cameron's and Stan Winston's whole motivation for founding the company in 1993. In the early days of planning Digital Domain in late 1992, Cameron had written a "Digital Manifesto," a passionately argued thirteen-page document laying out where he expected filmmaking to go in the coming years. In his manifesto, the director described something called "performance capture," in which an actor would don a "data suit," sending a stream of information about the actor's physical movements to a workstation, where it would be inserted into a "synthetic environment." Artists would then use software to turn the actor's digitized performance into a fantastical character. "Jack Nicholson could create not just the voice but the total body performance of a demon, while puppeteers nearby cause his tail to lash and his pointed ears to furl and twitch," Cameron wrote. "The actor can truly 'become' his animated character." Having broken ground on *The Abyss* and *T2*, Cameron was rubbing elbows with the brightest minds in special effects, and this is the stuff they were talking about. "It all seemed pretty obvious from where we were sitting," he says.

To most of Hollywood, the possibilities of lifelike CG characters driven by human performances wouldn't be obvious for at least another decade, when a creature named Gollum first showed his pale, dessicated face. In the mid-nineties, video-game developers began to employ the performance-capture technique Cameron had described in his manifesto, although it was usually called motion capture, or mo-cap. In 1997, Cameron used mo-cap himself in a limited way to create the digital doubles that walked the decks of *Titanic,* and in 1999, George Lucas relied on the technique to animate the movement of his controversial Gungan character Jar Jar Binks for the *Star Wars* prequel *The Phantom Menace.* But it was in 2001—the year, not the movie— that a director first deployed mo-cap in a transformative way. Briefly in *The Lord of the Rings: The Fellowship of the Ring* and more extensively in the second and third movies of the fantasy trilogy, Peter Jackson created the most believable computer-generated character in a movie to date, the Hobbit Gollum. Shakespearean-trained actor Andy Serkis performed scenes as the amphibious villain while wearing a blue suit and a few hundred markers on his face and body. Then artists at Jackson's Weta Digital took the data from Serkis's performance and used it to create a wholly new character. Gollum looked like Serkis—he had his face, his body twitches, his pathos and rage—but he was the grotesque, froglike creature that J. R. R. Tolkien had written about in his novels. The merging of live performance and special-effects work was akin to Boris Karloff in *Frankenstein,* only instead of green greasepaint, the effects enhancing the actor's performance were zeros and ones painstakingly chosen by CG artists.

Forrest Gump director Robert Zemeckis employed a variation of the performance-capture technique to animate Tom Hanks in *Polar Express* in 2004, but his characters turned out creepily unlifelike. While Gollum, a nonhuman in a fantasy world, had come across as real, Hanks, who played five human characters on a train ride to the North Pole, appeared to be dead-eyed, wearing a mask. *Polar Express* crossed an important line, into the so-called uncanny valley, a hypothesis born out of robotics that holds that when facsimiles of humans look and act almost like actual humans, the effect is disturbing to an audience. Directors who stayed firmly planted in the fantasy world would have more success with motion capture. Jackson revisited the technique to animate the giant ape in *King Kong* (2005), and Gore Verbinski used mo-cap to give Bill Nighy his tentacled beard as waterlogged villain Davy Jones in the second and third *Pirates of the Caribbean* movies (2006 and 2007). By 2007, mo-cap was widespread enough to inspire a backlash—the credits of the Pixar movie *Ratatouille* boasted, "100% Genuine Animation! No motion capture or any other performance shortcuts were used in the production of this film." By 2009, seventeen years after Cameron's Digital Manifesto, there would be more than twenty special-effects houses offering some kind of motion capture as a service.

In 1996, Cameron wrote *Avatar* because he wanted to challenge Digital Domain with humanlike creatures that would require performance capture to realize. He deliberately focused his story on characters that fit within narrow design parameters: the Na'vi, a species of ten-foot-tall blue aliens with catlike ears and tail but humanlike features. "If they were more human, they could be done with makeup, which was boring, would not advance the cause, and had been done for thirty years in *Star Trek,*" Cameron says. "If they were less human, they could not have been performed by humans effectively." When the effects supervisors at Digital Domain broke down Cameron's early *Avatar* treatment, the consensus was that the movie would take a lot of time and money and would probably look fake. "It made them very uncomfortable, and they were fearful of it wrecking the company," Cameron says. While wrangling with Twentieth Century Fox to fund *Avatar*'s R & D, he got absorbed instead in *Titanic,* and his sci-fi epic slipped to the bottom of the pile. It would not be until after he saw Jackson's Gollum that Cameron felt up to the task of attempting *Avatar.*

The Prototype

In May 2005, Twentieth Century Fox agreed to a $10 million development budget for *Avatar* based on Cameron's treatment, which had changed little since he had written it nearly ten years earlier. The $10 million would cover his writing a script, a year of designing characters and creatures with a staff of artists, construction of a virtual studio in

Hughes's Playa Vista warehouse, and production of a prototype that Fox would use to determine whether to fund the film. *Titanic* producer Jon Landau nicknamed the endeavor "Project 880" to preserve some secrecy. Cameron had been trying to decide which movie to make next, and there was fervent interest in Hollywood and among the director's fans about his plans. The smart money seemed to be on *Battle Angel,* an adaptation of a series of manga comic books first brought to him by Guillermo del Toro and being written by Cameron and a little-known screenwriter named Laeta Kalogridis, who had penned a well-regarded spec script about Joan of Arc while attending UCLA. But *Avatar* had a better scene in which to test the technology—a five-minute mix of action and dramatic dialogue between two CG characters—so Cameron decided to start with that one. "It didn't occur to me that this decision would essentially be the decision of what film would be made first, but that's what happened," he says.

From his roughly sketched treatment, Cameron wrote a five-minute scene in which the human-alien hybrid hero Jake (then named Josh) meets Na'vi woman Neytiri (then named Zuleika). In the test scene, the Na'vi woman defends the hero from some terrifying creatures called viper wolves, prays over the animals' dead bodies, knocks the hero down and berates him; then he follows her onto a log bridge. Incidentally, this is as close to "meet cute" as Cameron gets—in his last movie, the lovers had bumped into each other during her attempt to commit suicide off the edge of a boat, and in *The Terminator,* they were united by the impending nuclear holocaust. For the prototype footage, the director cast Korean American Yunjin Kim, who was fresh off the first season of J. J. Abrams's drama *Lost,* and a young actor named Daniel Best.

In August, Cameron shot the prototype in a day and a half using a number of new technologies and techniques. In addition to mo-cap suits like the one Serkis had worn as Gollum, the actors donned head rigs Cameron had designed with little boom cameras that tracked their facial expressions. Shooting with a virtual camera, Cameron was able to see the actors not as figures in suits but as crude versions of their alien selves. "It's very difficult for a director to work in a CG environment," explains Rob Legato, who helped Cameron develop the virtual cinematography system. "If he can shoot it just the way he would shoot it if the ten-foot-tall blue alien were there for real, then there's a live, organic quality that you get. It's not intellectually wrought, it's viscerally wrought." Cameron created terrain with ramps and risers and had the actors run on a tape line to simulate the surface of a rounded log.

Once he captured the performances, he started to experiment with virtual production, in which he could replay the scene and shoot it again, from any angle he wished, without having to bring the actors back. He could change scale, smooth out his motion, even move characters around. He got accustomed to walking through plants and people-like ghosts and to the quirks of the virtual camera, which lagged two hundred milliseconds behind the action. Every shot was also tested in 3-D. Cameron and Vince Pace had developed their 3-D cameras to shoot the *Ghosts of the Abyss* documentary in 2001, used them again to film *Aliens of the Deep,* and lent them out to Robert Rodriguez for some scenes in the third *Spy Kids* movie, but the technology was still nascent. The 3-D added two more weeks to finishing the test, as Cameron encountered all kinds of new problems he hadn't anticipated relating to focal-length selection. Finally, the five-minute prototype was cut. Despite the crudeness of the models, lighting, and environments, the footage had a cinematic feeling. "We thought it was the bomb," Cameron says.

The next step was to take the scene to full resolution, hopefully getting the CG characters in impressive enough shape to convince Fox to fund the movie fully. Cameron selected a thirty-seven-second chunk—

anything longer would have taken too long to achieve—and enlisted Industrial Light & Magic to tackle it. The initial results were devastating, particularly for the Na'vi woman, whose color was off and lips were fake looking. "She looked like a dead carp that washed up on a beach," Cameron says. Somehow his bold vision, laid out so emphatically in the 1992 manifesto, looked like a bad 1980s video game. "I lost all hope in the project."

Over the next three months, ILM would bring all its years of CG savvy to bear on the thirty-seven seconds of footage. By Christmas, things were looking a little bit better. Slightly encouraged, Cameron went to his vacation house in Crested Butte, Colorado, to work on the script. After New Year's, he relocated to his ranch in Santa Barbara County to continue writing. (Some writers move their laptop to another coffee shop when they need a change of environment; when you're king of the world, you can shift among your multiple idyllically located homes.) Wherever he went, Cameron faced his usual writing demons. "I'm not one of these guys who can write from nine to four every day and have a normal family or social life at the same time," Cameron says. "I need to completely isolate and think about the piece 24-7. This gets harder later in your career, when you're multitasking on lots of projects, and having five kids doesn't help. I still need to bunker completely to get anything good written."

As he wrote, he conferred with ILM by iChat, slogging away to get up to some level of reality in the characters' skin tone, eyes, lips, and lighting. Best's character was turning out well, because it had been designed around him, but Kim's character had been designed before she was cast and didn't physically resemble the actress at all. "We believed it didn't matter in the case of the Na'vi if they didn't resemble their characters," Cameron says. "Wrong. That was an important lesson." The actress's mouth was so different from her Na'vi counterpart's that it turned out to be difficult to make the CG mouth hit the correct shapes when she spoke. When Cameron ultimately cast the Na'vi, he would have to choose actors who physically resembled their characters.

Finally, a 3-D test clip was finished and a screening was held for executives at Fox, who were wowed. Studio cochairman Tom Rothman asked to watch the footage over and over again, and then to see it in 2-D, to make sure the movie would be good in either format. It was. The proof of concept was a success. There was only one problem. It had taken several months of minute changes and countless iterations to deliver six CG shots. The final movie would contain more than 2,500 of them. How was Cameron going to achieve his goal of making a whole movie this way and surpass the prototype's level of reality?

Good News/Bad News

The director began refining his process for making this technically arduous film. He chose a mo-cap provider, Giant Studios, which had worked on the *Pirates of the Caribbean* films, and signed on the company that had delivered Gollum so beautifully, Jackson's Weta Digital. In May 2006, he turned in a first draft of his script to Fox. As much as it liked the prototype, the studio disliked the script. "They had a lot of notes and basically acted like it was a complete shambles," Cameron recalls. The draft was too long—153 pages—and a work in progress, which is how Cameron usually writes, continuously editing as he goes, incorporating material from rehearsals with actors. But in the ten years since *Titanic*, "they'd all forgotten that that's how I work." From Fox's perspective, things looked grim. After nearly a decade of waiting for their star director to climb out of his sub and get back to work on a film set, the studio was not thrilled with the result. Here was an ambitious project with a lot of risky elements, including unproven technology and blue main characters with tails and a script the executives didn't get. As usual, Cameron planned to cast no-names. Oh, and by the way, the movie would cost at least as much as *Titanic,* which had nearly doubled its initial budget. "When you get Jim to say yes to a movie, it's a good news/bad news scenario," says Peter Chernin, who was then president of the News Corporation, having been promoted since he had overseen the roller coaster of making and releasing *Titanic.* "When Jim first pitched *Titanic,* he pitched it as a more modestly budgeted movie. With *Avatar,* we went in knowing it was going to be extraordinarily complicated." So complicated that at first Fox passed on the movie.

Over the summer of 2006, Cameron reworked the script with the help of Kalogridis, his cowriter on *Battle Angel.* He collapsed two characters into one, a scientist named Grace Augustine, making her stronger and more central, and added an opening series of scenes on Earth to build up the hero character, the paralyzed marine now named Jake Sully (there were too many guys named Josh working on the movie, so Cameron changed it to "Jake" to avoid confusion). Some of Jake's opening scenes would end up on the editing-room floor in the summer of 2009, but they seemed to make Fox happier at the time. Nevertheless, on September 11, a day that marks strange milestones in Cameron's life, Chernin drove to Lightstorm himself to deliver the news: Fox was officially passing on the movie. Chernin wanted Cameron to hear it from him so there was no illusion that this was a lower-level decision. Immediately, Cameron approached Walt Disney Studio chairman Dick Cook, with whom he had a bond over their shared belief in 3-D. Disney had been a partner on Cameron's two 3-D IMAX documentaries and the previous year had released *Chicken Little,* the first feature film to be projected in digital 3-D. Within two days, Disney was on board to make *Avatar.* In particular, the executives loved the script. Then Fox, Cameron's studio home, with whom he had a first-look pact, decided to reconsider the project. Cameron made some concessions in his personal deal and cut out a couple of CG scenes, and, in October, Fox green-lighted *Avatar.*

He Had Me at "Uh-Huh"

As Cameron worked on the script, a University of Southern California linguist named Paul Frommer had begun creating the Na'vi language, mixing bits of Polynesian and African tongues. This would be Cameron's Klingon—a constructed, fictional language—and the actors he hired to play Na'vi characters would have to master it. For *Avatar*'s casting, Cameron reteamed with his partner since *T2,* Mali Finn. Sick with melanoma, Finn would retire in 2005, before she could finish *Avatar,* and die in 2007, making this her last film. Before she left the production in the hands of casting director Margery Simkin, Finn found Cameron's leading lady, a then-little-known actress named Zoe Saldana. Raised in Queens, New York, and the Dominican Republic, Saldana is the daughter of a Dominican father and a Puerto Rican mother. She studied ballet as a child and broke into show business at age twenty-one via a forgettable dance movie called *Center Stage.* Saldana's unique beauty and athleticism would later earn her small roles in big movies—as the lone female pirate swashbuckling alongside Johnny Depp and Geoffrey Rush in *Pirates of the Caribbean: The Curse of the Black Pearl* and as an officious airport worker in Steven Spielberg's *The Terminal.* She would get a bigger part as Bernie Mac's daughter dating Ashton Kutcher in a 2005 reenvisioning of the groundbreaking 1967 racial drama *Guess Who's Coming to Dinner* called simply *Guess Who.*

In 2004, while still a relative unknown, Saldana gave a cheeky interview about action roles, saying, "I'd rather quit this business than constantly play the girlfriend of the action hero. In real life, if Spider-Man always came to the rescue, after a point I'd be like, 'Come on, man, I can do it myself.'"[2] A year later, at age twenty-seven, she would find herself at Lightstorm, reading for Cameron and Simkin for the part of Neytiri, a Pandoran native. Cameron and Simkin were both won over at the same moment, when Saldana spontaneously snarled like a cat in the middle of a scene. "It was completely improvisational and utterly what Neytiri would do," Cameron says. "Her beauty, her graceful feline movement, the power in her voice, her emotional range, everything said Zoe was the one." The production of *Avatar* was so lengthy that in the midst of it, Saldana was cast in an iconic role, as Uhura in J. J. Abrams's *Star Trek* remake, released in the spring of 2009. In the widely praised relaunching of the sci-fi franchise, Saldana played the competent communications officer of the USS *Enterprise,* translating Klingon and harboring a crush on young Spock while wearing a minidress and boots, but not, alas, kicking any butt. In *Avatar,* she would get her chance to rescue the hero, entering the movie by saving Jake from a pack of viper wolves.

Cameron first saw the man who would play Jake Sully on a poor-quality casting tape with twenty other actors on it made in Sydney, Australia. "I didn't need just a guy that girls would swoon over," Cameron says. "I needed a young man that men would follow into battle." Sam Worthington, a native of Perth, Western Australia, was working as a bricklayer in Sydney at age nineteen when he went along to a drama-school audition as moral support for his girlfriend. He got in, she didn't, they broke up, and Worthington embarked on a path that would lead him to Cameron's door a decade later. He performed in some theater and TV and had small parts in Australian movies before breaking through there in an independent film called *Somersault,* as a hunky and vulnerable rancher's son opposite then-unknown Abbie Cornish. *Somersault* got noticed at Cannes in 2004 and its rugged male star made it onto a short list for the new James Bond before Daniel Craig was cast in 2005. When he auditioned on tape for Cameron, Worthington had no idea what the project was. Even by Australian standards, he was extremely casual that day. "I thought it was another waste-of-time project that you tend to get in Australia," Worthington says. He was playing a scene in which the paralyzed marine meets a scientist, with another actor reading the scientist's lines off camera. Worthington watched the actor with steely indifference and, instead of the "yeses" the script called for, he grunted his replies. The actor's aloofness, born in part of not knowing he was auditioning to play the hero in a James Cameron movie, happened to be exactly what the director was looking for. "He had me at 'uh-huh,'" Cameron says. "He just seemed so hardened, so insular. He was an old-school tough guy, the kind Hollywood hasn't seen in a while."

Cameron had Worthington work with an acting coach—"His accent was thicker than Crocodile Dundee's," he says—and then flew the actor in for a series of auditions over a six-month period. "Twice a month there were act-offs with other actors," Worthington recalls. Fox saw the Australian's potential but was interested in a name, suggesting Jake Gyllenhaal or Matt Damon, "both of whom, mercifully, passed," Cameron says. It came down to Worthington and two other actors, including Channing Tatum, who went on to appear in *Stop-Loss* and *G.I. Joe: The Rise of Cobra*. It was on a *Braveheart*-esque scene where Jake rallies a group to battle that the studio was won over to Worthington. In January 2006, Cameron called the actor to let him know he had outlasted all the challengers and urge him to get on a plane to L.A. as soon as possible to start shooting on the performance-capture stage. Worthington was standing barefoot in a coffee shop in Sydney when he got the call, and his response suggests he didn't quite know what was coming. "I told Jim, 'I gotta get the brakes fixed on my car 'cause I'm gonna give it to my girlfriend, and I've gotta help my mate move his fridge, and then I'll be there.'" Overnight, merely by being cast in *Avatar*, Worthington became the biggest star no one had ever heard of. As her coveted role had for Saldana, playing Jake Sully would lead to another noteworthy part for Worthington before *Avatar* was finished, in a series Cameron had originated. *Charlie's Angels* director McG tapped Worthington to play a machine man in *Terminator Salvation*—his two-fisted performance was singled out above that of his far-better-known costar, Christian Bale.

Cameron's cast would include another actor who had proved her mettle to him and to Fox twenty years earlier. For feisty botanist Grace Augustine, the scientist who runs the Avatar program on Pandora, he returned to his first alien-fighting heroine, Sigourney Weaver. It was a role he had originally written as two characters, at least one of whom he had hoped would be played by Morgan Freeman, but had combined into one in an effort to simplify his sprawling script. "I've teased him that I'm playing Jim Cameron in the movie," Weaver says. "The character is driven, idealistic, perfectionist, but with great heart underneath."[3]

The Volume

Cameron's last movie had involved creating the largest and most meticulously detailed set ever made, a scale replica of the *Titanic*. By contrast, *Avatar*'s performance-capture soundstage, which is called "the volume," looked like a *Saturday Night Live* skit about postmodern theater. The warehouse environment was so bizarre and spare, it seemed as if Mike Myers would bound out in a black turtleneck at any moment, demanding to have his monkey touched. Instead of sets, gray-painted triangles and polygons and the occasional tree were moved around to create topography for the actors to navigate. Cameron used more refined versions of the technology he had tested for the prototype. For the CG scenes, which would make up about 60 percent of the finished film, the cast wore clingy Lycra bodysuits covered in markers that were recognized by the 102 cameras on the warehouse ceiling. They donned skullcaps rigged with tiny cameras that imaged their faces. Weta software created blends of their eyebrows rising or lips curling, which were applied to Giant's body capture and streamed to Cameron's monitor. There the actors appeared, in real time, as their blue, alien counterparts.

It took creativity to place the cast emotionally inside the environment of Pandora. Cameron brought the actors to Hawaiian rain forests and shot reference footage for them to use as sense memory when they returned to the volume. To help them feel an explosion, he boomed a noise over amplifiers, threw foam particles at them, and whacked them with a padded jousting pole. When Saldana was "riding" a flying creature, she clung to a giant gray hobbyhorse rocked on a gimbal by grips. For one gag, a stunt double clung to the back of a three-hundred-pound Samoan galloping around the stage. To approximate the planet's slippery, moss-covered terrain, Cameron laid plastic sheets on the floor, forcing the cast to walk gingerly. When a group of child extras playing Na'vi children were supposed to follow Jake Sully like a pied piper, Cameron taped a name to Worthington's chest, the kind of word a seven-year-old finds hilarious, like "buttface," and told the actor to conceal it from the kids on the stage. The director changed the word on every take. In take after take, the children ran after Worthington, giggling, to try to discern what his sign said. Eventually, Cameron got a magical scene. "I found the whole way of working very freeing," says Worthington. "All you've got to be is a five-year-old kid and jump into that world full-tilt boogie." It's the kind of filmmaking environment where it helps to have both imagination and patience. The learning curve on the new technology was steep. A crew member wrote a set catchphrase on a whiteboard: "It's Avatar, dude, nothing works the first time."

Some scenes were a combination of live action and CG. For those, Cameron used a new tool called the Simulcam, which allowed the director to see live-action actors in real time playing regular old human beings in exotic CG surroundings. They could be flying in a fully built prop helicopter on a soundstage, with Pandora's floating mountains visible outside their window in Cameron's Simulcam view. It's the kind of detail that helps a director compose a shot and preserve his own visual style. Cameron's goal was to make Pandora feel as real as possible, to shoot as if he were filming a documentary on another planet. That natural look is tricky to achieve in CG, which can feel sterile and too perfect. Most real-world filmmaking is about losing choices—the light is changing, the wardrobe is fixed, the set is only so large. In a CG world, the number of choices is potentially infinite—you can move your characters around, shift a tree to the left, add some afternoon light pouring in. "In theory, you should be able to make a better movie," Cameron says, in the midst of adjusting his camera angle on a third-act battle scene, on the 212th day of shooting his marathon film. "It forces you to really have your narrative ducks in a row. It forces you to think through every shot."

In late 2006, the Playa Vista set had some high-profile visitors when Steven Spielberg and Peter Jackson came by to kick the tires of Cameron's virtual camera and production pipeline. Jackson had visited Cameron at Lightstorm in 2004, when he was considering filming *King Kong* in 3-D, and gotten a quick tutorial on the 3-D cameras Cameron had used for his documentaries. The *Lord of the Rings* director felt it was too close to the start of production to introduce the new technology, but he and Cameron formed a bond over their appreciation of each other's pioneering work. In 2005, Cameron had signed Jackson's company to help realize his Pandoran world. By 2006, Spielberg and Jackson were in preproduction for a series of animated feature films about Tintin, the Belgian comic-book character, with Spielberg set to direct the first movie and Jackson to produce it. Looking for the most photo-real way to depict Tintin, they headed to Cameron's workshop, and three of the most elite directors of their generation stood around a dusty warehouse taking turns playing with a camera. As twenty-first-century filmmaking moments go, it was as if Matisse, Picasso, and Monet had gathered to compare paintbrushes. Jackson and Spielberg spent a week at the stage using Cameron's equipment and crew, who were on hiatus, to film a prototype for Tintin, as Cameron showed his colleagues how to pan and tilt within a virtual world. "He was helping us get our heads around the equipment," says Jackson. "Jim is very generous in the way he shares knowledge and information. He doesn't jealously guard technology and secrets."

Cameron's tendency to become absorbed in the details of filmmaking was indulged on the unique environment of the *Avatar* set, in which he could go back and reshoot elaborate action scenes endlessly from umpteen angles. An Avid editing suite was set up at the stage so that he could review each shot immediately and make changes. Instead of dailies, he had constant feedback on how his movie looked. Hours were spent on aircraft landing precisely right, a particular obsession of Cameron's. "To fully appreciate this movie, you have to like helicopters," he admits. The *Avatar* crew devised a way to let their director know when his next shot was set up—they played a deafening submarine sound that someone had downloaded from the Internet. Sometimes Cameron still didn't hear it, so intent was he on reviewing his footage.

The *Avatar* set was a very different environment from *Titanic,* not just because of the style of the filmmaking, but also because of the demeanor of the man running the show. Cameron had changed in the years since he sunk his big boat, thanks in large part to the experience he had had on the expeditions. The tight-knit crew at the Playa Vista stage was not unlike the small groups he led on the *Keldysh.* "We were out in the wilderness working far beyond the borders of the known. We were making technology and seeing it work. We were doing extraordinary things that outsiders would not even understand," Cameron says. "All these things bring you together." Sigourney Weaver, remembering Cameron tearing around England's hoary Pinewood Studios, told fellow cast members the filmmaker had mellowed. Worthington, a Cameron virgin, found in his director the kind of man he had been asked to play—a guy you would follow into battle. "I was at a point in my life where, fuck it, I was looking for someone to stand next to me," Worthington says. "I was looking for someone to give it all I've got to." There would be low-morale days, especially when trying to make a deadline to turn over shots to the film's various special-effects houses. A core group would repair to the "Hometree Bar," actually a visual-effects artist's office on the set, for morale-boosting shots of tequila. "I have my bad days, and on my best days I'm no Ron Howard," Cameron confesses. "But I tried to bring a new spirit of leadership."

Weta

With more than 2,500 special-effects shots, the bulk of the man-hours on *Avatar* were spent not on a stage but in a dark viewing room in Los Angeles, teleconferencing with Weta artists in Wellington, New Zealand. Peter Jackson and two other New Zealand filmmakers founded Weta the same year that Cameron founded Digital Domain, in 1993. One of the company's first tasks was to create the elaborate fantasy sequences in Jackson's macabre drama *Heavenly Creatures*. The shop went from Kiwi boutique to Hollywood powerhouse with the *Lord of the Rings* trilogy, earning an Academy Award on each film and another for *King Kong*. In many ways, Weta is what Cameron wanted to create with Digital Domain, a risk-taking, director-centric company.

In May 2009, Cameron and a half dozen L.A. crew members were conferring with their Wellington-based counterparts over a Pandoran jungle scene. "It looks like fantasy van art, man," Cameron said, wielding a laser pointer emphatically. "Get rid of that cliff." The Weta crew was nothing if not accommodating, adding light here, moving tree limbs there. By this point they had been working on shots for more than two years and were accustomed to Cameron's intense, detail-oriented personality and to his particular likes and dislikes. One of the trickier quirks for the Weta artists to nail down had been "Jim Cameron blue," a cyan lighting that has appeared in the night shots of all of Cameron's films.

Perfecting special-effects shots requires a constant back and forth between artists and filmmaker. In this case, the director had seen the images in his head for thirty years and produced templates with carefully chosen color, light, and composition. "I saw the flowers as much more translucent, with a lot more transmuted light," Cameron said, reviewing one shot. As always on a Cameron film, the real world was being used to inform the fictional one. Cameron encouraged an artist trying to get a creature right to "reference a rattlesnake skull and look at the quadrate bone." A six-legged horse was made shinier because "real horses are shinier." An energy map of the Pandoran forest was modeled on some rat neurons. As shot after shot was brought up on the screen for Cameron's appraisal, the smallest details garnered his attention. Hours were spent on getting alien sap to drip precisely right. When a shot from a battle scene went by with few changes, Cameron was pleased. "See, I'm low maintenance," he said, drawing weary laughter in both hemispheres. A column in one shot annoyed him. After fifteen minutes debating its placement, he declared, "That column is worth fifty million dollars of the domestic gross!" shaking his head at his own obsessiveness. "No one will notice. Well, I'll notice."

The postproduction on the film would be a lengthy and elaborate process, with Cameron again being a full-fledged member of the editing team. He brought *Titanic* composer James Horner back to write the music, a combination of ethereal choirs and ethnic instruments meant to sound both organic and otherworldly. In September 2009, *Avatar* took over two mixing stages at Fox. One was used for sound mixing and the other as a CG review stage, where Cameron sifted through the images flowing in from nine special-effects vendors, including Weta Digital and ILM. The idea of an "image mix" similar to a sound mix was one Cameron had detailed in his Digital Manifesto. One by one, he was living out his plans.

Avatar Day

Avatar would prove nearly as complicated to market as it was to make. With no preexisting intellectual property, there was no built-in fan base to harness, other than fans of Cameron. This was a movie designed expressly to lure audiences to giant 3-D cinema screens, but first Fox would have to sell it in the two-square-inch box of an Internet trailer. In May, seven months before the film's release, Peter Chernin was concerned and was considering not producing a traditional trailer at all. "It feels so revolutionary. A trailer almost diminishes it," he said, days after having seen a rough cut of the film for the first time. Audiences got their first look at twenty-five minutes of footage in July at Comic-Con, where Cameron was greeted as a conquering war hero in the San Diego Convention Center's cavernous Hall H, which had been specially equipped to show 3-D footage for *Avatar's* presentation. At Comic-Con, Cameron announced a unique marketing strategy—August 21 would be "Avatar Day," on which Fox would debut the film's trailer and 131 IMAX theaters would screen sixteen minutes of select 3-D scenes for free in the United States, while another 300 screens showed it internationally. When the trailer went online, demand was instantaneous, quickly making it the most-downloaded trailer at Apple.com. The *Avatar* footage triggered a record four million streams in its first day.

But the reaction wasn't all glowing. Some commenters likened the Na'vi to George Lucas's reviled CG character Jar Jar Binks, others to the eighties TV cartoon *ThunderCats*. A particularly hilarious viral video rewrote the subtitles to the climactic scene of the World War II movie *Downfall* to have Hitler raging about his disappointment in the *Avatar* trailer. "This is a fucking joke! I wait ten years for fucking Captain Planet with cats!" howled the Führer, a Cameron diehard who has even seen *Xenogenesis* and *Piranha II.* Audiences who saw the footage in theaters were considerably more impressed than Hitler, but Chernin's original fears about marketing an untraditional movie in a traditional way had been validated. The initial hype and interest that had surrounded the project were giving way to a backlash. This was a place Cameron had been before, on *Titanic,* only instead of online bloggers and commenters, back then it had been mainstream media who snickered at his ambition. He handled any buzz, good or bad, the way he always did, by throwing himself into his work.

In July, Cameron convened an unusual meeting in a conference room at Lightstorm. He sat at the head of the table surrounded by a botanist, a physicist, sci-fi and archaeology writer Charlie Pellegrino, *Avatar* cowriter Laeta Kalogridis, friend and frequent collaborator

Randall Frakes, and a journalist named Dirk Mathison. In case there was any doubt, Cameron donned a blue baseball cap with "HMFIC" printed on it (Head Mother Fucker In Charge). The questions the group debated—What is the lifespan of the average Na'vi? What is the composition of the atmosphere on Pandora? Why does unobtanium float?—would fill *Pandorapaedia,* a thick manuscript Mathison was maintaining about the plants, creatures, and properties of Pandora that would be used as a reference for any sequels or ancillary properties like video games. Though the first movie was nearly finished, the group was reverse engineering a mythology for it, putting great thought into the science of each question they pondered.

Unobtainium

One script element that Fox had initially objected to was Cameron's failure to explain unobtainium, the precious resource that sends humans to Pandora to strip-mine the planet ruinously. "Unobtainium" is a joke term engineers have used for decades to describe any needed material that is rare, costly, or difficult to obtain. "Unobtainium is beaver pelts in French colonial Canada," Cameron explains. "It's diamonds in South Africa. It's tea to the nineteenth-century British. It's oil to twentieth-century America. It's just another in a long list of substances that cause one group of people to get into ships and go kick the shit out of another group of people to take what is growing on or buried under their ancestral lands." For Cameron, the specificity of unobtainium is not important. He likens it to the precious briefcase John Travolta and Samuel L. Jackson retrieve in *Pulp Fiction*—you don't need to know what's in it, just that people are going to die for it. Despite Fox's objections, he never explains in the movie what makes unobtainium worth the trouble of interstellar travel. But the answer to that question is that the substance's room-temperature superconducting properties make it the key to cheap power generation back on Earth, where all the oil has run out. Unobtainium is crucial to running ships like *ISV Venture Star,* which delivers the humans to Pandora. The unfortunate irony is that the more unobtainium humans mine on Pandora, the more they will be able to travel there. It's a devastating feedback loop.

Like all of Cameron's movies, *Avatar* can be watched as pure escapist entertainment or as a dire warning about humanity's current path. This time he is cautioning not about a nuclear holocaust but about an environmental one. "All life on Earth is connected, in ways which human science is still grappling to understand," Cameron says. "But our industrial society is impacting that web of life at a rising rate, which will inevitably lead to a severe degradation of biodiversity and ultimately to a serious blowback effect against humanity. We have taken from nature without giving back, and the time to pay the piper is coming."

In this movie, as in every one from *The Terminator* to *Titanic,* he offers us characters who preserve their spirit in dangerous times, from a wounded warrior to a wizened scientist to a whole species of survivors. "The Na'vi are humanoid because the audience is invited to relate to them, not as aliens but as creatures which express some aspect of ourselves which we admire and aspire to," Cameron says. "They are emotional, spiritual, and physically accomplished. They are brave and unafraid of death because they know it is part of a greater cycle. They live in harmony with nature, not in some idyllic hippie fantasy but in a realistic way, meaning they know that they can be hunted as well as being the hunter, and they know they must not use technology to disturb the balance and must only take what they need." With *Avatar,* for the first time Cameron's future vision has not been limited by the strictures of a real-world movie set. The result is his most fantastical film, one that hews to the rules of science in its creatures and environments but not to the limitations of the physical world of props and the human body. Rather than diagramming the future, Cameron is expressing his present fear—that we might ruin our planet. *Avatar* is Cameron's spiritual and ecological call to arms disguised as an adventure about a planet with ten-foot-tall blue aliens.

Warp Speed or Blade Running?

Futuristic visions tend to fall neatly into utopian or dystopian categories. Some, from Plato's *Republic* to Gene Roddenberry's *Star Trek*, envision a society in which life is better than it is today, one where we have achieved enlightenment or peace or, at long last, can travel at warp speed. Others, from George Orwell's *1984* to Philip K. Dick and Ridley Scott's *Blade Runner,* depict a world of totalitarianism, anarchy, or robotic assassins. As a futurist, Cameron has tended to be a bit of both optimist and pessimist. In the first Terminator movie, Arnold Schwarzenegger's motorcycle-riding cyborg is our enemy, while in the second he's our savior.

In his films, Cameron has shown little faith in society's ability to adapt to a changing world. Yet, perhaps because his own story is so improbable, he exhibits great confidence in our potential to advance as individuals. The imaginative and worried boy from Chippawa forged his own unlikely path to Hollywood, the deep ocean, and the exotic other worlds of his own creation. Cameron gives us a future that is unfixed, one that is a dark highway at night, ours alone to navigate.

Acknowledgments

James Cameron generously granted me access to his set, his intimate circle of colleagues and friends, and his brain. His thoughtful, detailed, and frank answers to my relentless questions far surpassed anything I expected when I requested his cooperation on this book. When *Avatar* entered its final stages of postproduction and the already vast demands on his energy increased, he continued to make time for my project, because he said he would. I'm grateful for his keeping his word and sharing his most precious resource, his time.

Jon Landau opened the door. Besides fielding my requests with unwavering patience, he made things happen, as all great producers must. His steadiness and good humor in the midst of completing a dizzyingly complex movie is one of *Avatar*'s truly special effects. Rae Sanchini is another lobe of Cameron's brain. To have had her time and insight in researching his career was invaluable.

Several people helped me understand Cameron's contributions to the art and science of filmmaking. Peter Jackson, Guillermo del Toro, and Steven Soderbergh provided the crucial perspective of fellow directors, while Dennis Muren patiently walked me through the early years of CG, and Rob Legato thoughtfully explained the intricacies of performance capture. John Rosengrant provided a critical tether to the special-effects legacy of Stan Winston Studios, Al Giddings described the delicate art of underwater cinematography, and Vince Pace guided me through the 3-D advances.

Many of Cameron's creative and business partners shed light on his career. Gale Anne Hurd carefully advised me on his early years, as did Roger Corman. Stephanie Austin detailed the kinetic sets of *Terminator 2* and *True Lies*. Peter Chernin brought me on the roller coaster of making *Titanic,* and Jim Gianopulos, Tom Sherak, and Larry Gordon all shaped the tale from the studio executive's suite. His writing partner on *Avatar,* Laeta Kalogridis, sketched for me Cameron's life as a writer. Sam Worthington provided insights on his work with actors. Josh McLaglen, Jimmy Muro, Russell Carpenter, and Peter Lamont helped me understand the passion and endurance of a Cameron crew, while James Horner, Conrad Buff, and Gary Rydstrom described his postproduction style. Don Lynch, Ken Marschall, and Robert Zubrin brought an outside-Hollywood perspective to Cameron's projects.

Cameron's friends are a fiercely protective lot. That so many shared so thoroughly was crucial to my understanding of him. Randall Frakes and Bill Wisher brought the knowledge of thirty-eight years of friendship, while Tom Arnold, John Bruno, Lance Henriksen, Bill Paxton, and Arnold Schwarzenegger spoke with the insight of colleagues who had become comrades. The director's family is as smart, interesting, and no-nonsense as he is, and his parents, Philip and Shirley, and his brother John David gave me countless funny and illuminating stories about Cameron before he was king of the world.

.   .   .

A book, like a movie, rests on the shoulders of many people. My agent, Ed Victor, has been a smart and indefatigable supporter, shamelessly fun to work with from our very first meeting. My editor at Crown, Sean Desmond, championed this project through every twist and turn with a preternatural calm and optimism. I'm thankful for the agile team at Crown, who treated me and my manuscript with warmth and care. Michael Gruskoff, a genuine Hollywood gentleman, helped me find the right advocate for my book, and Zack Norman, one of my dearest friends, pushed the idea before there even was one.

My father, Charlie Winters, was the first person who thrust science fiction into my hands and asked me big questions. I am grateful for the artistic and loving home he and my late mother, Justine, and sister, Amy, created for me.

My husband, Martin, believed that I could write this book before anyone else did, including me. He read every page, often in the wee hours of the morning after hours bent over his own writing, and offered precious insights with his usual energy, wit, and wisdom. I love him dearly.

Notes

Author interviews conducted with Jessica Alba, Stephanie Austin, Jeff Berg, Michael Biehn, Kathryn Bigelow, John Bruno, Conrad Buff, James Cameron, John David Cameron, Philip Cameron, Shirley Cameron, Russell Carpenter, Peter Chernin, Roger Corman, Guillermo del Toro, Bert Fields, Randall Frakes, Jim Gianopulos, Al Giddings, Larry Gordon, Richard Harris, Lance Henriksen, James Horner, Gale Anne Hurd, Peter Jackson, Laeta Kalogridis, Peter Lamont, Jon Landau, Robert Legato, Joe Letteri, Don Lynch, Ken Marschall, Josh McLaglen, Dennis Muren, Jimmy Muro, Vince Pace, Bill Paxton, John Rosengrant, Gary Rydstrom, Rae Sanchini, Arnold Schwarzenegger, Tom Sherak, Steven Soderbergh, Anne Thompson, Bill Wisher, Sam Worthington, and Robert Zubrin.

CHAPTER 1: A BOY AND HIS BRAIN

1. Marc Shapiro, *James Cameron: An Unauthorized Biography of the Filmmaker* (Los Angeles: Renaissance Books, 2000), p. 48.

CHAPTER 3: KICKING IN THE DOOR

1. Nigel Andrews, *True Myths: The Life and Times of Arnold Schwarzenegger* (New York: Bloomsbury, 2003), pp. 120–21.

2. Steve Daly, "No Pity, No Fear, No End," *Wired,* April 17, 2009.

3. Christopher Heard, *Dreaming Aloud: The Life and Films of James Cameron* (Toronto: Doubleday Canada, 1997), p. 41.

4. Stan Winston, "Commentary," *Aliens,* collector's ed. DVD, directed by James Cameron (Los Angeles: Twentieth Century Fox, 2003).

5. Heard, *Dreaming Aloud,* p. 77.

CHAPTER 4: THIS TIME IT'S WAR

1. Paul M. Sammon, "Mothers with Guns," in *Aliens: The Illustrated Screenplay,* by James Cameron (London: Orion Books, 2001), p. 20.

2. Sigourney Weaver, "Commentary," *Aliens,* collector's ed. DVD, directed by James Cameron (Los Angeles: Twentieth Century Fox, 2003).

3. James Cameron, "Commentary," *Aliens,* collector's ed. DVD, directed by James Cameron (Los Angeles: Twentieth Century Fox, 2003).

4. Ximena Gallardo and C. Jason Smith, *Alien Woman: The Making of Lt. Ellen Ripley* (New York: Continuum International Publishing Group, 2004), p. 106.

5. Stan Winston, "Commentary," *Aliens,* collector's ed. DVD, directed by James Cameron (Los Angeles: Twentieth Century Fox, 2003).

6. Ibid.

7. Ibid.

CHAPTER 5: STARING INTO *THE ABYSS*

1. *The Abyss,* special ed. DVD, Disc Two (Los Angeles: Twentieth Century Fox, 1993).

2. John H. Richardson, "Iron Jim," *Premiere,* August 1994.

3. *Under Pressure: Making "The Abyss,"* special ed. DVD, Disc Two (Los Angeles: Twentieth Century Fox, 1993).

4. Martin Kasindorf, "Fox Plunges into 'The Abyss,'" *Los Angeles Times,* August 6, 1989.

5. Aljean Harmetz, "'The Abyss': A Foray into Deep Waters," *New York Times,* August 6, 1989.

6. *The Abyss,* special ed. DVD, Disc Two.

CHAPTER 6: AND THEN THERE WERE TWO

1. Christopher Heard, *Dreaming Aloud: The Life and Films of James Cameron* (Toronto: Doubleday Canada, 1997), p. 166.

2. Richard Corliss, "Why Can't a Woman Be a Man?" *Time,* August 5, 1991.

3. Heard, *Dreaming Aloud,* p. 174.

4. Tom Gliatto, "Problemo Child," *People,* August 5, 1991, p. 40.

5. Nigel Andrews, *True Myths: The Life and Times of Arnold Schwarzenegger* (New York: Bloomsbury, 2003), p. 215.

6. Jody Duncan, *The Winston Effect: The Art and History of Stan Winston Studio,* (London: Titan Books, 2006), p. 127.

7. James Cameron, "Commentary," *T2,* Extreme DVD (Santa Monica: Artisan Home Entertainment, 2003).

8. Duncan, *Winston Effect,* pp. 130–31.

9. Ibid., p. 133.

10. Peter Plagens, "Violence in Our Culture," *Newsweek,* April 1, 1991, p. 46.

11. James Cameron and William Wisher, *Terminator 2: Judgment Day: An Illustrated Screenplay* (New York: Applause Books, 1991), p. 8.

12. Ibid, p. 259.

13. Janet Maslin, "In New 'Terminator,' the Forces of Good Seek Peace, Violently," *New York Times,* July 3, 1991.

14. David Ansen, "Conan the Humanitarian," *Newsweek,* July 8, 1991.

CHAPTER 7: MYTHS AND *LIES*

1. John Lippman, "It May Be a Classic," *Los Angeles Times,* April 23, 1992.

2. Kathleen O'Steen, "Arcara Files Countersuit in 'Crowded Room' Flap," *Daily Variety,* January 7, 1993.

3. James Cameron, *Strange Days: You Know You Want It* (New York: Penguin Books, 1995), p. 13.

4. *True Lies,* DVD (Los Angeles: Twentieth Century Fox, 1999).

5. Kenneth Turan, "The Secret Life of 'True Lies'," *Los Angeles Times,* July 14, 1994.

6. Roger Ebert, "True Lies," *Chicago Sun-Times,* July 15, 1994.

7. Caryn James, "The Woman in 'True Lies': A Mouse That Roared," *New York Times,* July 17, 1994.

8. Brian Lowry, "True Lies," *Variety,* July 11, 1994.

9. James, "Woman in 'True Lies.'"

10. "'True Lies' Protested by Arab Groups," *Hollywood Reporter,* July 18, 1994.

11. Michael Hiltzik, "A Tangled Web of Deal-Making," *Los Angeles Times,* August 29, 1998.

12. James Cameron, "Spider-Man Scriptment."

CHAPTER 8: THE UNSINKABLE

1. Paula Parisi, *Titanic and the Making of James Cameron* (New York: Newmarket Press, 1998), p. 168.
2. Ibid., p. 39.
3. Ibid., p. 43.
4. Steven Smith, "Ship's Star Trouper," *Los Angeles Times,* December 14, 1997.
5. Ibid.
6. Kate Winslet, *Titanic,* special collector's ed. DVD, Disc One (Los Angeles: Paramount Pictures, 2005).
7. Smith, "Ship's Star Trouper."
8. David Gritten, "Making Titanic," *Los Angeles Times,* May 11, 1997.
9. *Titanic,* special collector's ed. DVD, Disc Two (Los Angeles: Paramount Pictures, 2005).
10. Linda Hamilton on *Larry King Live,* aired October 14, 2005.
11. Roger Ebert, "Full Steam Ahead: The Masterful Epic 'Titanic' Pulls into Port," *Chicago Sun-Times,* December 19, 1997.
12. Janet Maslin, "A Spectacle as Sweeping as the Sea," *New York Times,* December 19, 1997.
13. Kenneth Turan, "'Titanic' Sinks Again," *Los Angeles Times,* December 19, 1997.
14. Douglas Jehl, "Why 'Titanic' Conquered the World," *New York Times,* April 26, 1998.
15. Karen Schoemer, "Our Titanic Love Affair," *Newsweek,* February 23, 1998.
16. Natasha Stoynoff, "Champagne Breaks on 'Titanic,'" *Toronto Sun,* November 24, 1997.

CHAPTER 9: A MODERN-DAY MAGELLAN

1. Carl DiOrio, "Cameron Sinks Board Role at Digital Domain," *Hollywood Reporter,* August 20, 1998.
2. "Man Overboard," *People,* May 11, 1998.
3. Linda Hamilton on *The Oprah Winfrey Show,* aired April 5, 2005.
4. Don Lynch and Ken Marschall, *Ghosts of the Abyss* (Toronto: Madison Press Books, 2003), p. 89.
5. Ibid., p. 95.
6. James Poniewozik, "2020 Vision," *Time,* October 2, 2000.
7. Maureen Dowd, "Dead Heat Humanoids," *New York Times,* October 5, 2000.

8. Interview with James Cameron and Simcha Jacobovici, MSNBC.com, March 4, 2007.

9. James Cameron, "The Drive to Discover," *Wired,* December 2004.

CHAPTER 10: PROJECT 880

1. *American Heritage Dictionary,* 4th ed. (Boston: Houghton Mifflin Company, 2004), p. 98.

2. Elizabeth Weitzman, "Zoe Saldana: Beware, Silly Superheroes: This Tough-Talking Damsel in Demand Can Take Care of Herself," *Interview,* July 1, 2004.

3. "Talk of Retirement Is Alien to Sigourney," *Scottish Daily Record,* August 5, 2008.

Index

ABOUT THE AUTHOR

As a Hollywood-based contributor to *Time* magazine, Rebecca Keegan has profiled actors and directors including Francis Ford Coppola, Will Smith, and Penelope Cruz. She has written trend stories about 3-D, horror auteurs, and fanboy culture and penned play-by-plays of the Oscars, the Sundance Film Festival, and Comic-Con. She spent seven years in *Time*'s New York bureau covering breaking news stories such as 9/11, Osama bin Laden, and the Catholic Church sex-abuse crisis. She has appeared on CNN, Fox News, MSNBC, and NPR. She lives in Los Angeles with her husband.